Of

BATTENBERG,
BOMBAY AND BLAG

*Tales of a Club
Cricketer Gone Rogue*

Vic Mills

First published by Pitch Publishing, 2022

Pitch Publishing
9 Donnington Park,
85 Birdham Road,
Chichester,
West Sussex,
PO20 7AJ
www.pitchpublishing.co.uk
info@pitchpublishing.co.uk

ISBN 978-1 80150 136 1

Typesetting and origination by Pitch Publishing
Printed and bound in India by Replika Press Pvt. Ltd.

Contents

To my Mumbai support team of Ramu, Suby, Satya, Kartik, Kicha, Anil, Ram, Doc Bharat, Kannan and Hushang.

Introduction

HALF A century ago, when a Game Boy was nothing more than a plucky young shaver and an Xbox was a cardboard construction sold at the Post Office, the youth of the day found entertainment and enlightenment through Owzthat. The perfect antidote for a rainy Monday afternoon in the school hols the game, housed in a box an inch square by half an inch deep, consisted of two six-sided pieces of metal: the smaller half-inch piece had stamped on its sides 1, 4, 3, 2, 6 and OWZTHAT; the sides of the three-quarter-inch metal dowel read BOWLED, NO-BALL, CAUGHT, STUMPED, LBW, and NOT OUT. Add into the mix a scorebook and blue biro and you had all the technology to keep you entertained for hours if not days on end, while at the same time playing matches against some of the strangest of bedfellows.

My own preference, using the England touring party of 1932/33, was to pit Douglas Jardine and his victorious Ashes-winning XI against all-comers. Now this is where it starts to get a bit blurred and grainy. For in the haze of pre -and post-pubescent discovery, the opposition XI used, in the main, to consist of females. Indeed, for those who recall the BBC's *Come Dancing* programme, it was not uncommon for me to unleash the combined might of Larwood, Voce and Bowes against the Frank and Peggy Spencer formation dance team or against a composite XI of Pans People and Legs & Co.

On a really wet day the opposition would rarely stray beyond the Dagenham Girl Pipers, all of which were swept aside by the new ball attack with or without the need to resort to leg theory. And if the opposition did post a sizeable total, then the likes of Herbert Sutcliffe, Wally Hammond and Maurice Leyland would take little time in knocking off the required runs.

In an effort to give the touring party a more thorough workout I resorted to the *Encyclopaedia Britannica* in an effort to raise an XI of strong-minded females that would test even the cold Caledonian countenance of Jardine. The final selection promised some enticing match-ups including Eva Perón and Herbert Sutcliffe, Queen Victoria and Wally Hammond, Emily Pankhurst and Douglas Jardine, Jane Austen and Hedley Verity and, perhaps most mouthwatering of all, Boudica and Harold Larwood. While the scorecard has long since gone the way of dust and decades, a reproduction is just an Owzthat away.

Helen of Troy	b Larwood	3
Eva Perón	c Ames b Larwood	19
Queen Victoria	c Ames b Bowes	14
Margot Fonteyn	b Verity	33
Emily Pankhurst (c)	lbw b Larwood	7
Joan of Arc	not out	81
Jane Austen	lbw b Verity	0
Marie Stopes (wk)	c Paynter b Voce	4
Golda Meir	c Wyatt b Larwood	39
Boudica	b Larwood	5
Barbara Castle	lbw b Bowes	2
Extras		8
TOTAL		215

Larwood proved the pick of the England bowlers with 5-37, along with two each for Bill Bowes and Verity. It was left to Bill Voce to end the stubborn resistance of Marie Stopes. Margot Fonteyn displayed some nimble footwork during her innings, repeatedly dancing down the wicket to force Verity through the covers. The innings was built around a stoic performance from Joan of Arc who displayed immense courage especially against the short stuff from Larwood. It was left to Golda Meir to hit a flurry of late boundaries as the innings closed on 215.

After a lively opening burst from Boudica and Castle – the former causing consternation and a delay to proceedings for repeated use and damage to the outfield from her chariot – England's openers settled in and comfortably took the score into three figures before Jardine (39) and Sutcliffe (64) fell in quick succession to the flighted, if not flighty, off spin of Jane Austen. Hammond (45) steadied the ship before falling leg before to Emily Pankhurst, leaving Leyland (35) and Wyatt (30) to see England home by a convincing seven-wicket margin.

When not using Jardine's Bodyline team I would settle on the Bobby Simpson-led Australian tourists to England in 1964. This was of special significance as the opening Test in late June at Trent Bridge was, courtesy of Uncle Harry and Aunty Vera, my spectating Test debut. There was another debutant that day in the shape of the bespectacled Yorkshire opener, Geoffrey Boycott. Whatever happened to him?

That I was in the middle of something approaching a hormone overload that summer can be gleaned from my selection for the opening fixture against Simpson's tourists. Indeed, what other conclusion can be drawn from the choice of Christine Keeler and Mandy Rice-Davies as openers with Diana Rigg (Mrs Peel in *The Avengers*) to occupy the crucial number three spot? A year or two earlier I had something of a crush on my red-headed Sunday School teacher. For the sake of anonymity, she appears in the XI as RHSST. So too my first love, Jennifer S. I was a bumbling ten-year-old, she a far more mature 11. It was not destined to last. The remainder of the XI ranged from Violet Elizabeth Bott to Julie Christie and Glenda Jackson via Shula Archer. A decidedly odd summer for sure and with a scorecard to match:

Christine Keeler	c O'Neill b Hawke	40
Mandy Rice-Davies	lbw b McKenzie	29
Diana Rigg	b Veivers	73
V.E. Bott	c Simpson b Veivers	7
Glenda Jackson (c)	not out	107
Elizabeth Montgomery	c Grout b Corling	19
Jennifer S.	c Redpath b Veivers	62
Julie Christie	not out	58
Shula Archer (wk)	Did not bat	
RHSST	Did not bat	
Valerie Singleton	Did not bat	
Extras		14
TOTAL		409/6d

An adventurous opening partnership from Keeler and Rice-Davies – well, they would, wouldn't they – was followed by a dashing innings of 73 from every schoolboy's dream, Diana Rigg. The only blott, or Bott, on the landscape was a show of dissent by Violet Elizabeth who threatened to scweam and scweam until she was sick on being given out caught at slip off a thin edge. Thereafter Glenda Jackson dominated the innings with an undefeated 107 along with significant contributions from Jennifer S. (62) and Julie Christie (58).

Losing the early wickets of Lawry (17), Simpson (4) and Redpath (19) to the fire and brimstone of the RHSST, aided and abetted by some fine glovework from Archer behind the timbers, left the Australians with a mountain to climb. O'Neill (51) and Burge (38) stopped the rot, but when they fell to Singleton and Christie respectively, the writing was on the wall. A bewitching spell of 4-11 in seven overs from Elizabeth Montgomery took the game away from the tourists, who lost by a humbling 213 runs. With hindsight it was as much the onset of puberty and rampant hormones as Montgomery's bowling or a wearing pitch that did for the Australians. Still, the Chappell brothers along with Lillee and Thomson were on the horizon, but so too were Felicity Kendal, Helen Mirren, and Virginia Wadeeeeeee!

If Owzthat was my starter kit for the amateur game, then 30 years of club cricket completed the puzzle albeit at the cost of consuming a mile or so of Battenberg cake, a market garden of tossed salad, and the equivalent of the Manchester Ship Canal in stewed tea. A decade on from my club debut I found myself on the run from the law. That might need a little rephrasing. I found myself on the run from the legal profession. Better. In an effort to put a few miles between myself and a career I headed to Australia. They wouldn't find me there.

Despite an early encounter in the art and craft of sledging, this was the start of a love affair with country, climate and cricket that endures to this day. It also enabled me for much of the 1980s, with an innocent assist from the editor of *Wisden Cricket Monthly*, David Frith, to blag my way into and out of every Test ground in the country using a construction industry union card as a press pass. By way of stopover en route to Sydney I began a dalliance with India. This started with backpacking, progressed to paid employ for the *Times of India*, and ended with a decade-long NGO project to establish and run a cricket academy for the children of the Dharavi slum in Mumbai. This has since morphed into the Brexit-busting support of refugee cricketers in the UK, Germany, France, and Lebanon. A lockdown literary romp across the decades, *Of Battenberg, Bombay & Blag* represents a window into a rogue cricketing life from the erratic to the bizarre and all points in between.

VM, Berlin, January 2022

Gully Boy

FRESH-FACED, LONG-LEGGED, gym-skirted, and not long out of teacher training college, you may have an inkling where this is heading. If so, you'd be wrong. More inclined to sugar beet than sexual revolution, the 1960s rather passed Lincolnshire by. Evidence of this is that the arrival of our new gym mistress, Miss Chatterton, caused little if any groin-stirring among the rag-tag assembly of 11-year-olds. We cared little for her fresh face, gym skirt and long legs that particular May morning, but were drawn instead to the wicket sets she was carrying. Adhering strictly to the then sporting calendar, the weekend's FA Cup Final brought a civilised end to the football season and heralded the start of a summer of cricket.

A child of the '60s, knee- and navel-related matters paled when compared to the burning desire to kick with my left foot (still to be achieved) and land my off breaks on a length (patchy at best). That said, Miss Chatterton and Westgate Junior School did more in a week and a half than 30 years of club cricket by providing me with the one cricketing stat that I truly cherish. Under her watchful eye I batted undefeated during that period, encompassing several PE lessons and a few hours at the crease. This stat remained with me for decades. Until, that is, I happened upon Jack Fingleton's book *The Immortal Victor Trumper.*

The fact that Trumper and I share a Christian name is neither here nor there. That I lived for many summers in Sydney's Surry Hills close to the adjoining suburb of Paddington and Trumper's family home is, again, nothing more than coincidence. In conversation at the Sydney Cricket Ground one lunch interval, cricket historian and writer David Frith and I speculated whether there might still be a desk, long since consigned to storeroom or cellar, at Crown Street Public School with the initials VT carved into its wooden ink-stained work surface. Had this been a lengthy rain delay and not luncheon then the short walk to Crown Street was a distinct possibility. Of his early schooldays, Fingleton recalls that Trumper batted undefeated for FIVE WEEKS at Crown Street Public. His father's first question as the young Trumper entered their Paddington home, 'Still batting?' The reply, music to the ears of father and son, was affirmative, 'Still batting.'

In providing me with a long-cherished memory, Miss Chatterton was also responsible for a far more controversial piece of history that would take another 14 years before bursting into and on to the collective sporting psyche. It was the policy of Westgate Junior at that time to occasionally relocate to the sports fields of the nearby Bishop Grossteste College to participate in the very English game of rounders. Having already displayed a degree of hand-eye coordination, rounders offered me a further opportunity to put bat on ball. While all very promising, it was destined not to last.

The problem, and a painful one at that, arose post-swing. Unfortunately for me, but more so Miss Chatterton, I proceeded – the ball disappearing into the outfield, and me haring to first base – to blindly hurl the truncheon-shaped bat behind me, in the process occasioning a nasty thwack on the ankles of the nearby teacher in her role as umpire. Unimpressed and a tad sore, she let it slide and the game continued. When next at the plate the same scene played out: I hit the ball, hared off to first base, only to hear the soft thud and accompanying groan as the bat cannoned into ankles protected only by a pair of functional white gym socks and plimsolls. The third time I barely made it off the plate before being summarily dispatched to the sidelines, there to sit cross-legged, pink with rage and regret, and ruing the consequences for self and team. Fourteen years ahead of her time, Miss Chatterton had issued the first and probably only red card in the history of rounders.

* * *

Easter 1967: as if the prototype Adrian Mole, I am 15 and a half years old, have zero qualifications, and am about to leave Rosemary Secondary Modern School. On the plus side: I'm not down a mine, up a chimney, or working long hours, for starvation wages, in a Lancashire cotton mill. I also had, although unbeknownst to me, someone fighting my corner. Gerry Knox was a music, history, and occasional games teacher at Rosemary. He'd tried, but ultimately failed, to enlighten and enhance our lives with Gilbert and Sullivan. A commendable effort, but he might have had more luck with Cowdrey and Dexter or Trueman and Statham (three little maidens?).

The previous summer he'd stopped me in the corridor and congratulated me on scoring a fifty in a match against St Giles School. A match it may have been, but the fixture, pitting tough secondary modern against frighteningly tough secondary modern, was about as far away from the Eton and Harrow match as you could possibly imagine. I remember little of the innings itself other than a straight six that clattered into the gym wall at deep long-off. The same gym that months earlier – in an inter-school after-hours basketball match – had to have its doors bolted and windows locked to keep local ruffians out. A timely act, but it didn't stop the barrage of abuse or our growing fears for the journey home.

There was a degree of payback in the fifty as, two years earlier, as a pencil-thin 12-year-old centre-half for Rosemary's under-13 team we'd played St Giles in a school cup final on Lincoln City's St Andrew's training ground. At full time the score stood at 1-1. We wanted a replay. They wanted extra time. Extra time it was. We lost 5-1! The St Giles umpire that afternoon was teacher Fred Green. He generously offered 'well batted, lad' when I reached 50. Years later Fred joined the Lindum Cricket Club and became a resolute opener for the seconds. A dedicated counter of runs, it was not beyond him to cross-examine the scorers during the tea interval or at the close of play if he thought they'd missed a single or two. When not wielding a Senior Counties bat in the manner of his hero Tom Graveney, he could be seen in clubhouse or pavilion smoking Senior Service and hunched over the *Daily Telegraph* crossword. I used to irritate the living daylights out of him by wandering over and explaining that six down in every crossword (and this is true) was rattlesnake otherwise they simply didn't work.

In the last week of term before my Easter departure, Gerry sought me out and said I was to meet him at the Lindum Sports Ground on the coming Saturday. He was refereeing a rugby match and wanted to see me after the game. With handshakes and three cheers on the final whistle, players and officials made their slow, muddied way back to the Nissen hut and waiting bath. Barely off the pitch, Gerry spotted me, called me over, and introduced me to one of the Lincoln players, Ray Ingram, a local solicitor, and Lindum Cricket Club secretary. I stayed on until both had bathed and changed. We talked again outside the clubhouse. Gerry explained that

I had just left school, was a promising cricketer, and in need of a club.

More than provide me with an introduction to the club, Gerry went the extra yard and actually paid my first year's subscriptions of ten shillings. Years later, and privy to the club secretary's files, I found the actual piece of paper detailing that meeting. The note is signed by the club secretary and dated 10 April 1967. Fifty-five years on it would be fair to say that this simple yet lasting act of kindness is still paying dividends. A couple of weeks later I attended my first net practice. The *Lincolnshire Echo* just happened to be on hand to record the session and duly photographed the young off-spinner in action. I hope Gerry saw the picture.

* * *

Lindum Cricket Club in April 1967 was an engaging mix of ancient and modern. The new clubhouse was a joy to behold with plans already drawn for the second phase which would include tea room, changing rooms, showers, squash courts and gym. These would be a year or two coming, but most were happy to have a new clubhouse in which to chorus and carouse. The ancient came in the form of an old Nissen hut that housed a shower unit for those so inclined. As difficult as it is to comprehend, personal hygiene back then ran to little more than a bar of Lifebuoy soap and the club towel. The shortfall was aided and abetted by a daring blitzkrieg of talcum powder and Old Spice deodorant.

The jewel in the Lindum crown, albeit fast-fading, was the old-style wooden pavilion. The more charitable would say it had character; those less so that it should be put out of its misery. Having survived Hitler, its main threat now appeared to be dry rot and reluctant drains. A devotee of the faded and fusty, it was love at first sight. The uncomplaining carpets, arthritic chairs, rust-stained washbasin, and feisty floorboards meant it was the ghost of cricket past. In its pomp, the pavilion housed changing rooms, kitchen, bar, and tea room. The bar had been lost to the new clubhouse, but the rest was still functioning albeit wheezing and watery-eyed.

While 1967 marked the start of my playing days, I had been a regular Lindum attendee for the previous four years. With sandwiches, cake, crisps, and a drink in my school satchel, I'd begin the long march through Newport cemetery, down Nettleham Road, into The Grove and finally through the car park entrance. With vantage point selected, and play under way, afternoons would melt into weekends and weekends into long, idyllic summers. Still several years away from league cricket, matches were self-styled friendlies and, if the side batting first had not been bowled out, required a sporting declaration of sorts on the part of the captain. Friendlies they may have been, but the games, featuring county second XI and minor counties players, were not without edge.

The fixture list in those days would see us heading over to Nottingham most weekends or further afield to Sheffield and Derby. These were always hard-fought games, against good opposition, on picturesque grounds. Entry into the South Lincs & Border League in the early 1970s, while a necessity for the club's survival, brought an abrupt and somewhat sad end to many of these long-established fixtures. A regular feature in the late 1960s was Lindum's annual six-a-side tournament. Local clubs and village sides were invited to participate in a competition consisting of four groups, three teams in each, with semi-finals and final to be held early evening. On a sunny Bank Holiday Monday there was no better place to be.

To encourage big hitting – an incentive years ahead of its time – the groundsman reduced the boundary size. To further embolden pursuit of the maximum, a bottle of beer was awarded to the batsman for every six hit; a tactic that the IPL would do well to adopt as they look to narrow the gap between bat and ball. The day was also a much-needed fundraiser. As befits a club day, there was a raffle, food and drink stalls, and a lucky programme draw. On what would turn out to be a memorable Monday, I was fortunate to bag the latter's first prize of a transistor radio. A pivotal moment in my cricketing education, the transistor was immediately tuned to *Test Match Special* and there it stayed!

This was vintage *TMS* in every sense of the word with classic commentary courtesy of John Arlott, E.W. (Jim) Swanton, Alan Gibson, and the early chirpings of the Lesser Spotted Brian Johnston. It was still Johnston in those days and not Johnners. Indeed, the style of commentary was chalk and cheese to the vaudeville of today. This was austerity airtime; a simpatico union of lbp (language, binoculars, and pipe) with lbw. The prospect of cake or clotted cream entering the commentary box was still a decade or more away. The picture-painting all the better for an absence of sponge, scone, and slice.

* * *

I made my Lindum debut on 29 April 1967 in a first XI fixture at Grantham. The town was still some years away from being voted the most boring in Britain by the *Today* programme listeners. It was also still untainted by anything remotely Thatcheresque. The cricket club shared its ground in those days with Grantham Town Football Club. The football pitch was at the far end of the paddock and ran east to west. The cricket square nudged a relatively straight touchline and was north to south. Behind each goal and along the northern edge of the ground stood dilapidated stands, far from grand, which housed Town's faithful few. Not everything, however, was breeze-block bland. A paint-peeling hoarding, as if offering insight into Grantham's Tory roots, advertised dressed crab. During that first afternoon in the field, and as much as my concentration levels were focused on play, I couldn't help but wonder what on earth was dressed crab? Dressed how? Why? And for what?

As the junior member of the XI I was called upon to do very little during the innings. I didn't bowl and, positioned out of the firing line for long stretches of play, was left ample time to consider the fate of crabs, dressed or otherwise. Not that I was completely idle. Towards the end of the Grantham innings, I was walking in from mid-on when the batsman launched an Exocet straight drive with its coordinates locked firmly on the bowler. Heroically, and without perhaps quite thinking it through, he planted a sizeable right boot in its path. The ball – after contact with ankle bone and following an impressive scream that would have warmed the cockles of Edvard Munch – ricocheted to my right. Instinctively I hurled myself crab-like down and across, managing to arrest its progress with a juvenile claw. Returning the ball to our now hobbling bowler, I dusted myself down and thought no more of the incident.

This was not the case in the pavilion bar after the game. In fact, I walked straight into a discussion about the very episode itself. Although time distorts memory, I believe it was the first time the Lindum players had seen a fielder – the folly of youth – dive to stop a ball. Although never mentioned, I suspect that some saw my actions as not really in the spirit of the game as it deprived the batsman of full value for his shot. We were still some years away from the fielding revolution championed by Derek Randall, Ross Edwards, and Jonty Rhodes. Colin Bland roamed the cover region for South Africa and could hit the stumps with a direct throw seven or eight times out of ten, but I can't ever recall him diving to stop a ball.

Fielding was a far simpler skillset back then. A stop was required if the ball was hit straight at a fielder; either side and a bend or stretch was expected as a sign or signal of intent. If beyond the realm of bend or stretch then pursuit was the order of the day. But on no account was a fielder expected to throw himself at the ball in order to prevent accumulation or gain. Of course, the added bonus to such an approach was the fact that, with limited contact to grass and outfield, it was possible for a pair of fielding flannels to last an entire season without recourse to twin-tub or Tide. It would be too sweeping a generalisation to say that this single piece of fielding brought a premature end to the careers of several of those watching, but there was certainly a degree of concern in the bar that night. Had they witnessed the future? More to the point perhaps, did they want to be part of it?

* * *

The outdoor nets that springtime were situated about 30 or so yards from the clubhouse steps, flush with the tarmac car park, and facing the square. This had the twin benefits of being within a short sprint of the clubhouse or car should the weather turn inclement and also within easy reach of liquid refreshment. Not that rehydration was a high priority in those far-off cricketing days as what focus we possessed was firmly centred on mastering the intricacies of bat and ball. The positioning of the nets proved absolutely crucial that late spring as before the end of the month we were snowed off! And there the nets stayed for several years until a flurry of top edges, all of which landed on the roof or bonnet of nearby cars, brought a hasty relocation to the far side of the ground.

Hard as it is to imagine looking at the ground nowadays, in 1967 the northern and eastern edges were flanked by towering elm trees, all of which sadly went the way of the chainsaw as Dutch Elm disease took hold. The high-end housing estate that today occupies a significant part of the eastern side of the ground was a paddock back then occupied by an old grey mare. The horse was in no danger of injury until the day John Harris took it upon himself to bludgeon a quickfire century against a strong Peterborough side. To this day it remains the best amateur innings I've ever seen. Not a graceful knock of timing and technique but a brutal, violent innings that had the grey horse constantly on the hoof as Harris peppered the paddock with furious flat sixes.

Seen by many around that time, and even still today perhaps, as the club for toffs, the Lindum suffered from this thinking for all my playing days. This was fostered by the fact that many of its members were local businessmen or from well-connected families. Add in Lindum's winter sports of rugby and hockey and you could understand the reasoning. Indeed, with the ground ringed by spectators for an Albion Cup Final we would always work on the fact that around three-quarters were there to watch Lindum lose. The most picturesque ground in both city and county, the Lindum could easily have passed for a first-class venue. Appearances, however, can be deceptive. For a quick scan of Lindum's balance sheet – the club barely making ends meet – told a different story. In fact, we were totally dependent on the six-a-side and minor counties games to balance the books. Indeed, in my second season at the Lindum the committee came up with the idea of holding a jumble sale in the still standing, but only just, pavilion. With leaflets delivered to surrounding houses, players could be seen in the weeks leading up to the event scouring the neighbourhood for anything we might recycle as jumble. The event proved a roaring success with a long queue formed well before the doors opened. Hardly the stuff of toffs.

A keen Lindum cricketer in the 1950s and early '60s was the then Lincoln City FC manager, Bill Anderson. Every August, as part of their pre-season training, Bill would bring his Red Imps squad to the ground to challenge a club XI. This too brought a large crowd keen to see their heroes with bat and ball along with the chance of an early autograph. So, a busy, colourful summer for the newly arrived 15-year-old and a lot to come to terms with from a first season of senior cricket. I remain indebted to the many players who took the time to improve my game, to offer advice, and to generally point me in the right direction. In the interests of balance, it would be remiss of me not to mention those Lindum characters who were only too keen to point me – God bless 'em! – in the opposite direction.

* * *

As hard as it is to imagine, there was a time when a club cricketer's lot did not revolve around mobile phone, bluetooth, iPad, and internet connection. But how to inform a player of his selection if not by text, social media, or web page? A good question and one that involves a variety of components, not least imagination and left field. What has to be factored in at this point, and again this may seem astonishing when compared to the situation today, is that few players in the late 1960s had a home telephone on which to be contacted. Back then, the person assigned to collect match fees would also be tasked with noting availability for the following weekend. In the grand scheme of all things selectorial, this scrap of paper was crucial. For depending on where both the first and seconds were playing on a Sunday, it might be possible for the respective captains to hold their weekly selection meeting that night. If not within striking distance, then selection would be held in the clubhouse on the Monday evening following the latest net practice.

With captains and, on occasion, vice-captains in attendance, their number would be augmented by the honorary team secretary, a role occupied in the summer of 1967 by none other than Lindum legend 'Big Jim' Quincey. During a 64-year association with club and ground, Quincey turned his hand to many roles from player to committee man to scorer to groundsman before moving upstairs to president. With selection points chewed over, and fates decided, a list of the various weekend XIs would be pinned to the noticeboard in the clubhouse entrance. But what of those who couldn't make net practice and didn't have a telephone? By way of backup, it was then the job of the secretary, with support from the massed ranks of the General Post Office, to inform players of their selection by means of – POSTCARDS!

For the record, historical or otherwise, postmen were delivering twice a day in the late 1960s and were, near as damn it, as regular as clockwork. Which was one of the reasons why, along with your dustmen and paperboy, that postmen were considered worthy with the onset of December of a Christmas tip. It's worth mentioning too that there were no first- or second-class stamps in those days. The GPO compensated by the fact that, with a legion of postmen at their disposal, deliveries would, within perhaps a small margin of error, arrive the next day. Detailing the opposition, venue, meet time, and whether the first or second XI, the postcards would come complete with a threepenny (d as opposed to p) stamp along with a youthful picture of Her Majesty.

As with all such systems, especially those that rely on both paperwork and outside agencies, the Lindum's method of Presence by Postcard left itself wide open to cock-up and calamity. This would manifest itself on a Friday evening in frenzied (press button B) phone calls from players yet to be informed through one medium or another of their selection, and club captains who feared, rightly so on occasion, that they may be setting off for a difficult away match with fewer than the required 11 players. If it was a home game then there was always someone who could be called upon to make up the numbers. This was not the case, however, should you find yourself already heading down the A46 to Nottingham and facing the prospect of a long afternoon of leather chasing.

As to the season's cost for such a system, I can report that the Lindum CC final accounts for the year ending 30 September 1967 included a figure (for those who still function in pounds, shillings and pence) of £17-12-5 for postage and stationery. This from a balance sheet registering the total expenditure for the year of £587-17-8. As a sign of the times, I can further reveal from the same yellowing and dog-eared annual report that the expenditure included the sum of £15 for an end-of-season dinner for the tea ladies and a £5 gratuity for the groundsman. Proof, if such were needed, that as valuable as players and postcards happened to be, they were just part of the support cast when set against tea ladies and groundsman.

* * *

It was a simpler world back then, even the world of club cricket. Fifteen and in the first XI, the game was not without standards, rightly so, and not least on the dress front. Evidence this with a friend and club colleague promoted to the firsts after a seven-fer in the seconds at Burghley Park. Not standing on ceremony, he promptly took a five-fer on debut against a strong Peterborough side. Approached by the club captain after being applauded off the pitch, and expecting further praise for his efforts, he was simply informed that if he wished to play for the first XI next week he would need to clean his boots!

Thus it was that the first job on a sunny Saturday morning, having first breakfasted on marmalade sandwiches and tea, was the cleaning of boots. The ritual was to span three decades and two continents, but mercifully not the same pair of boots. My cricket bag was still an anorexic affair in those days. Not one of today's monsters that can only be manoeuvred or reversed thanks to a pair of training wheels. If only running between the wickets came with a similar pair. Expecting nor deserving to bat any higher than 11, or ten if the skipper was in a charitable mood, I did not have the need for a bat or pads and thus, should the need arise, was more than happy to delve into the bag of 'club kit' to find the necessary. With helmets not an option in those far off days, one simply ducked, took a stroll to square leg, or prepared for A&E.

But boots, being virtually the one compulsory item, were a must as was the cleaning. I would thus troop from kitchen to garden, boots in hand, together with a tube of Meltonian whitener. Dispensed through a small sponge pad, the ritual whitening had to wait until dirt or mud was removed from the studs followed by a wipe with a wet cloth. Liberally doused in whitener, the boots would then be left to bake in the morning sun. When of sufficient merit with bat to warrant a pair of pads these too would be sponged free of marks and scuffs before whitening.

Back inside the house, and to avoid any last-minute panic, shirt and flannels were located and laid out ready for packing. With that, the pre-match ritual was complete. With the morning still young, I headed along Newport and into Bailgate. Around 100 yards past the cathedral at the top of Steep Hill stood a row of second-hand bookshops. The sort of establishments that announced entry courtesy of a bell above the door. And there I would stay for the next hour or so digging around the shelves, threatening lungs with mustiness and mildew, in search of treasure. Whether propped, piled, stacked or free-standing, the treasure was there albeit that pursuit might occasion the odd close encounter with small furry animals, dust mites or a trawl or two of silverfish.

Once located there was the shiver of anticipation as you thumbed the inside cover in search of the obligatory pencilled price. Some of the finds remain with me today: the autobiography of Neville Cardus with torn and sellotaped dust cover published in 1947, Charlie Macartney's *My Cricketing Days* circa 1930, *Playfair Cricket Annuals* from the 1950s, and two lovingly preserved publications – *How to Watch Cricket 1949* by John Arlott and of similar vintage *Armchair Cricket (a BBC guide to cricket commentaries)* by Brian Johnston and Roy Webber. The jewels in the crown, however, remain Douglas Jardine's account of Bodyline, *In Quest of the Ashes*, and to provide balance if nothing else, 'Tiger' O'Reilly's travels with the 1948 Australian tourists, *Cricket Conquest*. Treasure, real treasure!

With the clock nudging towards midday, and content with the morning's swag, it was time to tear myself from must and mite and head home for lunch and then the walk to the Lindum ground. If the morning's booty was too exciting to wait then I'd toss one of the finds into my cricket bag for the hours of inactivity until called upon to field, bat or bowl. Simple, sunny, summer Saturdays, these. No manic callisthenics before the start of play. No team huddle. No mass outbreaks of high-fiving. No boorish chi'acking of opponents. And no tattoos, sunglasses, or earrings. Just unfussy flannelled friends and the English game at its most pure. As for what might pass as cause for concern? Unfurrow the brow and look no further than a temperamental tea urn.

* * *

Five minutes before the Sunday tea interval during the third England vs Pakistan Test at the Ageas Bowl in 2020, *Test Match Special*'s Jonathan Agnew stated that Joe Root had dispensed with a gully, confirming moments later that the position is now out of favour. Sense at last. Sense at last. Thank God Almighty we have sense at last. Apologies to the late Dr King for a slight corruption of his words, but the news from Southampton sent shockwaves through every strata of the game, nowhere more so than at club level where many cricketers still bear the scars, both mental and physical, from a far-too-close encounter with gully on entering senior cricket.

As a pale youth of 15 I recall being advised by the first XI skipper that, along with the intricacies of bat and ball, I should seek out a specialist fielding position and make it my own. With that he promptly dispatched me to gully – née Shell Alley – for the remainder of the season. The cosy, comfortable, leather on willow impression of gully is of innocuous looping edges gleefully seized upon by the innocent and untainted. In reality, gully can only stand and ponder the Meaning of Life as the batsman rocks back and unleashes a full-bloodied, pigeon-scattering square cut that lasers past (or through) him before crashing into boundary marker or picket fence.

The cricketing equivalent of a Victorian child chimney sweep: gully fielders are young, work in a confined space between fourth slip and cover point, and are constantly under threat from the proximity of action and environment. Lucky to pouch one in ten, the minimal returns from player and position elicit few if any expletives should a chance be shelled. In contrast, a catch taken will signal an outpouring of hugging and high-fives of near bacchanalian proportions.

Consultation of the Laws of Cricket reveals a shocking absence of anything in the way of human rights pertaining to gully fielders. It is a similar situation in the case of parliamentary statutes and international relief agencies. Adrift on a tide of indifference and inhumanity, the forgotten few go quietly and uncomplainingly about their work, pausing occasionally to suffer the breaks and bruises of outrageous fortune. However, as decreed by *Test Match Special*, their suffering may soon be at an end with gully rapidly falling out of favour with captain, and coaches alike. A humane decision, long overdue, but one that will do little to heal the scars of several generations of gullible gully boys.

* * *

It wasn't compulsory in the late 1960s to have a cockney rebel in your first XI, but sometimes it just happened. Given that most Londoners suffer increasing bouts of vertigo the further they travel outside the capital, few if any were game enough to venture beyond the North Circular. One to undertake the long march to Lincolnshire was rugby-playing cricketer Ken Lynn. A bit of a speed merchant, Ken spent the winter plying his trade on the wing for Lincoln RFC and was good enough to be capped by Notts, Lincs & Derby XV.

He saved his cockney credentials, however, for the summer months, when he was considered of sufficient nuisance value to be entrusted with the new ball. This did come with conditions, for what he lacked in pace he made up for with the gift of the gab. Before the first ball was bowled, he was already in conversation with captain, fielders, and batsmen. Not in any dark arts sort of way, more as a means to pass the time and have some fun along the way.

His best lines, however, were saved for his blossoming relationship with umpires. Indeed, Ken would quickly inform the umpire after his first appeal of the afternoon that the ball was in fact spearing down the leg side. The next appeal would follow a similar format only this time the ball had pitched outside the off stump. His next appeal, and by some decibels his loudest, was followed by an all-enveloping silence. The only conclusion the umpire could draw from this was that it must have been hitting middle and up came the finger. The circumstances were never fully explained to me, but it seems that at one away fixture at Skegness, Ken enraged the local burghers and assorted watching holidaymakers by bowling underarm. I suspect there was nothing untoward in this other than Ken getting a little bored with proceedings and looking to enliven both day and play.

When called upon to bat, he played the numbers game of block, block, swing, and any permutation thereof. In my first season in 1967 he and I shared a last-wicket partnership of 50 away at Normanby Park. While I played nothing more adventurous than a forward defensive, Ken went on the attack with mighty heaves into his arc between long-on and deep midwicket. At one point he cleared the boundary with the ball landing in a field still awaiting harvest. As an increasing number of the home side searched in vain Ken, not wanting to miss a trick, ventured that they might have more luck exploring an area a further 50 yards into the vegetation. Batting at the death that summer he amassed five not outs over 11 visits to the crease. Although only compiling 167 runs, his adjusted average of 33.40 was enough to win the Wells-Cole first XI batting trophy. This led to a rule change shortly after with qualification for the averages requiring ten completed innings. At the AGM that autumn Ken milked the presentation for every last drop, his smile as wide as the Thames Estuary.

Smaller and no less talkative, but decidedly grumpier, was another dual sportsman, Peter 'Piggy' Moore. In his case it was hockey in the winter with the Lincoln Imps and cricket during the summer. When not appearing at the Lindum his smallness of stature enabled him to ride out for a local flat racing trainer. He also blew the horn for a local dance band and could occasionally be seen in the orchestra pit at Lincoln Theatre Royal.

A decent egg at heart, Piggy's persona, like many others before, changed dramatically on crossing the boundary rope. There was nothing malicious in his sniping other than to be on the winning side and to get the best out of his team-mates. An inveterate grizzler, it was worth misdirecting a throw or bowling the odd delivery down the leg side just to keep him simmering on gas mark seven. A more than adequate wicketkeeper for the seconds, he cut a curious figure behind the stumps: bearded, brooding, cap pulled piratically low, the whole topped off with glasses and polychromatic lenses as dark as sin. Had he swapped orchestra pit for stage, he would have made the perfect, albeit diminutive, pantomime villain.

In July 1967 Piggy and I were selected for a first XI away fixture against a strong Peterborough side. Another member of that team was RAF wallah and Somerset seconds player Brian Lewis. Bowling off the wrong foot at pace, Brian blew away the opposition for a little over 70. Called upon as emergency opener, Piggy trotted out to bat. Keen to make early inroads, Peterborough opened with a fast and nasty former Sheffield Collegiate professional. His mood was not helped by Piggy who, rocking back to short-pitched deliveries, proceeded in chipping him repeatedly over gully to the boundary. Today this would have been lauded as a ramp shot. In 1967, for a diminutive piratical horn player, it was instinct born out of a deep desire for self-preservation.

* * *

The Lindum dressing room in the late 1960s was not short of characters. With the Scampton and Waddington air bases still operational we, along with both the rugby and hockey sections of the club, could always count on a regular supply of service personnel to supplement an XI or XV. Dennis Carter fell into this category. A solid second XI player, his forces fitness added greatly to the team's mobility in the field. He was, as you would expect of an RAF wallah, immaculately turned out. Had there been a prize for best dressed player on the paddock then Dennis would have won hands down and turn-ups up. But it was not his sartorial presence that intrigued me, rather his pair of batting pads. They were, to cut to the chase, enormous! An impression further enhanced by his tall, pencil-thin appearance. With no rules or regulations detailing the size, shape or material for pads, Dennis's did seem to flout both custom and convention. Indeed, the collision between ball and pad when he thrust his left leg forward made for an odd hollow sound, the sort a bass drum would make if covered by the regimental goat and then struck.

If his forward play was a cause for concern, this was nothing when set against his expansive backward defence. This would see him parallel to the stumps with both pads facing down the wicket. The initial impression, with Dennis almost lost behind the huge surface area, was of those grainy black and white pictures of the Berlin Wall. An optical illusion, no doubt, but the first impression was that both the wickets and wicketkeeper had disappeared from sight, and that first slip, and leg slip were also in peril of blending in with the off-white canvas. On days of indifferent light, it was not beyond the bounds of possibility for an entire slip cordon to be lost from view behind Dennis and pads.

Unlike opposition slip cordons, there was no chance of Lindum's mystery spinner, George Leachman, fading from view. If not readily identifiable, you only had to wait for his inbuilt GPS or smoker's cough to kick in to get a firm positional fix. One of the truly great smoker's coughs, it would start somewhere around his ankles and gradually work its way northwards before, with face contorted and changing colour from green to amber to red, it would explode somewhere around backward square leg.

George's large family house backed on to the ground. He would thus arrive in the dressing room pristine and primed for action. Below his statutory butcher's belly George sported a pair of drainpipe-thin legs, made all the thinner by a tight pair of flannels worn in the style of Max Wall. There was little chance of George over-stepping or no-balling as his stomach broke the popping crease long before that of his left foot. He had a curious action, too, in that the ball was spun out of the front of the hand thereby allowing him to bowl off and leg breaks with equal dexterity and little if any change of action. I dare say he had a doosra in his bag of tricks, but that was far too much trouble for both George and English club cricket in the late 1960s.

As savvy as they come, he was well aware of his ability to build pressure on the batsmen by wheeling quickly through his overs. As with all such mystery spinners, his action was not without speculation in that his straight right arm would barely pass his ear – no more than half past one on a timepiece – before being swung forward and the ball propelled teasingly on its way.

I recall a mid-season fixture at Cleethorpes when, from my vantage point in the back of his roomy estate car, I looked on pale and unblinking as George, a gifted multitasker, cornered at around 70mph while simultaneously lighting a Senior Service, coughing, laughing, and holding a conversation. At the close of play, George was often to be found behind the clubhouse piano belting out the tunes. One particular evening, John Harris, in black tie and en route to an RAF ball, dutifully bought his gallon of ale for his century earlier in the day. Not a great lover of bitter, George, seeing Harris disappear with his date, wandered to the bar and quietly ordered a gallon of Guinness, took it back to the piano, and played on. When Harris, still in black tie, appeared at the Lindum the following lunchtime, he was met by the club steward and presented with the chit for George's gallon. Done up like a kipper, he sportingly paid up before fading from view behind Carter's veritable Ponderosa of pads.

Mammoth Woolly

IT CAME as a bolt from the blue one winter's weekend. Lincoln City Council had converted a cavernous hall and changing area at the Sobraon Barracks into an indoor nets facility. We were truly blessed. Not quite as blessed as we initially thought, however, as there appeared little difference in the temperature inside to that of the ice and drifting snow outside. As if a chapter from *Cricket in a Cold Climate* we hurriedly donned as many sweaters as could be found in kit bags last packed amid sepulchral September gloom. While some smiled smugly under three sweaters with a combined wool content of a flock of prize-winning Merinos, there were others who had naught but anorexic cotton shirts and homemade short-sleeved sweaters. To combat the threat of hypothermia we batted and bowled at a lively lick, a plucky effort considering the season was still 11 weeks away. Not that all was frostbite and front foot. The temperature rose a degree or two when a club stalwart and local deputy head managed to snag his right foot (one of a pair that would have registered ten to two on a time piece) in the side-netting resulting in a perfectly executed triple Salchow.

While indoor nets were a first for juniors and seniors alike, few if any saw fit to change their habits. Thus bowlers chuntered, batsmen replaced imaginary divots, box and thigh pad adjusters adjusted, bat twirlers twirled, caps were pulled low to combat glare from lights and bowlers, grizzlers grizzled, stonewallers stonewalled, optimism for the new season abounded and, with muscles and backs mercifully free of tweaks, tears and pulls, we rejoiced in the absence of showers and dashed from nets to car to fireside. Lincolnshire used the venue for youth and senior sessions shortly after. At one such Sunday morning gathering the selectors – a motley crew with collars, ties, and grim expressions (hardly surprising since they hailed from Grimsby) – watched on as I bowled the then county captain, Joe Price, twice in consecutive deliveries with gentle off breaks that apologised for hitting the stumps. The following year, at a similar gathering at Stamford School, county legend and acting coach Harry Pougher pointed out that my version of the long barrier combined a left-handed thrower's knee placement with a right-handed throw. Ah, t'was ever thus, Harry, t'was ever thus.

* * *

When the amateur game was in full flow it was possible – playing two games a weekend, Friday friendlies, Bank Holiday matches, representative games, Gents fixtures, and midweek league and cup matches – to clock up over 70 appearances a season, all of which put considerable strain on groin, gusset, and groundsman. Twilight games of 16 eight-ball overs were a particular favourite especially if pitted against village teams with feisty wickets and teasing outfields. Taken out of our comfort zone of flat tracks and far pavilions, such games tested instinct and imagination to the full, not least as the requirement for midweek sides was not so much ability as availability. One match in particular deserves mention as we travelled a few miles out of Lincoln to the village of Fiskerton. During their innings, a batman arrived at the crease still dressing after a sudden clatter of wickets. When eventually zippered and buttoned he took guard. The left-arm Lindum bowler, military medium in appearance and manner, trundled to the wicket and released a delivery of such benevolence that a headwind might have prevented further progress.

Deceived by the absence of pace the batsman, looking to turn it on the leg side, took it high on his right thigh. I trotted in from gully to retrieve, at which point the batsman dropped his bat, took several paces away from the wicket, and started to beat his thigh furiously. A reasonable decision in the circumstances as grey smoke was now emanating from his flannels. Had this been Vatican City then we may well have been able to name the next Pontiff. As it was, those nearest – as if re-enacting a scene from *The Wicker Man* – joined in the ritualised beating of flannels and thigh. With the smoke now little more than a few tell-tale wisps it transpired that the batsman had omitted to remove a box of matches from his pocket when hurriedly dressing for the crease. The Lindum bowler, not noted for either pace or accuracy, had hit the box head on, causing the spontaneous combustion. Mercifully, the thigh pad prevented any serious injury other than a mass outbreak of laughter from home and away teams that continued in the Carpenters Arms, long after stumps. The incident proved beyond all reasonable doubt that smoking is hazardous to health, wellbeing, and attempted back foot shots through midwicket.

* * *

It is difficult to put an actual date on just when cricket dressing rooms became more fragrant. All we know is that there is a direct correlation between Pears, players, and pavilion. The Lindum pavilion in the late 1960s – a cousin many times removed from that in The Parks at Oxford – was high on history, and low on amenities: dressing rooms were functional with just a hint of health hazard, the kitchen was modest and put the gal in frugal, while the elongated tea room was early Trestle in period. The communal area was populated by wicker chairs dating back to the Siege of Lucknow, so too the woodworm-devoured bookcase and moth-eaten carpet. The bare floorboards in the home dressing room cried out for caution and tetanus boosters. Beyond a door in the far corner stood an ageing toilet circa late Armitage before he joined forces with Shanks. The one concession to soap and water was a sad, rust-stained washbasin above which hung an apologetic mirror. Those who needed a shower were required to make their way to the nearby Nissen hut home of Lincoln Wellington Athletics Club.

The lack of facilities fostered a minimalist wash and brush-up approach that evolved around a club towel and bar of Lifebuoy soap. To combat sweated endeavour most resorted to talcum powder, the mass use of which led to a pavilion pea-souper of pre-war proportions. Mercifully, help was at hand. The second-phase development to the Lindum clubhouse in 1969 brought the demolition of pavilion and Nissen hut, and the addition of squash courts, gym, dressing rooms, and copious shower facilities including a huge bath for those rugby players requiring more intimate bathing options. As if to celebrate the new surroundings, 'Big Jim' Quincey appeared one Sunday afternoon sporting not only his kit, but also a mysterious brown case. For we impressionable – and soon to be sweet-smelling – youths, the case contained a bonanza of Boots toiletries: a family size bottle of Vosene, soap other than Lifebuoy (we didn't know such existed), exotic rose-scented talcum powder, and a heady mix of deodorants including Old Spice *and* Brut!

No longer the domain of blood, sweat and beers, dressing rooms metamorphosed overnight into one part hair salon, one part Heathrow Duty Free, and one part Milan fashion week. Nor did it end there. As each season passed the more daring added hair conditioner, aftershave, and moisturiser. Players were now spending so much time on post-game preening that an addition to the hours of play was considered. This moved a step closer with the onset of blond highlights, earrings, and designer shades. In defence of club cricketers, they were only aping the professionals who appeared more than keen to swap bat and ball for designer watches (who fields in a watch?), A-list sunnies, and a selection of tattoos worthy of a Groucho – 'Oh Lydia, oh Lydia, say have you met Lydia?' – Marx song. Australia, who let us not forget put the man in Manly, stood firm for many years, preferring instead to apply only sunscreen and fly spray. But even they buckled as Warney took centre stage. As the seasons passed, and cricket became a game for the shampooed, the tattooed, and (following the tears of Kim Hughes, Steve Smith, and David Warner) the boo-hooed, I can't help but think back to that first perm of mine in the late 1970s. Did I start the avalanche?

* * *

They say – they who know about such things – that you never forget your first kiss or first girlfriend. Which is fine and dandy if you're prone to fresh underwear, reciting poetry, and taking your drink in small glasses. As you might expect, sporty types have their own version of caress and consort which – with slightly more mud and adjustment of box and thigh pad – centres on a first goal in school colours and a first fifty in senior cricket. Of the former I cite Westgate under-11s vs Monks Road Juniors on the Greetwell Road ground next to Lincoln prison.

Westgate wore replica Ipswich Town shirts – blue with white sleeves – and I, being tall and with all the fleet-footedness of the alpine cod, held the coveted number nine (Ray Crawford) jersey. More free-range than free-scoring, I saw my job as keeping an eye on our wingers. If they took off out wide, I followed suit down the middle. It was my job then to get on the end of any cross. That I chose to do so that particular Wednesday afternoon with a header surprised everyone: teacher, team-mates, opposition goalkeeper and, not least, myself! After the game, the teacher asked if I might have been standing offside before starting my run into the box. Offside? Football becomes a much simpler sport, and for that very reason far more enjoyable, if through nothing more than innocence you disregard the occasional rule.

As for a first club fifty, look no further than Yorkshire! A first-class county in every respect. Something we in Lincolnshire, a poor waif of a minor county, can only but aspire to. So, yes: Yorkshire, Abbeydale Park, and against a strong Sheffield Collegiate side. I was aided and abetted in the elevated batting position of four by the fact that when the toss was made only one of three cars that had set off from Lincoln had arrived at the ground. My game plan, when called upon to bat, and with one eye on the pavilion car park, was first to occupy, and then to nudge, nurdle and, in true Yorkshire fashion, make a complete and utter nuisance of myself. On a day of landmarks, the Abbeydale fixture included not only tea, but lunch! Runs and roast beef: not a bad return for a day in the Sheffield sun.

* * *

As the 1960s drew to a close the Lindum threw open its doors to welcome members of the Ramblers Cricket Club. This proved hugely beneficial for both parties in that the Lindum were desperately short of players, while the Ramblers were *sans* ground and set to wander the cricketing wilderness.

Before a ball was bowled the following summer, Lindum's second XI was re-named the Lindum Ramblers. As you might expect, the incoming players were not without their share of characters. Local councillor Ralph Clapham moved easily and happily between firsts and seconds. Dashing good looks and a persuasive manner, allied to sartorial elegance, made him an instant hit around club and bar.

Ralph and I shared a match-saving last-wicket partnership against one of the Nottingham clubs in late summer. At one point during the rearguard action, I was struck in the chest by their quick bowler. With barely enough ribs to call my own, my juvenile chest sagged, and I followed suit. Ralph rushed up and *sotto voce* urged me to stay down. By the time a glass of water arrived, and the colour had returned to pale cheeks, we'd managed to reduce survival time by another couple of overs. Without further drama we extended the innings to close of play and claimed a worthy draw. Our skipper was so delighted by the outcome that on retiring to the nearby Chateau public house he ordered 11 pints of beer. It being *that* sort of an establishment, the steward politely pointed out that they only served halves. Undaunted, and without missing a beat, the captain called for the pouring of 22 halves which were duly lined up in single file along the counter.

John Skinner was another Rambler who graced the second XI and committee room for many a year. While a steady enough cricketer, he was easily outshone off the field by his wife, Bridget. Barely a month or two into the new season and her cakes were the talk of the club. Forty years or more before baking would become a televised sport, Bridget was turning out prize-winning cakes at each appearance on the tea rota.

All of which left Nigel Lenton. Nige turned up at the Lindum in April 1968 in an ageing black Wolseley and sporting a farming college scarf of uncertain location and vintage. His languid manner on and off the pitch belied the fact that he was a dynamic, free-scoring centre-forward for the Lincoln Imps hockey club. Whether by accident or design he evolved into the first XI's utility player. He bowled leg spin, a discipline guaranteed to produce wickets in club cricket, could always be relied upon for valuable late-order runs, and was no slouch when pressed into service as emergency wicketkeeper.

As you would expect of a leg-spin bowler, his action was suitably eccentric. At the top of his ten-pace run-up he would encase the ball in a vice-like grip, grimace, and then start his trundle to the wicket. Nige had the polar opposite to a high action. He may have started upright but by the time he reached the umpire he was already stooping low, a downward path that continued through his release of the ball and beyond. If he had a knuckle ball it was only because his actual knuckles connected with the pitch in his follow-through. Unlike other leg-spinners he did not give the ball a violent rip, but more rolled the ball out of the back of his hand. He had a googly, but it was seldom sighted. For all his eccentricity of action he took 37 wickets at 16 in that first season, along with 318 runs, and five catches. His catch return might look a bit thin, but this had much to do with him fielding in the no man's land of gully.

While never first at the ground on matchdays, Nige could always be relied upon to be one of the last to vacate the clubhouse and bar on a Saturday or Sunday evening. Thank goodness these were pre-breathalyser days as, with the game long over and the bar shutters finally pulled down, he still had several miles to travel out of town. A country boy at heart, he nevertheless enjoyed the end-of-season jaunts to London. We would eventually get around to playing our last game of the season on the Sunday afternoon, but not before dipping a toe into London nightlife from Friday evening onwards. During a visit to the Whitehall Theatre to watch *Pyjama Tops*, Nige was tasked during the interval with purchasing ice-cream tubs for the XI. Sampling a pint in the foyer first, he arrived with the tubs stacked one on top of the other just as the lights went down and the curtain went up, revealing a couple of naked gals swimming in a large glass tank situated front right on the stage.

Momentarily disconnected with reality, Nige swayed one way while the ice-cream went the other. There ensued a minor disturbance as the players kept one eye on the stage while seeking out their now scattered ice-cream with the other. A year later, and in the relatively safe hands of Londoner Ken Lynn, Nige, sitting on the steps of Eros with the lights of Piccadilly Circus twinkling all around, held up his hands in defeat and appealed to Ken as to their current location!

* * *

I don't know what it is about the game of cricket, but it does seem to throw up more characters per clubhouse bar than any other sporting pursuit. One of the first to make an impression on me was the dapper Alwyn Shipton. By far and away the best-dressed man during the summer season, Alwyn was small of stature, quietly spoken, and with a neatly clipped moustache. An international hockey umpire in his day, he was a regular at the Lindum during both summer and winter whether attending meetings, running the line, or donning an umpire's coat. His officiating was of the minimalist – least said, soonest mended – style: firm but fair.

It was a view not necessarily shared by visiting bowlers, for Alwyn was one of the first local umpires to sport a pair of glasses with polychromatic lenses. As the sky darkened, so did the lenses. So much so in fact that his sedate journey to square leg – having turned down yet another vociferous appeal for leg before – saw many a piqued fast bowler heading in the opposite direction grumbling loudly about dark glasses, white sticks and tin can.

His move from umpiring to scoring brought a neatness and order to scorebooks not seen at the Lindum before or since. Unswerving in the rightness of a situation, it was he who walked determinedly out of the Sleaford pavilion during a tense final of the Pattinson Cup – Lindum thinking they had hit the winning runs with a ball to spare – to advise the umpires that the scores were in fact level. Set to face the final delivery, Lindum stalwart Steve Roberts enquired of his skipper, 'Big Jim' Quincey, what he should do. The reply was brevity itself. In rapidly fading light Steve returned to a crease encircled by Belton Park players intent on preventing the winning run. A hush descended. Pins dropped unnoticed. The bowler ran in. Over came his arm, after which we innocent bystanders heard two sounds: the first was the solid clunk of bat on ball; the next, a second or two later, was the rifle crack of ball hitting brick at deep long-on. Caring little for the drama of scampered single and full-length dive, Steve had hit the last ball of the match for SIX!

There is nothing quite as pure or quite as reckless as the amateur sportsman off the rein. Take a certain hockey chum of Alwyn's who, for reasons obvious, will remain nameless. By the way, those with a nervous disposition should look away now. For the more stout of soul, Alwyn told this tale of a player with a unique party piece. In those far-off days before breathalyser tests it was not unknown for hockey players to take a circuitous route home, calling at other clubs and pavilions along the way. A behaviour pattern that mile-on-mile increased the number of loo stops. Possessor of what can only be described as a prodigious bladder, this particular cove's party piece was to pee clean over parked cars. Not sideways, you understand (the car that is, not he of the prodigious bladder) but lengthways! We're not talking Minis here, either, but any vehicle that just happened to come within range. Undeterred by a lack of cars, he would simply pee from one side of the road to the other. Ah, the amateur game in full flow.

The best time to catch Alwyn in reflective mood was post-match with a half in his hand. I never once saw him with a pint. It was always a half before heading to the Conservative Club in town for a game of billiards. During away games I would corral him into a corner and get him to talk of his days cruising the South China Seas with the Royal Navy. In later years when he swapped his flat for a neat little room in a retirement home I would pop by for a farewell yarn before heading overseas. Even before the door had closed behind me, out would come the whisky bottle and glasses, leaving me to do the pouring.

* * *

In pursuit of burned-out Junes revived, I recall an image of Richie Benaud, the then Australian Test captain, keeping fit during the winter months by digging his garden. In light of the legion of support staff catering to the whims and fancies of the current England squad, it would be safe to say that the ECB has not gone down the soil and shed route. Shame. A year or two later, and with Richie in mind, I too embarked on a unique fitness regime. I refer, of course, to the Rambo of rubbish, the Garibaldi of garbage, the Tamerlane of trash: the bin man! With a distinct absence of wheelie bins and plastic sacks, this was without doubt the Golden Age for refuse and refuse collection. While Cardus saw English cricket's Golden Age as 1900–1914, we student bin men saw ours as somewhere between 0700–1500 on a Monday. Not your start of choice to a working week, but character-building all the same.

There was method to this manic Monday madness in that a solid day's work would free up time, and with it availability, later in the week for Gents' games and Friday friendlies. As a literary by-product of the work, it also enabled me to keep the first XI in *Playboy* and *Mayfair* magazines for the season. A few years later, by way of toe-dipping, I penned several thousand words of rampant raunch based loosely around Watergate and *Gardeners' Question Time*. A clue to its non-publication came from the editor of *Fiesta* who explained that my copy was rather too erudite for his readership. When not delving into the deep bed method or varieties of cumquat, bin life revolved around trying not to set fire with hot ashes to the lorry (failed), the calm removal of maggots from hair (succeeded) and avoiding close encounters with the local rat population (score draw).

On the plus side, the shifts left ample time and opportunity between house, passage and bin to fine-tune run-up and delivery stride, while the miles trod aided and abetted stamina. In many respects – rodents and personal hygiene apart – bin life represented the perfect fitness regime for the club cricketer. We were no slouches on the eco front, either. Indeed, in salvaging aluminium, copper, lead, wool, rags, and paper, we rightly saw ourselves at the vanguard of the recycling movement. By way of balance to an autumn term of legal text and tome there was also work over the Christmas holidays. This brought its own challenges, for in combating rain, sleet and snow we would slowly work our sodden way through the 30 or so mackintoshes recycled during the summer. As each mac became saturated we would replace wet with dry. The resultant collective break time funk of four damp and dripping bin men was, in every way conceivable, deeply, deeply disturbing.

* * *

And then there was the Oxford Summer Ball: a must for any bin man with an eye for superior refuse. Despite being paid by the city council until 3.30pm, most Friday mornings would see us showered, changed, and standing outside the Prince of Wales in Bailgate at one minute to 11 waiting, not for Godot, but opening time. On this particular Friday, however, I had other plans. Answering an advertisement in *The Times* I'd bought a couple of tickets for a summer ball. By mid-afternoon, and smelling far sweeter than a few hours earlier, I was in the care of British Rail and heading to the city of dreaming spires.

The bins were part of a grand plan to secure the necessary to embark on an I-can't-think-of-anything-else-to-do Master of Laws (LLM) degree. I'd already spent the winter as a furnace labourer in an iron foundry so bleak it would have shamed Dickens. Not what you'd call a natural furnace labourer, I was a regular at the nurses' station. On one grit-removal visit she suggested that I was not like my three co-workers. How so? Well, I hadn't been in prison. The work was only fit, or so it seemed, for ex-cons. Even then I had to disappoint her. As part of getting in touch with our inner con, we small band of law students had spent an afternoon in Wormwood Scrubs including afternoon tea with the assistant governor. I thought it best to keep this from my furnace colleagues.

Thanks to a glittering reference from my company law tutor, most of which would have failed a polygraph test, I'd had offers on the LLM front from the London School of Economics and University College London. I settled on UCL for no other reason than having scored runs the previous summer on their batsman-friendly wicket. But back to the ball.

My date for the evening was Louella, a fellow student now studying for the Bar. We'd always danced together at college discos and saw no reason to stop now. We met at

Oxford station: she having driven up on her motorcycle with evening dress under her leathers and me on the Birmingham connection a mere eight hours after emptying my last bin. We changed in the station loos and deposited our bags with left luggage. Georgie Fame (minus his Blue Flames) headlined the entertainment alternating with some noisy sets from the Glitter Band (mercifully minus Gary). The last tune before kedgeree and a slow clip to the station was Boz Scaggs's 'Lido Shuffle'. As Louella rode off into the sunrise, I settled back bleary-eyed to tick off the stations before Lincoln. Not that there was much time to recover. A cab home was followed by a frenzied bout of kit packing before a leaden-footed shuffle to the Lindum. We won the toss and our skipper, rather than allow me the luxury of an hour or two's restorative sleep in the dressing room, asked me to open. The biggest worry – 32 sleepless hours on from Friday morning's alarm – was the distinct possibility that, having taken guard, I might fall into a deep sleep once in my stance. I didn't, but it was a close call. To add insult to insomnia I remained at the crease for an hour before surrendering to medium pace and Morpheus.

* * *

I returned from the Oxford ball, not as Cinders but to cinders with another working week starting with the prefabs on Outer Circle Drive. A wet day: from dreaming spires to steaming driers and all in the space of 72 hours. Fallen crest! Not that there was time to mull over Oxford nights as, with summer negotiating with autumn, it was time to swap overalls for academia. With the money from my furnace labouring, the earnings off the bins and three modest cheques amounting to £250 from educational charities I had, come September, enough cash to survive the academic year. Unfortunately, my academic year lasted just three short weeks!

The warning signs were there from the start as the time-honoured boozy undergraduate reunion was replaced by a heavyweight faculty sherry party attended by the likes of Michael Zander and Lord Lloyd of Hampstead. There is little to show of the weeks in question other than a green entry card for the Institute of Advanced Legal Studies and a glass water jug obtained by a small act of petty larceny from the lectern of Professor Wedderburn at the LSE who, just minutes earlier, had delivered his term-opening lecture on company law.

The decision to bolt was not quite as clear-cut as you might imagine. At the sherry party I met a young Israeli student whose parents had bought her a flat in St John's Wood. The apartment just happened to overlook Lord's. Of all the apartments, in all the towns, in all the world, she had to have one overlooking Lord's. Had it been May and not October then this could have been the start of a beautiful friendship. As it was, three weeks after leaving, I was back in Lincoln. The only discernible difference being that from here on in I would spell career with a K! There was, however, to be no laurel-resting. Within a couple of days I was back with the usual suspects. Their take on the episode: we'll always have prefabs.

* * *

Some years ago, I turned up at an evening net session at the Lindum thinking I might have a hit. Looking around at the players and kit it felt like I'd just arrived from a different solar system. The fact that I carried my kit bag – and did not have one with wheels that appeared to need an HGV licence – quickly marked me out as from a galaxy far, far away. The other giveaway was a distinct lack of anything approaching Velcro. My pads had straps and buckles. Buckles, for heaven's sake! My thigh pad had tie-ups that secured the vital piece of equipment with a neat bow. As for

an elaborate truss-like device to house batting box? Look
no further than a pair of Marks & Sparks' finest. All of a
sudden, my Saturday morning ritual of whitening boots
and pads seemed positively prehistoric. A further scrutiny
of the scene suggested I was also short on club tracksuit,
helmet, arm guard, sunglasses, and designer stubble. And
to think I once saw myself as a trend-setter for sporting a
pair of sweatbands.

A sobering thought, but when no more than a callow
youth of 15 I innocently walked out to bat one early season
Sunday with a towel doubling as a thigh pad. And not even
a bath towel at that! Three firm eye-watering blows later
by the Norfolk left-arm quick Keith Rudd and I was ready
to make changes. The following lunchtime I limped into
Bycroft's Sports Emporium on Lincoln's High Street. You
know where you are with an emporium. Or so I thought,
until a pretty young female assistant enquired of my needs. I
stammered, blushed, mumbled something about leaflets and
fled. A chastening experience, but no more so than being
thwacked around the body by a minor county quick. A day
or so later I returned, was served by a male assistant, and
equipped myself with the necessary including a Litesome
Support (jock strap). The support proved just a tad more
technology than I was game to cede at that point in my career
and I soon reverted to bathers: remembering first to 'warm
box' before inserting.

As basic as my kit needs were during these formative
years, I was still some way ahead of Alan Harvey. 'Big Al'
turned up at the Lindum in the early 1970s. He had a fifty
at Lord's to his name for the Public Schools, had represented
Buckinghamshire while still in his teens, and missed out on
a blue at Cambridge due to a fine crop of young batsmen
that included the likes of A.R. (Tony) Lewis. Despite such

an impressive pedigree, he walked to the crease that day sporting a pair of green-pimpled batting gloves. There was hope for me yet.

During my seasons in Australia, kit needs, certainly on the clothing front, were very much a case of less is more. Little time or energy was devoted to fashion statements. Set to field for 80 overs in 30°C temperatures called for extreme measures. Designer stubble was positively encouraged as an extra layer to ward off the withering UV levels. Shirt sleeves were worn long and buttoned, collars up, and floppy sun hats pulled low and tight. What skin was open to the elements was generously smeared with sunscreen with the whole topped off by liberal doses of fly spray. And yes, although it seems strange these days, not a wristwatch in sight!

* * *

By way of an early season note to Lindum Cricket Club players their Facebook page recently posted a message stating that orders for new kit should be made to the club shop by the end of the month. The post also went on to remind all those members playing senior cricket that a playing shirt, training shirt and polo shirt were required as a minimum.

These are changing times. A century or two earlier when I started at the Lindum, we were more concerned with getting 11 players on the pitch come Saturday and Sunday and didn't give a second thought to the sartorial text or tone. Of course, where possible, white, off-white or cream was the order of the day. Occasionally the opposition would turn up with someone sporting a royal blue sweater. Word of warning: dismiss such at your peril. I recall a Pattinson Cup semi-final at Sleaford where this fellow ambled to the crease wearing a blue sweater and track shoes only to then launch several deliveries over the fence and into nearby allotments.

The only items with Lindum-branded colours at that point in the club's history were sweaters, both long- and short-sleeved, and the club cap. By no stretch of the imagination, however, were these considered compulsory by the cricket committee or players. By way of a counter movement to the club sweater – and every team had at least one – was the hand-knitted variety. You had to feel for the poor innocent in possession; the sweater having been foisted on him by way of birthday or Christmas. To seek a way out would only exacerbate the guilt of knowing that a girlfriend, mother, or grandmother had spent weeks if not months of serious RSI-threating knit one purl two to create this mammoth woolly. The only hope was that moth or mutt would do their worst during the close season, thus rendering it unwearable come April.

All trace of club colours stopped with the sweater. We thus had a free hand at choosing two or three shirts that would see us through the season. These would be left, along with green-stained flannels, undies, and socks for long-suffering mothers either late Sunday evening or early the following morning for the weekly Monday wash. Unfortunately for my mother, I was an advocate, one of the few in the late 1960s, of diving as a necessary part of fielding whether in the gully, covers or on the boundary. Choose any period in cricket history before this and it appears that a pair of fielding flannels could last the entire season without coming into contact with washing machine, soap, or powder. This was not the elaborate slide-dive you see today at club and county grounds accompanying every shot that pierces the infield, but more a lateral movement that a goalkeeper might employ at a penalty shoot-out. While my flannels were a contributory factor to my mother's washday red hands, it pales in comparison to today where flannels magically appear in utility rooms on a Monday morning more green than white. Mercifully, the improvement in ground fielding in recent decades has been accompanied by an equivalent advance in twin-tub technology.

Whether a tribute to W.G. Grace or the product of an expanding waistline I never discovered, but club stalwart Steve Roberts took the whole fashion/club colours thing to new heights by taking the field with his grammar school tie knotted around his waist. I liked the cut of his jib and, to be fair, it did the job while at the same time adding greatly to what was otherwise a mixed and slightly confusing ensemble of the home-knitted and shop-bought. All of which brings us neatly to the bag of 'club kit'. The recent Facebook post I note made no mention of players having to purchase bat, pads, and the like, it being accepted that no self-respecting cricketer would deign to turn up without such. Fair enough, but this fails to recognise the fact that not so long ago the bag of 'club kit' was as essential to the amateur game as that of tea urn or Battenberg cake.

There was a definite dressing room demarcation back then that ran along the lines of: batters batted, and bowlers bowled. So far so good. To this was added the caveat that anyone batting seven or below was not a) expected to bat or b) pursuant upon a) need not purchase either bat, pads, or thigh pad as these could be readily found in the bag of assorted 'club kit'. At the end of a day's play, it was the juniors' task to repack such kit which, by then, had been scattered to all parts of the dressing room as tail-enders frantically sought pads, gloves, box, and bat as the result of a middle-order collapse. The bag would then be buckled shut and dragged off to a cupboard or kit room there to remain until the following weekend. Although the term recycle was little used in those days, this was nevertheless the key to the content and upkeep of the 'club kit'. For as each April came around, and batsmen looked to replace or upgrade, so the items replaced quickly found their way into the free-for-all. As haphazard as it sounds, and albeit a country mile from the slick kit operation that now exists at the Lindum, we did manage to field tidy-looking XIs and, despite the odd renegade slipping through the net, most if not all opted for club sweater and cap.

On the Run

IN THE summer of 1977 I was on the run from the law. That might need a little rephrasing. In the summer of 1977, I was on the run from the legal profession. Much better. Having graduated two years earlier with a solid lower second law degree the pressure to enter the profession was mounting. My reluctance to so do dates back to a lecture in the first term of my second year when our space was invaded by a well-meaning fellow who described himself as a careers advisor. He didn't stay long. His message was simple: I hear you all want to become solicitors or barristers, so we'll leave it at that. At the conclusion of the lecture – another indecipherable hour of land law – I wandered down to the refectory mulling over my already decided career. Not happy, I booked an appointment with the guy for a few days later.

As his visits were few and far between, he was assigned a small, narrow office on the third floor of the Law Faculty. He asked a series of detailed questions, the answers to which, he said, would enable him to ascertain a suitable career path for me. The only path I felt we were heading down was the garden variety at the bottom of which I fully expected to find fairies. He concluded the hour-long interview by asking what I saw as my perfect job. On answering – a football commentator for BBC radio – he threw me out muttering darkly about a waste of time. His and mine!

By way of delaying tactics, and before sitting my finals, I asked my personal tutor her views on my applying to read for a Master of Laws. She was not very complimentary, suggesting I take a look at the male lecturers currently on staff. Men, she suggested, that had settled for academia as they couldn't cope with life in the outside world. Didn't see that coming. She nevertheless agreed to act as a referee in the application process, part of which included writing a stunning reference that had me contributing to the college law magazine and representing the faculty in mooting competitions. All of which was a country mile from reality. As it turned out my master's-delaying tactic lasted just three weeks before I saw the light and bolted!

The next option, in a fast-diminishing list, was cricket-related. A player who felt failure perhaps a little more than most, I was not one to hang around the pavilion feeling sorry for myself but would instead grab newspaper and book and relocate to the furthest point away from team-mates and pavilion and then to feel sorry for myself. Distance was the key. Once settled I could review the shot or delivery that had brought my downfall without being plagued by offers of sympathy or guidance. So maybe distance was the answer? But where? And how far? By a happy coincidence, the sports columns in the summer of 1977 were given over almost entirely to the proposed World Series Cricket tournament down under formulated and financed by Mr Channel 9, Kerry Packer. The official version, then, for my January 1978 exodus was to witness cricket's very own revolution. Unofficially, and whisper it softly, I was on the run from the legal profession. And 12,000 miles away, I would take some catching.

Content to be a foot soldier in the World Series Cricket-inspired insurrection, I was nevertheless determined to play some club cricket. This was more than evident at Heathrow's check-in where my 20kg baggage allowance was split evenly between clothes for my back and cricket gear. The day following my arrival in Melbourne's East Brighton I phoned the Victorian Cricket Association. They recommended half a dozen clubs. Scanning the local A-Z I saw that Brighton's ground, situated on the corner of South and Beach Road, was just a cover drive away from Port Phillip Bay. A happy coincidence, or so I thought, as any such problems with the heat and humidity would be more than countered by cooling breezes off the bay. A reasonable enough assumption, but one that foundered very early in proceedings.

I called the club secretary – attended net practice on the Tuesday and Thursday – and played my first game just six days after arrival. It was –2°C when I'd left Heathrow; the mercury was nudging 38°C when I stepped on to the Brighton Oval that Saturday morning. Having never sunbathed in such temperatures, let along chased a cricket ball, we're talking a steep learning curve that included shirt sleeves down and buttoned, collar up, floppy hat pulled low and tight, sun blocker liberally smeared, the whole topped off with half a can of fly spray. Little did I know or realise, but that was only the half of it.

Inadvertently adding fuel to the fire, I committed the cardinal sin of the pale Pom by walking out to bat in my borrowed black, green, and yellow hooped Lincolnshire Gents cap. BIG MISTAKE! This situation had pedigree. During the Bodyline series of 1932/33 arch-irritant Douglas Jardine had worn his Oxford Harlequin cap for the entire series, much to the annoyance of the Australians, only reverting to his England cap during the final Test in Sydney. Forty-five years on, I might just as well have painted a target on my forehead. If the cap hadn't alerted the opposition to my newly arrived status and nationality, then the five minutes it took to take guard – the umpire and I tangling over terminology – certainly did. And then the sledging started, which was all very odd as I hardly knew anyone in town and certainly none of the opposition players, and nor, to the best of my knowledge, had I slept with any of their wives, girlfriends, daughters, or mothers in the past six days. Not that they cared a jot as first the bowler, then wicketkeeper, then slips and finally cover point joined in a chorus of abuse. There was a degree of payback in that I managed to deposit their off-spinner on the nearby city to Sandringham rail line.

* * *

Unseasonal low pressure and late-summer rains brought a very English feel to a first summer of club cricket down under. Of more importance, however, it brought my paid employ as a beach cleaner to a premature end. There was nothing for it but to head to Sydney earlier than planned. It was a difficult decision as my club side, Brighton, had just reached the competition finals. In the end I was persuaded to stay for the play-offs. To assist my meagre finances, club members employed me to cut grass, clean windows, and spring-clean bathrooms.

The group semi-final against Dandenong produced a vintage piece of Australiana. The first ball of the match, Brighton electing to bat, saw the bowler start his run-up, increase his speed to the wicket and then, without missing a beat, produce the perfect thrown delivery! Hoots of derision emanated from the Brighton players who witnessed every sequence of the deceit. Fortunately it didn't result in a wicket, and a pitch invasion was averted. It had been a steep learning curve in the dark arts of Australian club cricket but this was off the scale. And yet I couldn't help but feel a grudging respect for the deed. This had been thought through, practised, and admirably executed. The choreography was precision-perfect even to the extent of being delivered behind the umpire, thereby restricting the vision of the official at square leg. It little aided their cause, however, as Brighton completed a comfortable victory by mid-afternoon on the second day thereby advancing to a group final against Malvern. By way of background: Brighton had played these same teams at the same stage of the competition the previous season. There had been much bad blood with scores left unsettled.

Positioned in the gully for much of the Malvern innings, I could do little but marvel at the relentlessness of the sledging and the quality and inventiveness of phrase. I fielded just a handful of shots during the 80-over innings but had little appetite that night other than for shower and bed. At the crease as our fifth wicket fell on the Sunday, the game – Brighton still 60 runs short and Malvern with the wind in their sails – was tantalisingly close. Enter Dr Rod Sitlington. In these days before helmet, chest protector and arm guard, it was always handy to have a medic at the other end. And so it proved as I failed to evade one of many short-pitched deliveries and could only watch and grimace as it cannoned into my ribcage. I took a knee and would have happily taken a bed in a side ward of a private hospital had it been offered, before standing and calling for water. At which point the opposition skipper barrelled up and starting to abuse me for not getting his permission.

Untainted by the goings-on the previous year, and cast as the Man on a Clapham Omnibus, I couldn't help but feel a little aggrieved. Now, now: don't get angry, get even. Rod and I dug in stoically for the next hour or so until I failed to get on top of a square cut. It mattered little as the scores were level and Brighton on their way to the Grand Final.

The three-day final against Balwyn was heavily rain-affected. To add insult to the inclement we lost out on winning the flag by just three runs. I again managed runs in a low-scoring game, but fell victim to a drying wicket and a ball that turned, bounced, and was gleefully snaffled by their skipper at short leg who saw the dismissal as the signal for another verbal volley. The following day I was set, cricket bag and all, to hitch to Sydney, only to find that my team-mates, in a final act of vintage Australiana – thankfully one that didn't involve expletives – had clubbed together and bought me an airline ticket. As to the message from this short, sharp, shock of an introduction to Australian club cricket? Easy. Harden the f**k up!

* * *

Eighteen months on from the Great Melbourne Sledging Summer of '79 and I was back in Oz. Having been a privileged spectator during the revolution that was World Series Cricket, I thought it only right and proper – there being nothing too pressing on the kareer front – to return for the reunification tri-series with Australia playing three Tests each against England and the West Indies. For reunification read sell-out: the Australian Cricket Board pocketing 30 pieces of silver in exchange for granting Packer's Channel Nine sole rights to televise cricket in Australia. Still mercifully a decade or more away from the Barmy Army, cricketing itinerants were few on the ground. So too affordable transport options, the sum total of which consisted of a multi-day Ansett Pioneer bus pass. That said, over a ten-week period I still managed to clock up 12,000 miles, spending 250 hours on buses, and watching over 200 hours of cricket.

I made my debut on Sydney's notorious Hill that southern summer: a day/nighter between Australia and the West Indies. An enticing enough prospect you would have thought, unless your sole aim – the cricket merely incidental – was to drink yourself into oblivion, a preoccupation for which the pyjama game was ideally suited. At that point in the ground's history, the bar on The Hill served only cans. No beer snake here, boys. And none of that low-alcohol nonsense! It all meant that come the evening session The Hill held all the appearance of Ypres or Passchendaele with sniping and scuffles breaking out all around. Meanwhile, in the soundproofed ABC commentary box, Jim Maxwell suggested that The Hill was a 'little lively tonight'. Lively? Jim, get real! If you managed to duck the flying cans there was always the likelihood of falling foul of a wildly thrown haymaker. And all the while NSW's finest, what few were in attendance, looked on with mild curiosity.

Not without its characters, The Hill between the wars was the domain of the legendary barracker Stephen Harold Gascoigne, aka Yabba. On seeing Douglas Jardine, Australia's main protagonist during Bodyline, swat away some flies, Yabba boomed out, 'Leave those flies alone, they're your only friends here.' The Hill was rarely if ever welcoming to visiting Poms. John Snow roused their ire during the final Test of the 1970/71 series. Following an altercation with a fan by the picket fence, England captain Ray Illingworth led his side off the pitch. In contrast to Test matches, Sheffield Shield days were more sedate, although heading to the ground on the morning after the Gay and Lesbian Mardi Gras meant a curious mingling of cricket's faithful with assorted dykes on bikes or (the still dancing) Qantas cabin crew en route from the all-nighter at the nearby Hordern Pavilion for a much-needed recovery breakfast. A sight to silence even the legendary Yabba? Perhaps.

Sydney remained my mailing address during the tour, along with a procession of floors, some with mattresses, all with cockroaches! Summer Hill, Petersham, Newtown, Ashfield; this was the wild west and with watering holes to match. The Summer Hill Hotel – chook raffle, meat tray and all – was the scariest of the lot. Fortunately Waldo, a local lawyer and buddy, was my ticket to safely and survival. Given the pub's reputation, a friendly local solicitor was always welcome. On the few occasions I found myself in town for the weekend Waldo and I would head to the North Shore and the fleshpots of Mosman: singlets and shorts not welcome! Tanned and toned with matching car and credit cards, the local gals – more lippy than lipo – were far scarier than the clientele of Summer Hill. In contrast to the resident rasmalai, Waldo and I arrived in a clapped-out VW with barely enough cash for a couple of beers and the petrol back west.

If asked to pick one highlight from the blur of cricket that southern summer it would have to be the final Test in Adelaide over the Australia Day weekend. Viv Richards scored two sublime 70s, at one point hitting the NSW quick Lenny Pascoe for four consecutive fours. The shorter and faster Pascoe bowled, the more languidly Richards deposited him into the picket fence between midwicket and backward square. But even this paled in comparison to Andy Roberts, who silenced a packed Australia Day crowd by dismissing the Chappell brothers in consecutive deliveries. Rumour has it that the only sound in and around the pavilion during this crucial period of play was Chappell the Elder's bat hitting the dressing room wall.

Having never won a series in Australia, Clive Lloyd not so much batted the home side out of the game as out of world cricket by leaving them a target of 574. At stumps on the fourth day Australia had limped to a miserable 131/7. The series over, I headed to the more calming waters of Canberra to make sense of the weeks on the road and to commit as much of it as I could remember to paper. I didn't manage to sell the finished manuscript – *Cricket on the Breadline* – but, in David Frith, found a friendly editor who published half a dozen extracts in *Wisden Cricket Monthly*.

* * *

Heading to Canberra at the tour's end, and in dire need of restorative funds, I was forced to use my law degree for the only time in my life and take work as a legal researcher. Prior to the job my Commonwealth Bank book (which I still have) listed a balance of just $20 followed by a withdrawal of $19. I was down every which way to my last dollar, no return flight, and no job! Desperate times call for desperate measures, hence a reluctant return to things legal. To add insult to insanity, I found myself in the Australian Capital Territory Land Titles Office and surrounded by wall-to-wall leases. Trust me, for someone who ploughed gamely through seven months of land law without understanding a single word, barely scraping a pass mark in the process, this was my worst nightmare. On the plus side, I was warm, dry, back in funds, and about to be introduced to the two-hour pub lunch.

Having survived the Land Titles Office, albeit only just, I was relocated to the National Capital Development Commission (NCDC) on Northbourne Avenue. I forget which floor and where I was sleeping at the time, but there is little doubt that when the call came to join a group house with Hels, Vinny, Trumpet and Fingers, I took it with both hands, a foot, groin, inside leg and pelvic floor. Just to clear up any misunderstanding: Fing and Trumpet were both called Sue, so we settled for identification purposes on their musical instrument of choice. If you think that a tad odd, then spare a thought for the house Labrador, Oshie, who was named after a very slow Japanese marathon runner in the Melbourne Olympics.

The property was U-shaped in design with a combined entrance and lounge leading to a large kitchen and dining area, the two arms of the U housing bedrooms, bathrooms, and studio. A sliding glass door led on to decking and an above-ground pool and garden. Of the pool, it took little time for the invention of a potential demonstration sport for the Sydney Olympics of Volleyduck. Ticking most of the IOC boxes, the sport seamlessly combined aqua fitness with green, environmental and wildlife issues. No ducks were harmed during the playing of this sport.

A friendly, drop-in, take us as you find us, sort of a house, the number for dinner could rise from two to ten while chopping veggies. An early visitor was Terry Arthur, who lived in Hong Kong. A fellow Pom, it was only natural that he and I should rendezvous in the early hours to watch the 1981 FA Cup Final replay between Spurs and Manchester City. With tea brewed, toast and marmalade readied, and a log fire roaring away for the second time that evening, we were joined by the ever-sociable Oshie. Delighted with another fire to flop in front of, he sighed, cast a cursory glance at the game, and set about hunkering down. And there he doggedly dozed until awoken by our hollering following Ricky Villa's stunning 76th-minute winner. The commotion duly woke household, street, suburb, and most of Canberra.

It was the practice of the NCDC at that time to host a happy hour - beers, wine, and party pies - after work on a Friday. With rolled suburban planning maps doubling as bats, scrunched paper as the ball, and waste bin as wickets, it was easy to turn boozy late afternoons into impromptu net sessions, after which my boss and I, his then wife owning an exclusive lingerie shop in Civic, would grab a six-pack and head for the storeroom where, surrounded by bras, panties, and suspender belts we'd partake of a few quiet ales. On the scale of does it get much better than that? Ask yourself. Does it really get much better than that?

On a slightly more serious cricket note, I was playing first-grade at the time for Woden. My skipper, Bruce Tapp, asked if I'd like to play a spot of Sunday social cricket for the Yass Golf Club. Sounded good to me. Or would have, had it not consisted of 60 overs a side, played during the heat of the day, and first entailing a car ride across the border into New South Wales. Lunch was invariably liquid and taken at a nearby pub, the sort of nearby pub with a corrugated tin roof. On one occasion sheep had to be removed from the paddock before the game could commence on a concrete strip painted green. At some point during the opposition innings a guy walked out to bat minus gloves and thigh pad; his demeanour suggesting that pads and box were a further imposition. He then proceeded to plant his front foot down the wicket and repeatedly crash the ball past me in the covers. Able to match tough with talent, we had in our ranks the teenage Peter Bowler (PB), who as a 17-year-old would score a fifty for ACT against Imran Khan's touring Pakistan side. He would later star for Australia in an under-19 Test series before turning his sights on England and a long and successful professional career as an opener for Leicestershire, Derbyshire and Somerset, scoring in excess of 19,000 runs with 45 centuries.

The open-plan dining room of our group house in Reid used, when the occasion demanded, to double as a dance floor. A handy feature for a party household. On one particular occasion we decided to host a *Rocky Horror* shindig. Thus, a little over an hour after walking off the field of play I was back home with cap replaced by platinum wig, shirt and flannels with a slinky black cocktail number, and Fingers and Trumpet applying a very passable job on the make-up front including black nail varnish. Whether by accident or design, but mainly the result of dress-up parties, I seemed to be sporting more than my fair share of frocks that summer. A point emphasised one day by a guy buttonholing me at the office and saying how good it was to see me in shirt and trousers for a change.

Late night turned early morning far too quickly and was accompanied by PB hammering on the front door for our 8am journey to Murrumbateman. There was just time to throw a little water over face, clean teeth, and grab a banana before heading out of the house and into the car. The game was already two or three overs old when we entered the fray. I headed for my usual position in the slips only to be summarily banished to the solitary acres of third man, to rue my late arrival and to further consider how I might remove the black nail varnish before being asked to bowl.

* * *

Having tired of titles and tie, I next found myself in Brisbane and, again seeking gainful employment, took work (along with 400 Vietnamese boat people) at the Golden Circle cannery. The train journey to and from the factory, with fellow workers hanging out of windows and doors, resembled a dizzying hack along the Mekong. I lasted for two weeks during which time I ate my body weight in pineapple and managed to all but halt production courtesy of caustic soda fumes and a following wind.

Back in Canberra, and thanks to a footy contact, I thought it only right and proper that I help build Australia's new parliament house. I was, at best, an average formwork labourer. The trickiest part of the job was Monday mornings. At that time, I was captaining a Portuguese football team. A no-nonsense, old-fashioned, English centre-half, most winter Sunday afternoons were spent kicking ten bells of shite out of nimble opposition forwards, a good many of whom I'd bump into around the site the following day.

During this six-month period I managed to stash enough cash to finance and follow England's exploits in the 1982/83 series down under. Returning to my Yarralumla lodgings following a last day on site I walked straight to the driveway dustbin and proceeded to deposit singlet, shorts, undies, socks, and finally boots before replacing the lid and walking bollock naked back into the house. After a long and decidedly alcoholic dinner with friends that night I was poured on to the early train to Sydney the following morning. My few belongings for a summer on the road had been throw into bin liners in the early hours and forced a bloodshot repack before arriving at Central.

Towards the end of the summer, I received a letter from my old Brighton skipper asking if I was available as ringer and in-house all-rounder for the NSW barristers' grudge game in Sydney against the Victorian Bar. The game offered a rare opportunity to play at the Paddington Barracks ground on Oxford Street. Of perhaps greater interest from a welfare perspective, however, was the post-match entertainment and I was set, albeit for just a few hours, to swap mattress for mansion. The evening event was at a huge house overlooking the harbour at Crow's Nest. My tactics were simple: eat solidly for an hour, drink for another, and then make polite conversation. A spectacular night in a spectacular setting, I recall at one point during the evening attempting to sell my law degree to a judge of the NSW Supreme Court.

As a result of that evening, I finished up playing club cricket for Lindfield – an XI once again top-heavy with the great and good of Sydney's legal profession – on the North Shore. One particular summer Lindfield rented the Bradman Oval at Bowral for an inter-club match with Australia taking on the Rest of the World. During the game I managed to clear the picket fence at long-off, the ball ricocheting off a mature gum tree. As I walked back to take guard the wicketkeeper mumbled, 'I bet Bradman hit that tree a few times!'

* * *

The Adelaide Oval in December 1982 was the ultimate in colonial chic: stylish wrought iron gates, the low-rise George Giffen Stand, manicured members' area, grassy banks at either end of the ground, an imposing scoreboard, and enough bare flesh, beer and barbies for the beach; add in the winding River Torrens, university parkland, nearby St Peter's Cathedral, and a backcloth of the Adelaide Hills and you had the most picturesque ground in world cricket. Two years after witnessing a historic first ever West Indies series win, I was back in Adelaide to watch England lose comfortably by eight wickets and go two down in the series after three Tests. While the action, from the tourists' perspective, was eminently forgettable, the Test would nevertheless change my cricketing life.

Prior to Adelaide I'd served a long and exhausting apprenticeship as a lone Pom against vastly unequal odds in the outer. The heat and dust you could just about cope with, but it was the flying cans and haymakers that added an extra frisson to the day. Remember: no plastic cups at this point in Australia's drinking history and NO light beer! During the previous couple of years, I'd had half a dozen or more articles published in *Wisden Cricket Monthly* by editor David Frith. We arranged a first meet during lunch on the second day. With bluff, bluster, and bull in equal measure he escorted me, not only into the members' area but into an altogether brave new world. A world *sans* singlets, shorts and flying stubbies. A world where conversation was courteous and cultured and could be conducted without fear of falling foul of a wildly thrown left cross. I had found peace, serenity and (arguably) civilisation. And wanted more.

Over dinner that night I settled on the ultimate blag. David's press pass was more or less the same size and colour as my Builders Labourers Federation (BLF) union card. The game was afoot. I arrived at the ground next morning dressed for the part: slacks, shirt, tie, jacket, briefcase, and the harassed look of a journo. Catching sight of Ian Chappell, I simply fell into step behind him and proceeded confidently through the press entrance showing only the briefest glimpse of my union card. Having cleared the first hurdle, there was still a further gate and steward before the inner sanctum. The same brisk, positive approach and I was through. My apprenticeship was over. And all thanks to a caring, sharing, construction industry union. The same union card continued giving for a further seven years before I secured a bona fide press pass thanks to the *Times of India*.

* * *

There is, to the best of my knowledge, just a single reference to Australia in the 56 Sherlock Holmes short stories by Sir Arthur Conan Doyle. In the *Boscombe Valley Mystery*, Conan Doyle introduces a bushranger by the name of Black Jack of Ballarat. It was precisely because of this literary reference, and the fact that the first ever English touring side to Australia in 1861/62 played in the Victorian country town, that I accepted an invitation to play against the Gentlemen of Ballarat for the Bar and Bench of Melbourne. The dusty old law degree coming up trumps yet again.

The non-playing captain of the Gentlemen was John (Spot) Hurley, a former World War II fighter pilot. Sporting a mop of hair and bowling off a long run-up, I might, in fading light, with myopic eyes, draw comparison with Bob Willis. Or so Spot thought – the impression helped by a four-wicket haul in the Ballarat innings – and promptly invited me back the following weekend to play for the Gentlemen against a St Kilda XI. During the post-match drinks, the Bar and Bench having recorded a comfortable win, I was summarily adopted by Spot's daughters and happily accepted their offer of a lift back to town. Wedged in the back with my kit, we hooned down the highway, the girls trying to make themselves heard as The Jam's 'Town called Malice' blared out of the Mini's game speakers. The return to Ballarat proved something of an anti-climax as we were soundly beaten by an experienced St Kilda side. Some 120 years earlier, the English tourists fared slightly better, although eventually running out of time while chasing victory against the Twenty-Two of Ballarat.

* * *

It has been a long-held opinion of mine that everyone, at some point in their life, should live above an Australian pub. Briefly homeless in the early 1990s, I took up residence at our Surry Hills local, the Shakespeare. While the combination of Tooheys and trifecta might have been a tad light on inspiration for the Bard, the pub nevertheless offered the chance to breathe deeply of vintage Australiana. For devotees of the TV series *Minder*, the Shakespeare proved an admirable replacement for the Winchester when the series moved for a couple of episodes to Sydney.

With time off for good behaviour I departed the Shakey, moving a few hundred yards to Phelps Street and a house share with an English cricketing buddy and gynaecologist. Word of warning: if placed in a similar situation, DO NOT read the textbooks harmlessly nestling by the telephone, and DO NOT on any account answer the phone when the nearby maternity hospital theatre sister is on the line and explaining that Mrs So and So is several centimetres dilated and would you pop along to the delivery suite. In between pub and placenta, Surry Hills proved the perfect location for easy access to the Sydney Cricket Ground (SCG).

While Test days filled the ground with a heady mix of outback and inner city, I leaned towards Sheffield Shield days when there was barely 1,000 in attendance and you could sit, sprawl, or sleep away the hours of play. The modest crowd saw the SCG Trust open only the members' area. The pavilion remained out of bounds, but that still left the Ladies' Stand and the sweeping expanses of the M.A. Noble Stand. The modest museum was also open at lunch and tea intervals or when play was a little too slow and the humidity a little too high.

In the late 1980s I met and became firm friends with Jack Blomfield. Jack was long time retired and a proud holder of the 50-year SCG membership badge. He would drive down from Pymble on the North Shore and park up close to the ground. He'd seen all the greats and was more than happy to yarn away a session or two. One particular morning we cared little for the play and instead pored over the local A-Z with Jack explaining the various tram routes and stops. That's the way cricket should be watched: on your own terms with not a fig for the players or state of play. Jack was a veteran subscriber to *Wisden Cricket Monthly* and was delighted when, during a Test in the late 1980s, I was able to drag David Frith away from his lunch to meet a loyal customer. It would have been good to sit them down and let them shoot the cricketing breeze, but the editor was always a stickler about not missing a ball of the action.

Shield days would see an appearance in the elongated press box at the back of the Noble Stand of legendary leg-spinner Bill (Tiger) O'Reilly. During a quiet Shield game, he was called by a sub at the *Sydney Morning Herald* and asked to compile his greatest ever Australian Test XI. O'Reilly happily obliged. With no constraints on selection his copy the following morning comprised eleven leg-spinners! That particular summer I'd brought my copy of Jardine's account of Bodyline to Oz with the sole purpose of getting O'Reilly, one of the key players in the five-Test drama, to autograph several pages and photographs. I buttonholed him on the concourse behind the Members. While signing he asked my name.

'Vic Mills.'

'Aren't you that fellow taking wickets over in WA?'

'I'm afraid not, that's Vic Marks.'

Ah, so near, yet so far.

Late leaving the SCG one evening, I spied the then South Australian coach Barry Richards heading towards the nets, bat in hand, with match-winning leg-spinner Peter Sleep. Sadly there was to be no cameo from the master batsman as Richards simply placed the bat on a length and instructed 'Sounda' to wheel away.

* * *

There is little doubt that in penning the line – four legs good, two legs bad – George Orwell had in mind a certain Blue Heeler by the name of Ziggy. An Australian cattle dog by profession, Zig found himself a much-loved member of the Gillard family of Brighton Beach. Spared the hard, unstinting work of cattle droving, he was more than happy to trade country for city, outback for armchair. Aware of his good fortune, he took to city living with all the grace and gusto he would otherwise have deployed chasing around a dry, dusty paddock or sitting imperiously among hay bales in the back of a ute. A sociable dog-about-town sort of a Blue Heeler,

Zig was, at best, a reluctant guard dog. And why not; there were always family members around or friends popping in for a glass of red. If that failed, then let's not forget he was a cattle dog. It wasn't his fault that the patio and tennis court contained zero cattle. Had the tennis court been grass instead of synthetic turf, and populated by Holsteins or Herefords, then I have no doubt he would have been up before dawn and herding to his heart's content. Well, maybe not. But a distinct lack of cattle for a cattle dog means only one thing: matinee time in Mooroolbark.

Not that his days were entirely sedentary. Fair go: there were always possums and postmen to chase. With no dogs allowed on Melbourne beaches after 7am, there was also his early morning hoon around Brighton Beach with a restorative dip in Port Phillip Bay to finish. Saturday morning there might be an excursion to Middle Brighton for coffee and conversation. In search of a small adventure one particular morning, he slipped the lead and finished up being fed from the breakfast table by local stars of stage and screen, Glenn Robbins and Eric Bana.

And, of course, there was always cricket. With floodlights around the tennis court, it would be fair to say that we were playing night cricket long before the IPL or Big Bash. And perhaps having a bit more fun, certainly if the noise level was anything to go by. So on came the lights, down came the net, stumps were pitched, batsmen took guard, bowlers measured their run-ups, at which point – as if to the accompaniment of a Boxing Day roar at 'The G' – Zig would saunter out to take up the fielding position he had made his own at deep long-off.

With a few too many legs to attempt the long barrier, he more than made up for it with his speed around the baseline. And if the ball was hit in the air a classic catch was not beyond him. Most of the time, however, he would nudge or nurdle a half chance into the side netting of the forehand court. Pleased with his efforts, he would grab the ball and, tail wagging, such fun, trot to the bowler where there would ensue a brief tug of war before dropping both ball and a liberal dollop of drool in readiness for the next delivery. Warney may have had much to contend with in his long and distinguished career, but never drool. And then, with little or no warning, Zig would tire of game and gallop. Unconcerned with the state of play, he would simply drop to his haunches and down tail: game over. No amount of cajoling could entice him back into the contest. And there he would stay, a distant look in his eyes, thinking not of a-droving down the Cooper, but the Fluffball he'd taken a fancy to a few blocks away.

Over and Out

CONTRARY TO public opinion, a club cricketer's lot is not all switch hit, scrambled seam, and scones. Ill met by sunlight, catastrophe and cock-up haunt the hours of play, while injury stalks cover point and crease waiting for its moment to break fingers, pull hamstrings, and tweak groins. In my own case it was a shoulder that merited not one dislocation – why bother to make the effort – but four!

In 1988, as part of Australia's bicentennial celebrations, an Aboriginal Cricket Association (ACA) team retraced the steps of a tour undertaken by their ancestors 120 years earlier. The itinerary of 1868 included a fixture against Lincolnshire on the Lindum. Lest it be forgotten another decade would pass before a white Australian XI toured England. During my Canberra cricketing days, I played against one of the ACA tourists, Neil Bulger. In the Woden vs Queanbeyan fixture that southern summer, Neil scored a mighty hundred on the first Saturday of the game and followed it a week later by bowling us out twice in the day, collecting a five-fer in each innings.

In the days leading up to the fixture I visited a local orthopaedic specialist with a troublesome knee. He declared the joint fit for play and mentioned that he'd be at the game. Matchday dawned bright and sunny, perfect weather for the 1,000 or so spectators who ringed the ground. Thrown the new ball, I achieved an early breakthrough having their skipper caught behind. Returning in the afternoon session, and seeking that extra half yard of pace, I conspired through a traumatic trifecta of rip, tear, and wrench to separate shoulder from socket. Where once upright and in delivery stride, I was now a heap and a decidedly crumpled one at that. From my vantage point on all threes life didn't look or feel too good. On the plus side, the contortionist in me – don't try this at home – now appeared able to lace my boots while bending over backwards with my arm between my legs. It was a slow and increasingly painful passage from pitch to pavilion. A call went out over the PA for a doctor. Who should walk into the dressing room a moment later but my jaunty jointster from earlier in the week? In urgent need of pain relief, and caring not for his healing touch, I offered a simple self-diagnosis, 'Knee? Fine. Shoulder? F**ked!'

* * *

Although I have no hard evidence to back this up, it is my suspicion that club cricketers feel failure and ill fortune far more than their professional counterparts. Of course, this could just be an urban myth put about by mythical urban cricketers, but I for one still suffer past failures far more than any success that might have come my way. As Cream and Jack Bruce ventured in 'Born Under A Bad Sign', if it wasn't for bad luck I wouldn't have no luck at all.

For instance, and thanks to a 1967 Lindum fixture card, I recall a first XI away game on Saturday, 1 July at Forest Amateurs. At 15 years and eight months I was, by some distance, the junior member of the side. No plea of mitigation, this. However, before the first hour was up, I managed to drop both openers who went on to post 170 for the first wicket. To compound the missed chances, I was called upon late in the innings to bowl youthful off spin, recording deeply unflattering figures of 6-0-46-1. A chastening afternoon and one that remains to this day. The fact that I took two screamers the next afternoon against a strong Cleethorpes side did little to lessen the hurt. If it wasn't for bad luck, I wouldn't have no luck at all.

On the basis that we all have a run-out tale – and here bad luck is the prime mover, or in this case remover – I was run out the following year in a second XI game on the Sobraon Barracks without facing a ball. By a country mile, this is the cruellest of dismissals. Poor calling, overzealous backing up, a slip, a slide, an expert pick-up and throw, you name it – the charge sheet is long and unforgiving. And all you can do, on an afternoon that offered such promise, is wander back to the pavilion, unbuckle your pads, and rue whatever deity it is that oversees club cricketers. If it wasn't for bad luck, I wouldn't have no luck at all.

Real ill fortune and with it lasting pain, however, can only be found down under. A first season of Melbourne club cricket in 1978 brought me into contact with a playing regime that basically involves your team batting one Saturday and the opposition the next. To this end, most games are drawn with points awarded on first-innings scores. An outright win is still possible should a side be bowled out twice and the required runs knocked off or an innings win recorded. A rare enough occurrence all the same unless, that is, the elements intervene. This was exactly the case during a fixture for Brighton Cricket Club.

By way of getting my retaliation in first, I should remind you that, despite this particular game, Brighton went all the way to the three-day Grand Final that season, missing out on winning the flag by just three runs. But on this particular day, having fielded all the previous Saturday, we set about our innings amid rain and bad light. By the time this had blown through we had already been bowled out cheaply. Asked to bat a second time, we were caught on a drying wicket with the obvious consequences. Having failed to trouble the scorers in the first dig I was a reluctant returnee to the wicket in the second. Pitch apart, the difficulty was compounded by a very good opposition leg-spinner. In fact, every side we played that summer seemed to have a very good leg-spinner. In a decade of club cricket at home I would have encountered no more than a handful of leggies and not terribly good ones at that. To cut a long and miserable story short, I did my bit for Anglo-Australian relations and dutifully bagged a pair. If it wasn't for bad luck, I wouldn't have no luck at all.

A few years later, now safely back in the UK, I was selected for a Lincolnshire A game at Bourne against a strong Northants second XI. To compound the potential for suffering and shame, my parents ferried me to the ground and stayed on to watch. As is the courtesy in such fixtures the county side is given first knock. This, I suspect, is no more than a ruse to take the game late into the afternoon and thus ensure that both lunch and tea, already bought and under preparation, will actually be eaten. With the new ball in hand, and nervous as a kitten, although that might be doing a disservice to kittens, I did my best to give the Northants openers the perfect start by barely managing to pitch a delivery on the cut strip. After posting figures of 6-0-38-0 I was mercifully taken out of the firing line much to the delight of first slip who had borne the brunt of my waywardness. Bad, but it got worse as, fielding at backward square midway through the innings, I managed to shell a straightforward catch from Robin Boyd-Moss. The well-timed pull shot lasered at my midriff was in, out, and grassed in the time it took to growl an expletive. The wretched day was rounded off by a brief appearance at the crease and a complete and utter failure to trouble the scorers. If it wasn't for bad luck, I wouldn't have no luck at all.

Three days later Bourne visited Lincoln for a South Lincs & Border League match at the Lindum. Posting around 150, we stared down the barrel with the visitors handily placed at 70/1. It was then that the skipper threw me the ball. It was he, by the way, who had been first slip and resident Aunt Sally against Northants days earlier. Having shortened my run-up to give what I hoped was added balance, I proceeded to bag 6-10 with a flurry of yorkers that had little to do with me and far more with a random evening up of fortunes by cricket's All-seeing One. Victory out of the jaws of defeat then and a modicum of payback for events of the previous Wednesday. Standing on the steps as we walked off was Bourne's former Lincs player, David Johnson. He'd been on hand to witness my shambles of a performance days earlier. I couldn't resist. I smiled, looked him straight in the eyes and offered, 'Funny old game, cricket.'

It's not always funny ha ha, but this ridiculous game does have its moments. As club cricketers we don't always get the chance to set the record straight; most of the time we just take it on the chin and look to the next game or weekend. But the hurt remains long after stumps have been drawn. Yes, if it wasn't for bad luck, I wouldn't have no luck at all.

* * *

By way of a window into cricket's past, I possess the last remaining Lindum Cricket Club blazer in existence. While not a stitch (or patch) on the Shroud of Turin, carbon dating nevertheless puts the blazer at somewhere in the mid-to-late 1930s. Which seems about right. I mean, with fascism threatening the world order, what else would you do other than nip down to your tailor and get him to run up a rather natty rainbow jacket? All very Bertram Wilberforce Wooster. By way of lineage, it appears the blazer was originally the pride of Lindum club member Fred Newsome. At some point in the 1950s he handed it on to my long-time mentor and mucker, 'Big Jim' Quincey. Thirty or so years on, although no money changed hands, I persuaded Quincey to part with the blazer for several pints of Foster's over several summers. By the late 1980s the wearing of blazers, MCC members apart, had long since dropped out of fashion. In their heyday – the unwritten rule being the more garish the better – blazers were worn before play, during luncheon and tea intervals, and after the game over a pipe and pink gin.

Without the cricketing wherewithal for such an appearance, I was nevertheless able to debut the Lindum blazer at the Henley Royal Regatta in the late 1980s. It proved the perfect event too in that stripy multi-coloured blazers were very much the rule as opposed to the exception. Having proved its worth in at least one social situation it seemed only right and proper to take the blazer overseas. First stop New Delhi, although as a tasty morsel for moth and mite it never left the secure environment of bag or hotel left luggage, as I backpacked around the subcontinent.

The next stop on the blazer's *tour de force* was Australia and Melbourne. As I waited for my press pass to arrive, and thanks to a kind invitation from the Gillard clan, the blazer headed off to the annual first Tuesday in November running of the Melbourne Cup. Five or so weeks of thin rations in and around India had little prepared either me or the blazer for a day-long picnic that started in the members' car park around ten in the morning. With a profusion of fine wines and fizz the strategy had to be one of moderation. By mid-afternoon, however, it would be fair to say I was flying and engaged in deep conversation about all things Indian with a teacher from one of the very best gals' schools in Melbourne. So, would I go and give a talk to her gals about India? While a room full of nubile sixth-formers was enticing, I did have just enough wits about me to decline the offer, citing the Test and one-day schedule.

Early in the following January the blazer made its debut at the Sydney Cricket Ground for a one-dayer between Australia and England. A curious occasion as, with borrowed MCC tie, the searingly colourful combination of vertical striped blazer and bacon and egg tie gave me the appearance of a Jackson Pollock canvas twinned with a malfunctioning early colour television. The blazer, and in particular the tie, led to many offers of drinks throughout the hours of play. Which in turn brought about the surreal situation of us drinking, talking, and watching the game on TVs in the members' bar, while no more than 20 or so yards behind us through ceiling-to-floor windows the action was taking place very live and very instant.

The blazer was to see many more Henley Regattas before taking a well-earned sabbatical. Indeed, the next time it surfaced was at 'Big Jim's' funeral. There was absolutely no way, after such a life lived as his, that I was turning up at the service in sombre black. So out came the blazer and with it a fitting send-off and celebration.

* * *

The problem with games against near neighbours Collingham started long before the toss and opening overs. They started in the car park. By that I mean it was useful, in judging the likely quality of the opposition, to take a quick peek for any vehicles bearing the Nottinghamshire County Cricket Club logo, it being the practice of first-class counties on non-matchdays to expect their contracted players to turn out for local club sides. On this particular day I spied three Notts fleet cars belonging to opener Paul Todd, all-rounder Kevin Saxelby, and young wicketkeeper Chris Scott. The omens were not good. A day of leather chasing looked on the cards.

A decade earlier Collingham had built many an innings around their captain, Dusty Hare, who just happened to captain Notts seconds at the time, farm the local Nottinghamshire countryside, and in whatever spare time remained play full-back for the England rugby union XV. Summer just wouldn't be summer if Dusty hadn't taken a hundred off us either at Collingham or on the Lindum. Downcast on spying the cars, it would be fair to say that depression had well and truly set in by the time I made the short walk to the dressing room. Much of this had to do with the fact that I'd be taking the new ball that afternoon and was in fact still licking my wounds from the previous season and another mauling from Mr Todd.

On that occasion I'd careened in enthusiastically off a 25-yard run-up only for Todd to plant a large front pad down the wicket and bludgeon the ball high past my left shoulder and at several times the velocity of myself as I, still in motion, wheeled away taking evasive action in the process. On a scale of worse things to happen on a cricket pitch, the lofted straight drive over the bowler's head ranks high on the Richter Scale of Disillusionment. Not that my bowling had much art or craft about it. This was a continuation from club cricket in Melbourne where to the surprise of many, not least myself, I'd been press-ganged into taking the new ball due to the absence and illness of others far more suited. Once back in Blighty, however, and denied the comfort of hard, bouncy Victorian wickets, my cover was blown.

I brought little to the new ball for the Lindum other than a willingness to the cause and a devastating naivety in the science of quick bowling. I simply ran in as fast and as balanced as I could and released the ball. End of story. If it swung, which it didn't very often, then so be it; if it moved off the seam, then three cheers for me. But none of this movement whether in the air or off the pitch was any of my doing. My follow-through was no less unplanned and chaotic as I wheeled away to the off, hair every which way, and spectacles perched precariously on the edge of my nose. I remember bowling uphill and into the wind at Spalding one early August evening and proceeded to deliver an over of perfect leg cutters. None resulted in a wicket, sadly, although it was worth the effort if only for the look of incredulity on the slips, wicketkeeper, and batsman. But don't get excited. For just as quickly as they came the leg cutters disappeared never to be seen again.

But back to the Collingham game. I forget whether we won or lost the toss; all I do remember is that we were soon in the field, and I was taking the new ball and marking my run-up. In an effort to reverse the previous summer's slaughter of the innocent I opted for the Pavilion End, all the while trying not to be intimidated by the Notts sweater and several thousand County Championship runs currently taking guard 22 yards away. Had I been thinking straight, or thinking at all, then now might be the right time to bring out that perfect yorker; to laser in an unplayable sand-shoe crusher with the new batsman yet to get a sighter or feel for pitch or play. Had I been a thinking sort of a bowler then that certainly sounds like a strategy. But I was not that thinking sort of a bowler and thus had no discernible strategy other than to careen in and let the delivery and devil take the hindmost.

The stunned silence that followed from team-mates as that first ball crashed into the base of the stumps remains with me today. We all, to a man, felt a strange kind of collective embarrassment. There was no wild whooping or hollering or high fives or hugging. Just an eerie silence. I felt as though I should approach the batsman and at the very least apologise, while at the same time explaining that other than the obvious, it was really none of my doing. The yorker, as if my mythical leg cutters, had come and gone, and most likely would never be seen again. But I didn't. So, we loitered awkwardly in the middle – small groups, hushed conversation – waiting on the next Notts sweater and the resumption of normal service.

* * *

The current first dictum of cricket is quite simply to keep your head while all around others are losing theirs. To assist in the art and craft of self-preservation batsmen now have a helmet to aid their cause. This was not always the case. The very first helmet I saw was in Melbourne circa January 1978 and was, you won't be surprised to hear, part of the hype and hoopla involved in Kerry Packer's World Series Cricket. Not quite the fashion accessory it is today, the early prototype looked as if it had just been stolen from the moped of a pizza delivery boy. White, no visor, and large chin strap; yes, it was that bad. However, when faced with the full force of the West Indian pace battery along with a supporting cast of Dennis Lillee, Len Pascoe, Mike Procter, and Imran Khan then anything was better than nothing.

Cricket equipment in general – and the helmet in particular – has come a long way since then, not least among the amateur ranks where they are all but compulsory nowadays and, you suspect, one of the first items to be packed. It was a rough ride, however, before they became universally accepted. The first one I came across in club cricket was the property of our skipper, 'Young Jim', son of 'Big Jim' Quincey. A talented cricketer, he played several seasons with both the Civil Service XI and Lincolnshire's minor counties side. Of course, once purchased, the helmet surfaced on every possible occasion, sporting or social, so that player and helmet could bond.

Unfortunately, the first time 'Young Jim' chose to wear it in a competitive game was an away fixture at Market Deeping and against the slowest left-arm spinner in creation. I couldn't bear to watch. Eyes covered, as if face to face with the Gorgon, I fled to the pavilion.

I was part of the crossover generation between non-helmet and helmet wearing, but didn't feel the need to acquire one. I was happy with my Lindum cap and happier still, being a natural hooker, to take on any short-pitched bowling whether at home or abroad. By way of backup, this being the 1980s, I also sported a head of permed hair. Critical data supports the theory that 'Big Hair', allied to near toxic levels of perming solution, combined to form the perfect headguard in the event of collision between cranium and Kookaburra (ball and bird).

In 30 years of club cricket I actually wore a helmet on just two occasions. The first involved the short trip to nearby Gainsborough for an Albion Cup match. Afternoon rain had conspired to produce a glue pot of a wicket: greasy on top, hard underneath. The opposition had a big unit of a bowler by the name of Pinder. Not quick, but tall, he was able to make the ball bounce disconcertingly. This he did early in the innings. I went back and across in readiness to pull only for the ball to stick in the surface. I was round on the shot before the ball arrived and it struck me on the back of the head. Although it was more glancing blow than direct hit, I took the mandatory eight count and then asked for a helmet. The very next delivery, again short, was duly dispatched.

The only other time a helmet was called for was in the far grander surroundings of Grace Road. I was a late replacement on the eve of the game for Lincolnshire A vs Leicestershire seconds. Seconds they may have been, but nine of the 11 on duty that day had current or past first-class experience including Test bowlers Les Taylor, Chris Lewis, and Winston

Benjamin. As all visiting teams do on such occasions, whether by accident or design, we offered first knock to the county pros. One of their number just happened to be my old mate from Canberra grade cricket, Peter Bowler. He and I had played Saturday club cricket for Woden and social Sunday cricket for the Yass Golf Club. PB sought me out before the game and we briefly caught up on old times. He then opened the innings and compiled a stylish 90 as Leicestershire posted 260/4.

Having only played a couple of these games before I was a little rusty on protocols. The protocol in question being that a club cricketer is deemed to be taking the piss, and lots of it, should he arrive at the crease without a helmet. The fact that I didn't possess a helmet was not up for discussion, there being no time as the first ball was already on its way. It would be fair to say that for one or two deliveries from Chris Lewis I didn't hit the ball. That is, the ball hit my bat. Seeing a short-pitched delivery, I moved back and was in the process of playing a defensive shot when the ball cannoned into my bat.

Trudging off at the tea interval, PB jogged alongside and asked if I had a helmet. No, but I could get one. I returned wearing one and to my surprise found every delivery from the faster bowlers in the post-tea session handily pitched in my half of the wicket. As a result, I compiled an artisan 42 before falling leg before to England under-19 quick Lloyd Tennant. With head still conveniently attached to body I set off for the pavilion. As I passed Chris Lewis at mid-off he turned and said, 'Well played.' Helmet by moonlight, indeed.

* * *

It was a wretched, desolate afternoon and early evening promised little improvement. That said, and as you might expect from a combination of cafeteria bowling and cotton wool clouds, it didn't start out that way. In actual fact the day, a July Saturday, dawned hot and expectant. For club cricketers countrywide it was the sort of day to win the toss, elect to bat, and then fill yer boots! And the Lindum did just that, posting a total of 240 something in the allotted 45 overs. A match-winning score and one to which I contributed the princely sum of just four runs. Thankfully, time has erased any possible plea of mitigation. Although, the club cricketer's locker is not short on excuses: the only ball to deviate all afternoon, a classic catch, a brilliant pick-up and throw, a lengthy partnership, and a long time with the pads on. It could have been any one of these or even a combination. The outcome, however, was still the same and saw me change quickly into T-shirt and shorts before heading towards the Lindum's Empty Quarter to quietly fume away the afternoon, taking the cricketing gods to task for my abject and acutely personal failure.

There would be little chance to address the situation with the ball, either, as the post-tea session would be dominated by the spinners with the faster bowlers tasked with little more than taking the shine off the ball. Banished, for my sins, to the boundary, I was left with even more time to reflect and repent. No bad thing as it turned out as, by stumps, my mood had lightened and, after a long shower, I was ready for clubhouse and conviviality. By a lucky happenstance, Lindum had scheduled a cheese and wine fundraiser that evening and a combination of fellowship and fromage amply fuelled by the fermented did the trick. So much so in fact that by the time the club steward started muttering about locking up and heading home we were the last group standing, or rather swaying. We numbered seven in total and had all supped well during the evening. As part reward and part bribe for vacating the premises the steward plated up and handed over the remains of the cheese and off-cuts of baguette.

Heading out of the ground, the clock nearer one than midnight, we made a noisy way up The Grove and on to Nettleham Road. Respect, here, to the lighting department of Lincoln City Council, for the street lighting was so bright as to unfurrow the brow of even Dickie Bird. The combination of light and a total lack of traffic (Lincoln having gone to bed hours ago) set an idea in motion. A veteran of many day/night matches down under, I saw no reason, in light of the favourable conditions, why we couldn't stage England's first ever limited-overs match under lights, right here, RIGHT NOW! With that I opened my kit bag and proceeded to pad up on the pavement, adding cap, thigh pad, and gloves for good measure and all the while explaining my idea to the rest of the guys and gals. The hidden agenda, of course, was an unexpected chance to right the wrongs of the afternoon and enjoy a second innings. A total lack of traffic cameras proved the only disappointment as there would be no permanent record of the play, performances, or potential for criminal proceedings.

Happy to join in the fun, Young Dicky was detailed as keeper behind imaginary stumps; Sue and Gary patrolled the off side in front of the red postbox, with Andy and Janey positioned at square leg and deep midwicket, respectively. Sacky, the Pride of Darlington, opted to take the new ball, or in this case the new cheese from the paper plate containing the redundant pieces. Although denied television coverage we did have commentary supplied by Radio Lincolnshire's very own sports presenter, Andy, recently back from a stint with the BBC World Service sports department. Alternating, as the play and Pinot took him, between his native Cornish and a passable impersonation of John Arlott's Hampshire burr, he seemed happy to add a professional touch to the otherwise decidedly amateur production unfolding before him.

Having arrived at the wicket I proceeded to do a spot of tarmacadam gardening before using the white lines as a guide to a suitable guard. Aware that to pitch the ball (sorry, cheese) would be an altogether counterproductive move, it looked like full tosses of varying height and speed would be the order of the night. To a now hushed crowd Sacky ran in and delivered a rotating chunk of mature Cheddar. In an effort to get an early feel for conditions I pushed solidly forward, bat and pad close together. While not exactly pinging off the middle – more my lack of timing than the quality of the deli or delivery – the slice hit the splice, teetered a little, and then reluctantly headed towards the tarmac. Indicating I was about to handle the cheese – I didn't want to join the admittedly limited list of those given out handled cheese – I picked it up, gave it a cursory squeeze, and threw it back. The next delivery was arrowed down the leg side and needed just a flick off the hip to send it high over backward square, pavement, and fence and on to the lawn of the nearby Bromhead private hospital.

Thinking he might have better luck with the baguette, Sacky positioned his fingers as if for an away swinger and set it in motion. Moving on to the back foot, I executed a passable – more than passable given the hour and alcohol intake – late cut and sent it skittering down a nearby gutter in the direction of Lincoln Cathedral. A second piece of baguette, delivered wider still, enabled me to throw the kitchen sink at it and slice it high over backward point, beyond a stone wall, and into the private garden of a very large house.

Having seen enough, Sacky collected his imaginary cap and sweater from the imaginary umpire and made his way to extra cover. Gary took over possession of the cheese plate and opted for a chunk of Red Leicester. Executing a well-timed slog sweep, this went the way of the Cheddar. With confidence high I used my feet to further floated offerings of Caerphilly and Cheshire and again sent them over the fence and on to the manicured lawn of the Bromhead. Adopting the clipped vowels of Trevor Bailey, Andy suggested that a change to a semi-hard Cornish Yarg or Wensleydale might prove more difficult to play. Undaunted, and making up for lost time and the afternoon's disappointment, cheese and baguette were sent arcing high over fence and wall. In a last-ditch attempt to unsettle and unnerve (bring forth the *fromage de belle France*) the two remaining pieces of Brie and Camembert (pasteurised? Yeah, but not intimidatory) were brought into the attack, but with little or no success.

With drinks called, and the remains of a showy little Chablis passed around, it was agreed to bring proceedings to a close rather than risk injury from an errant piece of baguette. With handshakes and hugs all round, the time now nearer two than one, we headed towards Newport Arch and our various beds. Thankful for the chance of a second innings, I didn't bother to remove my kit, but wandered happily off into the night: cap low, spirits high.

As to the lasting significance of the UK's introduction to night cricket? Other than several hangovers and the collective need on waking for strong coffee and aspirin, the consensus is – none whatsoever! But what of the lasting significance on the hospital's head gardener? This remains an open verdict. The scenario is of much head-scratching and chin-stroking early on the Monday morning as he surveyed his lawns and shrubberies now festooned with French bread and what looked like the contents of a cheese platter. A mystery of *X-Files* proportions, there is every likelihood that in a snug bar somewhere in Lincoln this very day, a still perplexed and now retired head gardener continues to tell his cheese story to the dubious and disbelieving.

* * *

I think it would be fair to say I was not temperamentally suited to captaincy. This may have had something to do with pushing a Burghley Park opener (a Burberry male model for those in pursuit of trivia) as he threatened to run into me while I stood in double teapot mode at the end of my follow-through; or for turning my back on a finger-wagging umpire at Bourne as he attempted to chastise me for kicking out at the pitch in frustration; or for telling Andy Afford, the Notts left-arm spinner, to 'go look at the f**king scoreboard' as he preened and postured at the popping crease after I'd swept him over square leg for six! While all are worthy of mitigation pleas, their combined worth more than accounted for the lack of approach by the Lindum committee for any proposed leadership role.

There was also the small matter of a captain's post-match responsibility of making polite conversation with the visiting skipper over beer. This might have been a little delicate if there had been an incident. Another incident, that is. An incident that, if not directly involved, I had been a far from innocent Man on a Clapham Omnibus. I was a dawdler too in that, an hour or more after play I could still be found in the dressing room mulling over the game before taking a leisurely shower, dressing, and packing. I would eventually head to the clubhouse, but with no particular itinerary other than paying match fees, giving my availability for next weekend, and thinking of food. Hardly the cut of a leadership candidate.

On the rare occasions I was handed the captaincy – just three instances over a period of 30 years – it was either for a Friday friendly against a touring team where limited availability meant a Lindum XI heavily reliant on juniors or on the odd occasion, last senior standing and all that, where the first team was hit by representative calls. Of the former

I recall a Friday game where, with six or seven juniors in the side, we had kept the opposition run rate in check during the afternoon with some courageous fielding under hot sun only for the opposition skipper to delay his declaration. Five o'clock came and went. So too five and ten past, at which point, feeling rightly aggrieved, I called loudly for a second drinks break, making the implied point in the process that enough was enough. There was also the very real prospect that any later and it would be bath and bedtime for some of the more junior members of the side. With the cordial barely opened and the Sandman stirring, a declaration was called.

There was, as far as I could see, no mid-point to the Art of Captaincy. On those rare occasions when called upon, I would continually hover between righteous indignation at some perceived breach of protocol by the opposition skipper or find myself in pursuit of a slice of Churchillian rhetoric to incite and inspire the troops. An example of the latter, a turn of phrase that I suspect the great man may have worked into one of his rallying wartime speeches had he ever found himself in the east of England, on a wet Sunday afternoon, confronted with limited playing resources, and heavy overnight rain having leaked under the covers.

So, there we were: Peterborough! The northernmost reaches of London overspill. If that were not bad enough, it was the sort of windswept afternoon that played havoc with the ears of a Basset Hound. Bad for the Basset, but not particularly good for Lindum as, with a decidedly lightweight XI, we were looking down the barrel. One of the few senior players on duty that day was an opening bowler of yeoman stock, Keith Smith. We walked slowly to the middle noting in passing the damp outfield, scudding clouds and, on reaching the pitch, an 18in square of wet wicket – the result of overnight rain and a malfunctioning cover system. The wet area was close to a length and as such offered promise and with it hope. With this in mind, and summoning all my Churchillian resolve, I placed an arm over Smithy's shoulders and offered the following words of inspiration and encouragement, 'Mate, you've had to sleep on the damp patch often enough, now try and bowl on it!'

* * *

For reasons that will become obvious there will be several redacted passages in the following tale. It is early September in Melton Mowbray, home of the pork pie. The first leaves of autumn tumble across the outfield. I decide on three sweaters for the post-tea fielding session and have already told the skipper that I will field only at mid-on and mid-off, third man and fine leg. In light of the afternoon's events, he agrees, and I shuffle off into the gloaming. It's not that my body is shutting down but, with no sleep in the last 36 hours, it is showing distinct signs of seizing up. I tried to grab a few minutes' sleep in the dressing room during the tea interval, but failed. A team-mate was kind enough to bring a mug of tea and a bun. I rallied briefly, just enough to don flannels and sweaters before treading a laboured path on to the outfield.

Twenty-four hours earlier: a Friday night in uptown Lincoln. I'd agreed a meet for drinks with REDACTED. She passed through Lincoln occasionally and it was our practice to get together for a catch-up. As the evening progressed, she suggested we get a room. REDACTED. We retired (no luggage) to a second floor not-quite-suite of the Tower Hotel in Westgate and, in the words of Ian Dury, she took me to the cleaners and other misdemeanours. It was a sleepless REDACTED sort of a night, there being the need to take a fresh guard on several occasions. While much of the evening is now a blur, I distinctly remember us taking a bath around six o'clock in the morning, which must have annoyed the neighbours no end, then we dressed, declining the early breakfast and preferring instead to motor around Lincoln's bypass to an American diner. I was eventually dropped off around 10.30am, giving me just enough time to pack and make ready for the journey to Melton.

Given that my eyes, as Shakespeare might have ventured, were like piss 'oles in the snow, my team-mate and driver soon realised there had been debauchery afoot. This was to be no kiss-and-tell car journey, though. So we skirted around the hours of darkness as I attempted but ultimately failed to sleep. All was not lost, however, as with a bit of luck our skipper would win the toss, take first knock, I could then bat down the order and try to get some restorative shuteye. We arrived a little late at the Melton Mowbray ground and bumped into the skipper who had indeed just won the toss. Following him into the dressing room he told me to pad up and open, and my team-mate/driver to take the first umpire shift. REDACTED.

To say that I batted in braille for those first few overs would be something of an understatement. Having difficulty focusing, let alone focusing on the ball, I pushed myopically down what I thought was the correct line. Sadly, in the words of Henry Blofeld, I was playing down the Piccadilly Line while the ball was actually on the Bakerloo. My chum in the white coat decided this was the funniest thing he'd seen all season and did little to hide it. And then, more by luck than judgement, bat and ball collided, and I was away. As if by magic the fog lifted, headache departed, eyes cleared, feet moved, and the adrenalin flowed. The early morning REDACTED left me mildly euphoric and arguably more relaxed than I have ever been at the crease. Amid all this unexpected well-being the runs flowed. I raced to a fifty, batted a little more circumspectly to a hundred, and at the start of the 41st over was 118 not out and looking at a 140 with a fair wind.

Sadly there was to be no fair wind. Reacting unselfishly to a hastily called single, and forgetting that non-strikers can still say no, I was run out by half the pitch. Not even in the frame. I wandered off heavy-legged, the early morning and late afternoon taking hold. Once in the dressing room I discarded my pads, box, gloves, and thigh pad, and curled up on one of the benches. I was conscious of congratulations and kind words but wanted only sleep.

I don't doubt for one minute that professional cricketers take such nights into day in their stride. But we amateurs are a different breed. For sure, we can have nights of excess. Afternoons too. But rarely, if ever, do we combine the two. And so there I lay, sleepless in Melton and aching from head to toe. Then the tea and bun arrived and life improved. Although it would be fair to say I was not looking forward to a couple of hours in the field, autumn closing in, muscles seizing up, vital functions closing down.

Fortunately for me, the bowlers did their bit and Melton were hustled out for just 61 in 26.2 overs; Lindum's winning margin was a healthy 149 runs. An anonymous figure in the gloaming, I was called upon to do very little during the mercifully short session. Back in the dressing room I even managed to shower and dress without any help before tumbling back in the car and dozing my way to Lincoln. Rather than drop me home we drove back to my chum's house. His wife put out a little supper and I started to perk up. Just then the doorbell rang. A shiver passed. No. Surely not.

* * *

It had been a long, slow decline into cricketing retirement brought about by injuries in general and a much-dislocated shoulder in particular. Not that I was too bothered at the death. Thirty years a first XI player meant that I was not going to linger in the seconds, although kudos to those who do. I'd never been a supporter of a play-as-long-as-you-can philosophy. If I couldn't come charging in from 25 yards or throw myself around in the field then to hell with it. I called time as a Lindum player and happily took my place on the other side of the boundary surrounded by books, newspapers, transistor radio and my treasured Sydney beach mat. And all was hunky dory until the phone went late one Friday evening in August. It was the first XI skipper. We're a man short for tomorrow's home game and would I mind stepping into the breach?

By the following lunchtime I'd located flannels, shirt, sweaters and all my batting paraphernalia. Time then to retrace old steps to club and ground. The dressing room was friendly enough, but it had changed since our heyday in the late 1980s, when the next party was just as important as the next wicket. It had been a raucous, free-wheeling time with a first XI to match. The philosophy, certainly among an enlightened few, was of an uncomplicated amateur game: 50 per cent played out on the paddock and 50 per cent in the bar! On this particular day – the content of the team, arguably more skilled than in our pomp, was aided and abetted by several minor county players – the dressing room seemed somehow more austere and far less fun and frivolous.

We batted first under leaden skies. The top order performed admirably and the last batting bonus point, the score reaching 200, was achieved easily inside the 45 overs. With a late flurry of wickets, I padded up as we started the final over. With a wicket falling off the fourth ball I collected my batting inners and gloves and started the long walk, the wicket being on the far side of the square, for what would quite definitely be the last time. During that long march I can't say that my years as a Lindum player flashed before my eyes. Far from it. With few spectators and grey skies, it was all very downbeat. There were no tears in my eyes, either, as was supposedly the case with Bradman at The Oval in 1948. However, at some point between pavilion and pitch I came to a quite momentous decision.

After three decades of batting as a right-hander I thought it would be fun, and somehow oddly fitting, to face the very last two balls of a long career as a left-hander. Approaching the crease, I nodded acknowledgement to our umpire. Addressing him politely but firmly I asked for two legs, spun around into the left-hander's stance, and proceeded to scratch and mark my guard. Given that we were still several years away from Kevin Pietersen's 'switch hit' it did feel slightly strange to get into my stance back to front. A bit of fun, maybe, but I was not about to throw my wicket away with a swing and a miss. If anything, and having had at least ten seconds to think this through, I settled on propping forward, bat and pad together, hoping for an inside edge down to fine leg. No such luck, I'm afraid. This left-handed caper was a little more difficult than it looked. There was to be no final addition to my name in the scorebook as the bowler adopted the perfect wicket to wicket line and tied me up in a confusion of bat and pads. Still, I survived, and the innings closed with Lindum a run or two shy of 250. A winning score in August just as it would be in April.

This, alas, was not the consensus with the collective and waiting minor counties players in the home dressing room. They were not impressed. Ooops! Couldn't see the funny side of it. Not even, as I took lengths to explain, that it was the perfect way to bring down the curtain. It shows strength of character, I continued. It was a statement. Not standing for any chaff or nonsense from the game. Going out on my terms. Even if those terms just happened to be cack-handed. With still no lightening of the mood I left them to dissect and debate and trooped off happily to the tea room. A last Lindum tea and with it the chance to show off my newfound dexterity by eating sandwiches, cake, and dispatching tea with both my right and my newly discovered left hand.

Flights of Fancy

Available on the NHS

CRICKET, AS a game, is not suited to change and certainly not at the pace we have today. As each week brings new competitions, formats, procedures, protocols, terminology, and personnel so this works only to corrode the very cornerstones of the game. The primary one of which is the inalienable right of the paying public or county members to slumber away a session or two during four-day Championship games, there being nothing better than a slow second afternoon's play between Somerset and Gloucestershire at Taunton to encourage heavy eyelids, a nodding head, and finally a deep and restful sleep. In today's society where sleep, for any number of reasons, is at a premium then the County Championship should be available on the NHS or prescribed by your local GP as the perfect non-addictive vehicle to refresh and restore.

From the restful white clothing of players and officials to the steady hum of expectation among the patrons as they grapple with four down in the *Telegraph* crossword, so the building blocks for an afternoon siesta are already in place. To this quintessential English scene can be added cricket's equivalent of two Mogadon and a glass of water: homemade beef and mustard sandwiches and a pint of warm local ale. For sleep to be guaranteed, however, there is a need, after the flurry of early wickets in the morning session, for a plucky albeit pedestrian fifth-wicket partnership to put the necessary drowsy ducks in a row. With that, sleep comes quickly and is only broken by the polite pavilion applause as the players troop off for tea. Now fully refreshed and eager to enjoy the final session, there is just time to stretch the legs and go in search of coffee and cake to fuel the remaining overs and the journey home.

In contrast to the four-day game, the limited-overs format of any variety is counterproductive to all forms of meaningful sleep. The garish coloured uniforms, anything but restful, work only to assault the senses. The combination of loud music, dancing girls, fireworks, and a public address system all but out of control only add to the growing malaise. Cheap fizzy lager and the saturated fats of on-site fast food further collide to amp up hyperactivity, sending attention levels through the roof. And if on the off chance your eyelids start to flutter, then expect the local branch of the Barmy Army to strike up with some inane serenading of a particular player or team. The nightclub effect – championed by pounding music at the fall of a wicket – is completed by the faux strobe lighting provided by the glint and glitter emanating from the players' gold bangles, earrings, and designer shades.

Twelve thousand miles away, the scene is no different as Sheffield Shield days offer more than ample opportunity to get your head down during an afternoon session. As with County Championship days the 1,000 or so spectators are lost amid the huge grandstands. While this might cause sound to travel and reverberate around the rafters it soon dissipates and all is quickly silent. Into the potential sleep pattern in say Sydney or Melbourne, as opposed to Southend or Maidstone, can be added temperatures contentedly nudging 30°C. No need to wrap up warm on Shield days. The combination of heat and humidity make dozing or a lengthier nap close to compulsory during the afternoon. The quality of sleep can be gauged by a total lack of stirring or twitching should an orchestrated appeal go up for a caught behind. Even the arrival of an errant fly on nose or ear is greeted with little more than a drowsy, reflex swat. The tea interval, as in the County Championship, provides the perfect wake-up call after which, and fortified by brew and bun, it is time to settle in for the final session.

Threatened by limited-overs cricket, the prospect of sleep is little helped by the current County Championship format of playing games both early and late in the season. The problem with early fixtures is the very real threat of frostbite or hypothermia should patrons fall asleep on the terraces in April or May. This is compounded late in the season by the prospect of a sudden cold snap in September. The lack of regular County Championship games through the summer may further confuse the already erratic sleep patterns of members. There is good news on this front, however, as the counties are set to market a new, eponymously named app, that re-creates the sleep-inducing sound of *Seagulls over the SWALEC*. By way of a bonus feature, those with a heightened sense of hearing may care to tune into *White Noise at Wantage Road*. In the interests of balance, other sleep-inducing sound apps are available including *Steady Drizzle at Scarborough* and *The Best of Boycott: batting for the bedroom*.

* * *

Short Leg's Short Legs

Of the many conundrums that beset world cricket, few rank higher or have caused the game's great thinkers more soul-searching than that relating to a certain close catcher. To wit: just how short should short leg's short legs be? Pivotal among attacking positions in recent years, short leg is now a key element in both the fast and slow bowler's game plan. Indeed, the advance in protective clothing, the helmet in particular, has allowed short leg to be on such intimate terms with the batsman as to warrant a column or two in the Sunday knee-and-navel publications. Out of sight, patiently willing the thinnest of edges, it is cricket's ambush waiting to happen. Whether bat-pad or pad-bat, the resultant commotion is enough to convince the most myopic of umpires that a catch has been taken. But what of the history of short leg, and what of its rise to prominence from parking position to that of prime (re)mover?

From Test arena to public park, cricket teams throughout the ages have searched for positions to place the inexperienced, aged, and infirm; mid-off, fine leg and third man spring most readily to mind. Into this retirement plan came the position of short square on the leg side. While not expected to make an active contribution, short leg nevertheless remained close enough to be of sufficient nuisance value should the occasion demand. Counted, if not counted upon, the position was accepted by all. All, that is, except Douglas Jardine, whose leg theory or Bodyline turned short leg into a specialist position overnight. Whether looping edge or out of the middle, here was a tactic and a field placement to gain advantage: and with Bradman the prize, this was all Jardine desired. That Bodyline all but brought the downfall of the Commonwealth was enough for the tactic to be abandoned and for short leg to return to the realms of dreamy inactivity. Indeed, a good many years passed before it was heard of again, and only then as a backcloth to the issue of safety in sport.

The prototype for protective clothing, short leg became the domain of the more portly or rotund, there being no better form of padding than that provided by nature. It was here that the late Colin Milburn found his ample girth a positive advantage. The Berlin Wall in flannels, his presence, a trick of the light, would effectively cut off all chance of gain between mid-on and backward square. With the odd catch taken, Milburn soon made the position his own and short leg was back in favour. The post-Packer arrival of the fielding (as opposed to batting) helmet gave players licence to stand as close to the batsman as the umpire and obscenity laws would permit. Evolution next took hold as coaches linked proximity to the bat with that of agility. Enter the smaller, more streamline version. No longer the haunt of the aged or overweight, short leg became an area of great profit.

Not a position for which to volunteer, David Boon and Augustine Logie nevertheless made it their own. Yet confusion remains over the ideal size for the position. Boon, similar in stature and just as permanent as Ayers Rock, was old school: the proverbial brick outhouse, his agility whether fielding ball, tinnie or hamburger nothing short of legendary. If Boon represents the past then Logie's career was very much a role model for the future: brave as a lion and with the reflexes of a title contender, Logie could catch flies. As a rule, few positions, whatever the sport, come complete with a ready-made description of the incumbent. An amalgam of the brave and the barking, short leg stands as the exception to the rule. For whether positive, as in the need for agility, or negative, as in the desire to make himself a smaller target, take it as read that the shorter short leg's short legs the better for all concerned.

* * *

Sway, Duck & Jerk

Full marks for imagination; none, alas, for accuracy. Sway, Duck & Jerk are neither a firm of hotshot city lawyers nor your friendly neighbourhood pawnbrokers. Cricketers with a keen sense of well-being, however, will recognise them, either singularly or collectively, as the accepted methods employed in the avoidance of short-pitched bowling. In a sport where self-preservation is of growing concern, the main aim is very much that of keeping your head while all around others are (in danger of) losing theirs. The more steely of nerve will thus sway nonchalantly out of line as the ball passes perilously close at whisker height. Those less confident will simply duck and accept the consequences. The most common method, however, is the reflex action or jerk and involves an undignified blur as the body is violently arched, heels kicked high with the head flung back in urgent self-protection.

As essential to the batsman as the cover drive or forward defensive, avoidance of the short ball is a key element in the art of survival and accumulation. Given the concentration of short-pitched bowling of late, supporters new to the game may be forgiven for thinking it a recent phenomenon whereas, in fact, it dates back to the inception of over- or round-arm bowling. The confusion over origin, although easily made, is linked to the increase in intimidatory bowling over the last 50 years. Hard as it is to imagine, but in the late 1960s the bouncer was still looked upon as a shock tactic. The success of Peter Pollock and Mike Procter in 1969/70 and of John Snow during the southern Ashes summer of 1970/71 led, certainly in Australia, to an urgent review of the length at which bowlers should seek to attack. There followed the bloody reign of Jeff Thomson and Dennis Lillee: a time of great carnage, with broken bones, bruised English pride, and a run on fresh underwear not seen since Bodyline.

Victim of these tactics in the mid-1970s, the West Indies went away and not so much refined this simple approach as, with the selection of Roberts, Holding, Garner and Croft, made it their own. Thus the short ball, lost amid arguments and accusations, underwent something of a role reversal. No longer the shock tactic, it became the stock ball; the fuller, drivable length now reserved for the surprise attack. The end result is that batsmen have been left to combat the short ball by their own devices. Test history suggests a variety of methods in operation.

The 'Boycott Method' is the ultimate in non-confrontational confrontation. The object is to remain rooted at the non-striker's end, running only twos and fours, or, if inadvertently left to face an over, to expertly steal a single off the first ball. Only when the bowlers tire or the wicket loses its devil should consideration be given to facing a delivery.

The 'Hick Method' demonstrates clear intent on leaving the dressing room, for not only is the pavilion gate left open but the batsman actually takes guard behind the square leg umpire. The safest of the alternative methods, problems do tend to arise when it comes to building an innings.

The 'Milburn Method' was nature's way of safeguarding batsmen before the invention of chest protectors and armguards. Patented by the late Colin Milburn, the thinking was that increased body mass, the product of a robust diet, would provide extra layers of padding to combat the rising delivery. The downside proved to be tours to the subcontinent where Milburn's appetite brought the very real threat of nationwide famine.

The 'Richards Method' is Caribbean in origin and played entirely on the front foot. Thus, length matters little as deliveries are either swung high over midwicket or dispatched on the up through extra cover.

The 'Gavaskar Method' dictates that size, or lack of it, is everything. For so small is the batsman, that a good length, let alone a short ball, passes harmlessly overhead. All other deliveries, the back foot prominent, are either hooked or cut.

The 'Close Method' is a painful reminder of yesteryear. Developed by the former Yorkshire and England captain Brian Close, the tactic is based on advance as opposed to retreat. Removing all trace of the bat from batting, the idea is to take every delivery on the body. This entails (entrails?) remaining at the crease until the bowlers tire or the match is deemed unsuitable for children.

* * *

Tail Twisting

Yet to become an Olympic sport, although this surely is only a matter of time, there is nothing we English like better than a spot of tail twisting, especially if it involves officialdom. And what better place to do just that than Lord's, the Home of Cricket. Recent downtime has seen a relocation to cricket's HQ for Middlesex County Championship games against Yorkshire and Warwickshire. The cricket apart, these visits allow, despite the imminent threat of excommunication (or worse), the chance to twist the tail of the pavilion stewards. A pavilion and stewards wherein photography is, to put it mildly, strictly VERBOTEN! Contravention of which is likely to lead to The Tower with charges of treason to trespass and everything in between. Indeed, to even entertain the prospect of taking pictures in the Long Room is the ultimate derring-do. However, for someone who spent much of the 1980s wandering in and out of Australian Test grounds using a Builders Labourers Federation union card as a press pass, then maybe not quite so derring and with hardly any do to speak of.

* * *

The Red Scorpion

No one arrives in the Philippines by chance. Manila is not for the accidental tourist. My excuse was a spot of R&R after six weeks backpacking around India. Frying pans and fires? Maybe. It certainly began to feel that way when, barely an hour in the country, news broke of a security alert around the embassy circuit. Local bad boy (and victim of too many B movies) the Red Scorpion had apparently threatened to bomb one of the foreign missions. A forgetful fellow, he'd been none too specific about which one. President Ramos, television personality and all-round good guy, was soon before the cameras, but he didn't know either. Welcome to the Philippines!

Safe in a gated community, our own residence was protected by a guard who, when not checking doors and windows, sat the night away with a shotgun across his knees. Trips into town were similarly protected with our own driver and a 4x4 with tinted windows. While not quite the wild west, there did seem to be a few more guns on the streets than necessary for the local Sainsbury's run. The occasional expedition apart, I stayed close to the pool, rested, read, and generally tried to get my head around India. When that proved too much there was always the sports pages. Sadly, they proved no less vexing than the subcontinent. For sandwiched neatly between the basketball and tenpin bowling results was an entire section devoted to cockfighting! Decide for yourselves where the carnage ends, and the sport begins. I did contemplate ringing the Philippine Cockers Club (yes, such exists) to enquire of the same, but didn't want this innocent bout of feather ruffling to get back to Old Red himself.

Sanity returned with an invitation of a game of cricket for the Australian Embassy. At last - overlooked for years by the England selectors - my first cap, albeit for Australia, and an Embassy XI at that. A green and sporty oasis among the mayhem that is Manila, the Nomads Club was a joy to behold. For here, at last, was reason, order, tranquillity, cold beer, and a pleasing absence of firearms. My last game had been in deepest Lincolnshire two months earlier in late September. A dismal, dank affair, play was abandoned shortly after tea amid Dickensian gloom and sea fret. Manila presented no such problems that steamy November Sunday morning. The only question, other than whether both sides could raise 11 good men and true, was whether the matting wicket would behave. Or more to the point, what to do should it misbehave. A couple of rearing deliveries on and it needed not so much a polite prod as a prolonged spanking. Batting first, the Embassy XI posted 194/8 (V. Mills retired 50) in 30 overs. A commendable team effort, not least as it took place against a backcloth of 747s departing the international airport just beyond the sight screen at long-off.

Lunch, as you would expect of any sporting contest involving Australians, consisted of chilled bottles of San Miguel. Fearing not the combination of heat, exhaustion, and alcohol – a rum cove, Johnny Asia – or the possibility of happy, errant fielders wandering between fine leg and third man singing rugby songs, the Embassy XI supped well. The Nomads, fresh from a recent tour of Hong Kong, began in spirited fashion. Steady bowling and inspired fielding, however, saw an end of their best batsmen and an Australian victory by 60 runs. With the game happily concluded by early afternoon there was ample time for a further assault on the San Miguel. Indeed, had I not been booked on a 10.45pm flight to Sydney, it's likely I could be propping up the Nomads bar to this day.

* * *

Keeping the Batsman Honest

It may be a generational thing, but I can't quite bring myself to consider the phenomenon we now know as a slow bouncer without first thinking LONG HOP. When still classified as a long hop there was more than an element of pantomime about the delivery. For while the ball was being retrieved from the midwicket boundary, garden or ploughed field, the poor wretch of a bowler would busy himself scratching away at the popping crease or rubbing his hand in the dirt in the hope of fast-fading mitigation.

The onset of Twenty20, however, and the rise and rise of the Indian Premier League have seen bowlers, hugely disadvantaged in this particular format, attempt to level the outfield by inventing all manner of mischief in an attempt to defeat the batsman. Taking pace off the ball has long been a preferred weapon. To this has been added the deceit of taking length off the ball. Enter the slow bouncer, a delivery that, at worst, will still soar high over the boundary and into an ecstatic crowd. So, nothing lost there. But at best, the batsman, already partway through his shot, will either sky the ball to midwicket or arc it slowly into waiting hands at cow corner or backward square.

Of course, as you might expect, there are slow bouncers and then, depending on the bowler involved, there are 'slow' bouncers. I mention this because, some years back, I was fortunate to play several games of club cricket in Sydney with former NSW and Australian Test batsman Peter Toohey. The same Peter Toohey who toured the Caribbean with Bobby Simpson's side in 1978. The good news of that tour from a selection perspective was that the Australian Cricket Board banned its Packer players from Test cricket, thereby leaving the door open for the likes of Toohey. The bad news was that for the first two Tests of that series the West Indies Cricket Board selected their full contingent of World Series players including Roberts, Croft and Garner.

Sharing a post-game beer with Peter, I mentioned that the last time I'd seen him was on the front page of Sydney's

Daily Mirror in a battered and bloodied state having lost an argument with an Andy Roberts bouncer during the first Test in Port of Spain. So: that bouncer? Toohey had hooked Roberts for four the previous over. This, he explained, was probably the slower of Roberts' infamous two bouncers. A natural hooker and puller, he set himself for more of the short stuff. Unfortunately for the diminutive right-hander, the ball, delivered at frightening pace, was on him in an instant and burst through his combination of attempted hook and blur of self-preservation.

Grateful that the ball struck solid bone, the injury required just three stitches. The head wound and a broken thumb saw him 'absent injured' in the second innings. He missed the second and third Tests but was recalled for the final two where, with the West Indian Packer players now also banned, a more humane series broke out. There was something of a happy ending too in that Toohey scored 122 and 97 in the drawn fifth Test in Kingston. So, there you have it. The slow bouncer is not quite the modern invention we might think. But, with Andy Roberts as a working model, it might be handy to have a somewhat faster variation to keep the batsman honest if not upright.

* * *

Hardly Rolex Science

Of the oddities that currently beset the game of cricket, surely the most curious is that of fielders wearing wristwatches. Why do players, whether at domestic or Test level, feel compelled to sport a timepiece during the hours of play? Given the regulated start times and two-hour sessions, a cricketer's wristwatch is about as useful as Lewis Hamilton attaching a Hotpoint fridge-freezer to his F1 Mercedes or Adam Peaty swimming the Olympic 100m breaststroke final one-handed while carrying a Deliveroo Domino's four seasons pizza in the other. From a club cricketer's perspective, taking anything on to the field of play that contains glass and metal – spectacles and pacemaker apart – seems a recipe for disaster. Of course, the easy answer is that the professionals have a lucrative sponsorship deal that obliges them to display such timepieces during the hours of play and beyond. If this is the case, then why not advertise something more in keeping with the game and its traditions?

The latest copy of *Wisden Cricketers' Almanack* would be ideal to throw at a sweetly timed cover drive to impede its progress to the boundary, while at the same time advertising the all-round merits of the celebrated publication. Bowlers, on the other hand, might care to discard wristwatch in favour of a portable wall barometer, thus enabling them during drinks breaks or at the fall of a wicket to explain just how and why the fluctuations in barometric pressure help or hinder the swinging ball. On the same lines, it can only be a matter of time before cricketers go down the same path as those walking billboards formerly known as F1 drivers. The dyke has already been breached in India where IPL teams sport a patchwork quilt of lucrative advertising on shirts, flannels, and sweaters. Thankfully, this has yet to permeate Test cricket where a solitary sponsor is still the norm.

A flight of fancy maybe, but when the England team sported the Waitrose logo, I did so want to believe that following a day's play the entire squad plus management and backroom staff would be bussed to the nearest supermarket outlet to embark on a spot of late-night shelf-stacking: tall fast bowlers restocking the top shelves with the more diminutive batsmen and wicketkeepers handling the lower shelves together with the glass cabinets in the deli and bakery sections. And what better way to promote the message of value for money than having Ben Stokes operating in the beers, wines and spirits aisle. In the meantime, and on those rare occasions when it's imperative that he knows the time, a fielder can always ask the umpire or simply glance at the pavilion clock. Hardly Rolex science. But, of course, it'll never happen. For the more cricket cosies up to television networks, the more sponsors and corporations will come a-calling.

* * *

Corpulent Crusaders
The Guardian; Friday, 11 September 1998

The selection of Leeward Islander Rahkeem Cornwall for the third Test at Old Trafford in July 2020 focused attention on a long-forgotten figure of the game: the corpulent cricketer. Weighing in at 22-plus stones (plus? Plus lunch!), Cornwall, a cricketing colossus, is a rotund reminder of a bygone age. The retirement a couple of decades ago of weighty Warwickshire opener Andy Moles brought the day of reckoning ever closer for cricket's remaining fat few. Stout, ample, plump, their kind strode large, very large, over the sport, leaving fond memories of an immense appetite for both game and life. To such men was attached a folklore as generous as their waistlines. Sadly, although the hunger remains, the diet has changed. As is the lot of endangered species, they have fallen foul of progress; of a relentless and fast-moving development which, in the case of cricket, is the limited-overs game.

Out of the glut of pyjama cricket has evolved the archetypal one-day player: sober and uniform, his athletic frame, stylish hair, and evenly tanned features are much cloned. Television coverage has revealed the 'new age' player as something of a hybrid. Cricketer he most certainly is – you can tell by the jewellery, tattoos, designer shades and mobile phone – but there is more than a hint of estate agent about his dress and demeanour. While he may harbour a passion for wine and wenching, the immediate impression is one of mineral water, early nights, and a calorie-controlled diet. No place here for the Jack Simmons *Encyclopaedia of Lancastrian Curry Houses* or Fred Trueman's *Guide to Strong Northern Ale*.

County grounds in the early morning no longer echo to leather on willow, but resemble instead some demented callisthenic heaven as promoted by Joe Wicks. In meeting the needs of the modern day, cricket has become grotesquely energetic, far too energetic, in truth, for the more rotund of shape. When our Falstaffian figures entered the game, cricket consisted almost exclusively of batting and bowling. Everyone took it upon themselves to field, but only as an afterthought. Savings on catering apart, the retirement of Moles and his like signalled the end of a century of Grace-like waistlines, together with a host of legendary feats with bat, ball, knife, fork, and spoon. Not always a king-size bed of roses, the downside to such men of size was the reaction – often unpredictable – that their appearance could generate. ting and subsequent abandonment of the Test.

Under the influence of Micky Stewart and Graham Gooch, fitness came before fried food and jogging before jam roly poly. During their austere reign, coach and captain toured county grounds and committee rooms preaching a gospel of practice and perspiration. Ian Botham and Merv Hughes, distinguished ambassadors for the fat few, championed a counterculture, but soon perished against unequal odds. The central pillow removed, there was much wavering among the corpulent crusaders. The hope of the subcontinent, Arjuna Ranatunga, an onion bhaji away from retirement, soon went the way of Moles, while an ambitious Steve Waugh put paid to the tenure of Mark 'Tubby' Taylor. With the writing on the wall, David Boon quickly threw in his lot with McDonald's.

With the odds, as if pancakes, heavily stacked against them, cricket's refuseniks numbered few and far between. One such, Lancashire's Ian Austin, lingered long at the tea table in an attempt to turn back the tide of maple syrup; there to be joined by Mike Gatting, firm of jaw, less so of stomach. Gatting's final Test century, at Adelaide in 1994, was a single-handed celebration of pies, puddings, curries, fish suppers and all manner of sticky desserts. A despairing effort, however, as he too went the way of Ranatunga, unable in the end to differentiate between long hop and lasagne. And yet, just when we thought their kind extinct, up pops Rahkeem Rashawn Shane Cornwall. In light of the current pandemic and the lack of workers to pick late-summer crops, it is perhaps just as well for the UK's food chain that the West Indies were only invited for a short tour. That said, Rahkeem remains a welcome addition to a game that appears intent on churning out a generation of Midwich Cricketing Cuckoos.

* * *

Celebration

The art and craft of celebration within cricket has advanced in leaps and bounds – make that hugs and kisses – in recent years. Hard as it is to imagine, but Don Bradman, for all his legion of achievements, received just three modest, rather formal cheers from the England team as he made his way to the wicket for the last time at The Oval in 1948. Twenty years later, Fred Trueman's 300th Test wicket, the dismissal of his old adversary Neil Hawke, drew naught but firm handshakes and a congratulatory slap on the back from his colleagues. Contrast these milestones with that of today where modest performers are hugged, kissed, and generally fondled as if some long-lost lover. Little wonder the modern approach is for containment rather than attack. Without wanting to appear prudish on the subject of body contact, one can only speculate, given the game's rapid evolutionary tendencies, of where it will all end.

Can we expect, for instance, mass groping of short leg's short legs with the snaring of a bat-pad catch? Is the day approaching when Sydney's Gay and Lesbian Mardi Gras will feature a float of Test cricketers re-enacting a Shane Warne hat-trick? Will third umpires attain icon status for their inventive use of slow-motion replays? And flushed with revolutionary zeal, will the MCC coaching manual contain a chapter on the use of massage oils at the fall of a wicket? While such examples tend towards the extreme, it must not be forgotten that cricket has sold its soul to television: a medium that, more than any other, encourages excess.

Spared the seedy antics of Anglo-Australian cricketers, the West Indies introduced their own brand of celebration: the high five, a practice now openly employed by all Test-playing nations. In the general scheme of calypso cricket, celebration is a key element. To this end, fielding is only tolerated, indeed only undertaken, on the understanding that madness and mayhem erupt at the fall of a wicket. The odd hiccup apart, high fives stand as the acceptable, if slightly boorish, face of celebration: a wholesome act at the fall of a wicket and one whose only apparent defect appears that of height. A gifted and instinctive short leg, Gus Logie was never destined for a long Test career. Surrounded by such tall timbers as Ambrose, Walsh, and Bishop, his tenure was brought to an abrupt halt by severe knee and ankle injuries – the result of repeated attempts to defy gravity. A tragic incident, yet one viewed as little more than an occupational hazard as high fives continue and, if anything, are more frenzied than ever: there being no better way to add insult to injured pride than to party, preen and parade every last drop of mischief out of the dismissal.

* * *

ABC

Sydney Morning Herald; Thursday, 2 March 1995

For two decades from the mid-1970s onwards the West Indies pace attack systematically demolished every batting line-up that dared turn up at the same ground. Indeed, it was only a matter of time before a Test-playing nation broke with tradition and sent a note: sorry, visiting sick aunt, entire country unavailable! And given the carnage of blood and broken bones, who could blame them? Throughout this period, the impression gained from Clive Lloyd, Vivian Richards and Richie Richardson was that, given the slightest encouragement, they would have gladly selected nine fast bowlers, before embarking on a frenzied island hop in search of a fast-bowling wicketkeeper. Exaggeration? Maybe. But so ill-matched had become the contest that respective boards of control no longer appealed to the ICC for a ruling on intimidatory bowling, preferring instead to petition direct to Amnesty International.

Within the rules, if not the spirit of the game, West Indian officials contended they were merely selecting those players that were available. Which translates roughly into never mind the quality, feel the pace. This little addressed the issue, however, of how they managed to continually mine such a rich vein of talent. Some years ago, Max Boyce unwittingly touched upon this cricketing conundrum when he wrote of a factory under the hills that produced outside-halves for Wales. Earlier still, rumour had it that England cricket selectors need only whistle down a mine shaft for a couple of fast bowlers to arrive in the next cage. Obvious when you think about it: from picking the seam to, er, picking the seam. It would be putting too much faith in the chain of causation to argue that pit closures and decline in the coal industry in the 1980s had anything to do with England's failure with the new ball. For to do so would suggest that salvation back then lay in the appointment of Arthur Scargill as chairman of selectors. An interesting thought all the same.

Sociologists and anthropologists provide several theories for this far from equitable distribution of talent. Yet such reasoning – poverty, self-expression, financial reward, national pride, or political statement – exists to varying degrees in all Test-playing nations. The answer, if one were to be found, quite obviously lay outside the confines of manly pursuit. After a long and detailed search, the answer appeared to have links with music; but not, as you might imagine, in calypso or reggae, rather that of country and western, and one song in particular. The lyrics of Johnny Cash's number, 'A Boy Called Sue', tell of adversity – by way of an unusual christian name – thrust upon a youngster. The outcome of which, bruised but happy (note here the key word), is maturity at pace. Using this as a starting point, further research confirmed that, in the case of Caribbean cricketing folklore, there was more than meets the eye.

Wind the clock back to the early 1950s and it appears that West Indian parents brought a touch of ingenuity to their adversity. Cricket represented a better life for their children. But how to ensure survival in the game, and then at the highest level? Deliciously simple, devastatingly effective, a random sample survey of opening bowlers produced the following results along with a quite distinct behavioural pattern: H.H.H. Johnson (Hophie Horace Hines), W.W. Hall (Wesley Winfield), V.A. Holder (Vanburn Alonza), A.M.E. Roberts (Anderson Montgomery Everton), E.A.E. Baptiste (Eldine Ashworth Elderfield), S.T. Clarke (Sylvester Theophilus), M.D. Marshall (Malcolm Denzil), F.d.C. Stephenson (Franklin da Costa), B.P. Patterson (Balfour Patrick) and E.L.C. Ambrose (Elcon Lindwall Curtley).

The rationale, let us call it Cash's Law, appears to be that the more curious and demanding the christian name, the faster and nastier the bowler. This would explain the rapid rise to maturity of the likes of Marshall, Patterson, and Ambrose, and, in a discipline where the norm is usually mid-to-late-20s. Batsmen, meanwhile, remained reluctant to approach the subject of short-pitched and intimidatory bowling or demand a fuller length as this would entail addressing the likes of Hophie, Theophilus or Vanburn.

The fact that the current West Indian side is in the cricketing doldrums suggests the collective eye of players, coaches, and parents in particular has been taken off the ball. The point is emphasised by the lack of fast bowling resources and a national game in decline. But all is not lost. West Indian dominance with the ball owes much to the foresight and imagination of parents and grandparents. All the more reason, then, to divert funding away from coaching and touring to those in the business of christenings and naming ceremonies. It's as easy as ABC: Alonza, Balfour, Curtly.

Footnote: Victor Stanley Mills was a moderately successful medium-quick.

* * *

Boxing Day Test

The Boxing Day Test at the Melbourne Cricket Ground is a must for all cricket lovers. The timing, however, still calls for the safe and seasonal navigation of Christmas Day. As a small, sleepy band of early risers we number just three, four if you count the resident Blue Heeler, Ziggy. After a restorative cuppa it's straight into chore mode. Outside, the patio and pool is tidied and shade-bearing umbrellas raised. Indoors, there are glasses to unpack, champagne to chill, and smoked salmon sandwiches to prepare. Not to be left out, Ziggy pads from room to room alternately sniffing and snuffling before signing off. By 10.30am there is just time to run and change before the first of the two dozen or so guests start to arrive.

Once up and running the morning is given over to making sure glasses are full and food is served. The guest list comprises the great and good of Brighton Beach: old money, new money and, in my case and just to give balance, no money! One particular Christmas morning, no names no pack drill, a house guest volunteers to cook the turkey in the gas barbecue. Brave man. Whether a malfunction on the part of the unit, faulty dials, or an error in calculating the weight/ cooking time ratio is never established. The outcome is a large turkey cooked to perfection by 11.30am and the chef pan-fried shortly after!

Safe in the knowledge that every dog has its day, Zig wanders around amiably stopping occasionally to have an ear scratched or submit to a life-affirming body rub. Few of the assembled know, however, that this is just canine cover, and a mass outbreak of crotch sniffing could erupt at any moment followed, by way of encore, with the vigorous humping of the nearest leg. Good boy, Zig! With lunch to cook most guests drift off after a couple of hours. This leaves time for celebrations to be transferred to the seasonally decorated dining room where the large table is already laid with white linen cloth and place settings worthy of a transatlantic crossing.

As the courses come and go Ziggy, ever the optimist, perambulates quietly between table and chairs. Despite the sort of temperatures that would cause even a Blue Heeler to question one hump or two, we move on to Christmas pudding with the added ingredient of silver threepenny bits. These, for the lucky recipients, their dental work still intact, can be exchanged at the meal's end for the going rate of a dollar a pop.

With presents opened, the choice rests between a well-earned small siesta or the chance to walk off bird and brandy sauce with a stroll on the beach. As traditional as the turkey itself, no South Road Christmas would be complete without a spot of night cricket on the tennis court. So down comes the net, up go the lights, and play begins. It is now that Zig comes into his own. With pitying glances at we poor two-legged wretches, he puts his four to good use skittering around the court in a fashion both festive and frenzied. Goodness only knows what the neighbours think as a combination of barking, whooping, and hollering offers little chance of anything remotely approaching a silent night.

The Boxing Day morning Sandringham-City light rail service is no less animated and provides a vintage slice of Australiana. The scene is helped in no small measure by hangover and medicinal hot pie. Thus, suits and blazers mingle happily with a green and gold army of shorts and singlets, the bonhomie and easy banter cemented by a common enemy in the form of local and visiting Poms. Arriving at Richmond station, the comrades part: suits and blazers heading for the members' area and all other ranks to the outer for a day of sunscreen, shades, and shrinking sobriety.

There is a brief flicker of hope on the way to the press box as high on a wall in the members' area is a large black and white picture of Wally Hammond putting Australia to the sword in the 1930s. Swapping past for present, the press box is all handshakes and hearty Christmas cheer. To celebrate the season of goodwill, sponsors walk among the hacks handing out souvenir Kookaburra cricket balls with the date and fixture printed on the side. In our hermetically sealed box, we little hear the pandemonium at the toss as 75,000 voices combine to create a rumbling, rolling thunder that reverberates around concourse and grandstand. And so it begins.

The journey back to Brighton Beach at the close of play is slightly more problematic in that a great many of this morning's passengers have spent the day soaking up both ambience and amber nectar in equal measure. By the look of it, the green and gold army has had a good day. A very good day. And is now totally pissed! Sufficiently so in fact to lose inebriated infantry and officers at each stop along the way home. Eye contact is not recommended at this point. An unfortunate combination perhaps, but now is not the time or place to be either sober or a Pommie bastard!

* * *

Batting for the Barberini

It wasn't so much a case of Last Exit to Brooklyn a few months back as Last Exhibition before Lockdown. So off to Potsdam, the Museum Barberini, and *Impressionismus*. While not overtly promised cricket in the exhibition, I remained Chocolate Lab optimistic of a find. Ask yourself: all those fields, gardens and groves, there has to be cricket, stands to reason. Then again, it's the hope that kills you. The museum missed a trick, I thought, in not advertising the event in Mark Knopfler's words as 'Monet for nothing and chicks for free'. But there you go. With a 3pm time slot, the good doctor leading, we worked our way through the 100 or so exhibits: Renoir, Pissarro, Monet, Sisley and Boudin; not a bad top order, with Caillebotte, Signac and Le Sidaner to follow.

Despite field following garden following grove there appeared no sign of play. Surprising when you consider the perfect conditions captured by Sisley in *The Meadow at Veneux-Nadon* (1881). There is a suspicion of play in Monet's *Under the Poplars* (1887), where a couple appear to be looking for a ball. Not easy given the lush vegetation. No doubt a working title of *Lost Ball* was on the tip of his brush. Boudin's *Sunset on the Sea* (1885), meanwhile, simply drips pity and pathos at a game of beach cricket lost to an incoming tide. By way of inspiration, there is little doubt that Renoir had cricket teas in mind when producing *Still Life with a Honeydew Melon* (1879). Indeed, with space to spare centre right, a plate of scones, Victoria sponge or a Battenberg cake would have worked to enhance the powerful image still further.

Rain stopped play would seem to be at the heart of Monet's *Water Lilies* (1914–17) although the overriding impression is of a man struggling with the masking tape. On a more optimistic note, his *Grainstacks* (1890) suggest close of play on a perfect summer's eve; while, with stumps drawn, Caillebotte's *Couple on a Walk* (1881) reeks of strong ale and mischief as spectators depart ground for nearby tavern. And with thirst quenched, what better way to relive burned out Junes than over supper in Le Sidaner's *Window with Carnations* (1908). Oh well, so much for cricket on canvas. Still, as that wag Pissarro might have ventured: yer pays yer Monet and yer takes yer chance.

Deepest apologies to all lovers of Impressionist Art. VM.

* * *

A Shot 4 a Shot

It is time, with another edition of the Indian Premier League come and gone, for world cricket in general, and the respective governing bodies in particular, to face up to the reality of saturation coverage and the increasing number of eminently forgettable matches and performances. That every Test-playing nation along with sundry interlopers now have their own Twenty20 competition means that on virtually any given day in the cricketing calendar it is possible to tune into televised pyjama play. Every which way, overkill is now a distinct possibility. All the more reason, then, to consider new initiatives to make this increasingly tired and troubled format that much more marketable and one set to attract yet another new audience.

Despite the innovative nature of Twenty20 and its continual quest for the novel and liberating, the game's powerhouses whether in Dubai or Delhi would do well to cast an eye over the past when considering the future. Indeed, to take this approach a stage further, to consider cricket innovation at grassroots level as opposed to the more rarefied atmosphere emanating from the corridors of the International Cricket Council or the Board of Control for Cricket in India. At the heart of this growing malaise is the fact that the current format is too heavily weighted in favour of batsmen what with reduced boundary sizes, free hits, fielding restrictions, limitations on short-pitched deliveries, and eagle-eyed umpires ever keen to signal a wide and with it an extra delivery.

Several decades ago, my own club, Lindum, held an annual six-a-side tournament on the Whit Bank Holiday Monday; with the wicketkeeper retaining the gloves and the other five players bowling an over, an innings would consist of just 30 deliveries. Light years ahead of its time, we too reduced the boundary size to encourage six-hitting. The only difference between this and the IPL format is that for each six hit the batsman was awarded a bottle of beer. While too late to be included in this year's edition, we respectfully suggest that this innovation be included in the 2023 tournament, but not without first being trialled in other countries and Twenty20 competitions.

So how would bottled batting work in a match situation? Although only at a feasibility stage, the idea is that not only would a beer be awarded for every maximum, but that the batsman would then be required to drink it at the crease before facing the next delivery. Studies suggest, albeit through increasingly blurred vision, that this would significantly reduce the current unacceptable gap between bat and ball, while at the same time adding still further to the fun and frolic of the occasion. Of course, not that you were in any doubt, the prospect of crease-consumed alcohol would offer further lucrative marketing opportunities from brewing companies to the hospitality industry and all points in between.

The minimal break in play to facilitate the arrival and consumption of the beer would offer yet another marketing opportunity, in keeping with the current sponsorship of the strategic timeout, if the occasion was christened something along the lines of the 'Mild and Bitter Maximum'. Conversely, this being one of the more democratic of sporting pastimes, those batsmen for whom the preference is for strong liquor would be offered the opportunity of indulging in a rum and coke, gin and tonic or vodka and lemonade thereby creating the equally marketable 'Shot 4 a Shot' advertising campaign. Of course, the only downside in this revolutionary proposal – in light of the 50-plus cans consumed by David Boon on a pre-Ashes flight between Sydney and London some years ago – is that it would offer the Australians an unfair advantage.

Footnote: in keeping with the best limited-overs traditions, this innovative IPL insight is brought to you by the makers of Foster's, XXXX, Swan, Tooheys, Coopers and Victoria Bitter. Remember: don't drink and (cover) drive.

* * *

Grassroots Reset for Test Stars

The recent palaver over Test matches done and dusted in sessions as opposed to days and the current comment-provoking practice of rotating international players has led many to the conclusion that the game of Test cricket in set for extinction in the not too distant future. While it's a clear over-reaction on the part of those who should know better, the current state of play does suggest that players and pundits need something of a reality check. And what better way to rethink and reset than by a return to the grassroots game and club cricket? It would make a refreshing change for instance if – rather than bleat about under-prepared pitches and Test matches over in two or three days – the teams in question offered to play a beer match in the remaining unused playing time. This would, at a stroke, pacify sold-out fourth- and fifth-day crowds, caterers, sponsors, insurance companies, advertising agencies, and TV networks. And what fun into the bargain: reverse batting orders, occasional bowlers, and a carnival atmosphere to match the fancy dress. A tad left field? Perhaps. But an outcome far preferable to disgruntled players, pundits and public.

While the 2021 Ahmedabad Test – when England were beaten by India before the close on the second day – was an extreme example of an early finish. This has been a growing trend of late with matches, sold out for the fourth and fifth days, falling foul of the perfect storm of poor batting, inspired bowling, and under-prepared pitches. It all cries out for recourse to one of the basic tenets of club cricket. And what could be more identifiable or recognisable to the paying and playing public than for those batsmen already dismissed or not yet required to pad up to do a ten-over stint on sight screen duty, especially if an opposition bowler is continually switching from over to round the wicket? The benefits of this would be twofold in that it would again put a more identifiable face on the Test player if he's seen to be mucking in and it would also free him up for more guaranteed brownie points in posing for selfies or signing autographs.

With a further eye to the club game, it would certainly help if some of cricket's superstars were seen getting their hands dirty once in a while. I'm thinking here of a little light groundwork in the week leading up to a Test: mowing the outfield, rolling the wicket, marking the boundary line, and putting up the nets. Rather than just turning up and playing, the time invested on club and ground would give the players a greater feel for their surroundings and supporters. As a preference, I would far sooner see my England team embarking on a spot of light groundwork on the morning of a Test than reaching for a football and instantly consigning several team members to the physio's room long before the toss has been made. And think of the added respect of the fans as they can actually relate to the actions and dirty fingernails of an international player.

With respect in mind, Test players would enhance their image and spectator appeal no end if, instead of dashing off to the pavilion and waiting mobiles and iPads during a rain break, they ran instead to the groundsman's shed where, growing increasingly damp and dishevelled, they helped push the covers on the wicket or position a tarp on the outfield. Given the vagaries of early season weather, the club cricketer continually lurches between the damp and the dishevelled. It is a look he can easily identify with and one he would cheer to the rafters should England players run on to the pitch at a rain break, instead of off it.

In the past decade, the emphasis for international cricketers has been on brand identification when perhaps they would have been better advised concentrating on game identification. And what better way to emphasise this than by the hero of the day's play declining an immediate post-play interview with Mark Nicholas or Jonathan Agnew and preferring instead to don a t-shirt and shorts and head off around the ground collecting boundary markers, stumps and run-up discs. While he's at it, and once returned to the dressing room, what could be more grounding than allocating him the task of collecting match fees and player availability for the next Test or series? No inconsequential task nowadays either given the intricacies of the rotation system.

With warm-down routines now an integral part of the modern game, what could be more fitting for the England XI than lending a hand to lunch and tea staff in taking down trestle tables, stacking chairs and even offering ten minutes or so to dry and stack dishes? We've all been there, and it proved as invaluable a rite of passage as anything involving bat or ball. From beer match to ground crew to tea room, any, or all of which would provide the perfect reset for a game and players that seem to get more detached and distant by the series and season.

* * *

Endangered Species

Another summer, another series, and the body of evidence continues to grow that the tail-ender (tail-gunner would be more apt) has, along with English leg-spinners and portly umpires, joined cricket's growing list of endangered species. The advance in protective clothing allied to the captain's insistence that every wicket including nine, ten, Jack, be sold dearly, has brought multiple confusions (make that contusions) to this once humble position. There was a time, not all that distant, when tail-enders little knew which end of the bat to hold, let alone where to strap the pads. More Barnum than Bailey (Trevor) their batting – muscular, funny, occasionally daring and always exciting – was pure circus. At the heart of this simple, uncomplicated approach lay an unswerving adherence to that most sacred of unwritten rules. To wit: only deliveries of full length should be bowled at members of the Fast Bowlers' Union. In return, and after the customary first-ball sighter, all further stroke play to evolve around the reliably rustic.

A simple existence, then, wherein each accepted his place, performed his duty, and was happy with the outcome. Until, that is, tail-enders decided, or had it decided for them, that such unwritten rules were not worth the paper they were not written on. The head-up, eyes closed, agricultural swat duly disappeared, if not overnight, then within a short space of time, to be replaced by a straight bat, staunch defence and, most worryingly of all, ambition. Moreover, the arrival on the equipment scene of helmet, chest protector and arm guard – removing at a stroke the prospect of serious injury – left them free to push, prod and generally infuriate to the close of play and beyond. Little wonder, given such flagrant disregard of the Tail-enders' Charter, that the 'no bouncer' rule fell by the wayside. While difficult to pinpoint the precise moment, few would argue that Dennis Lillee and Jeff Thomson were prime movers in this change of emphasis, aided and abetted by captain and resident *agent provocateur* Ian Chappell. With the West Indies pace battery following close behind, it soon became open season on rabbits.

In an attempt to counter intimidatory bowling at lower-order batsmen, the ICC has restricted bouncers to one an over. This little prevents bowlers from pushing the legislation to the limit with a barrage of short-pitched deliveries. Other than to petition the European Court of Human Rights or Amnesty International, it's difficult to see what else remains for the tail-ender. This is not to suggest he is without friends. Indeed, beyond the boundary, opinion favours a return to the old values, where batsmen batted, bowlers bowled, and everyone knew his place. For the current practice to be changed, however, a way must be found to remove the tail-ender without him appearing to lose face or, perhaps more to the point, his head. Failing that, and although a touch old-fashioned, has anyone thought of bowling a yorker?

* * *

The Hundred

If there is one word to describe the latest addition to the game of cricket – The Hundred – then it must surely be DUCK! No, really, do it! Do it now! Run! Hide! Just don't take your eye off the ball. To do otherwise is to risk serious injury as the sixes – replicating a scene from the Orson Welles-narrated *The War of the Worlds* – rain down. A suitable enough analogy given that, even before a ball has been bowled, we have a Code Red alert on the Health and Safety front. A mere 20 deliveries less per innings than a Twenty20 fixture, The Hundred nevertheless gives batsmen free rein to start targeting the boundary and beyond from the very first delivery. And if you think Twenty20 is a slog-fest then just wait for The Hundred. On a warm evening, with a batsman-friendly track, there can only be one outcome: carnage! It may also be one of the few sporting fixtures where the audience ends up wearing more protective equipment – helmets, arm guards, thigh pads, and chest protectors – than the actual players themselves. Fear not, though, for as these pandemic months have demonstrated, some UK firm or another, most probably owned by a Tory donor or having recently completed a multi-million-pound NHS PPE contract, will soon begin production of protective equipment for crowds of willing Hundred patrons.

Of course, given that cricket is in a constant state of evolution, I dare say that even as I type there is a young man or woman somewhere in the world – Australian outback, Himalayan mountain pass or African rift valley – perfecting the perfect disguised delivery to at least temporarily even up the grossly uneven contest between bat and ball. It will be short-lived, make no mistake, for just as soon as a new mystery delivery is conceived a counterstroke will be invented to again swing the balance heavily back in favour of the batsmen. Such is the way of the world as nothing pleases the sponsors or franchise owners more than the ball disappearing beyond the boundary every few seconds, the stroke to be greeted by a wave of rolling noise. Not from the crowd you understand, but from cash tills and online purchases of team merchandise and sponsors' products.

The added danger in this further-reduced format of the game is that there is also a significantly reduced opportunity for the consumption of alcohol. This will in turn lead to a review of both drinking habits, in particular speed of consumption and alcohol availability, and the always difficult decision of just how long a patron is willing to give to both watching the game and queuing for beer or fast food or, as may be the case, even faster fast food. These are all considerations that I suspect the average Hundred spectator has yet to either consider or come to terms with. With this in mind, ground authorities would do well to increase the number of both first aid stations and St John Ambulance volunteers as patrons are suddenly confronted by a host of difficult choices previously not encountered. For the very real threat exists that, in queueing first for drink, then food, then more drink, he may well miss a large portion of the match. The worst-case scenario being that by the time he makes it back to his ticketed seat, the stand is empty, the floodlights dimmed, covers in position, and post-match interviews all but complete. In terms of ticking boxes, he has supped well, eaten his fill, the only downside being that he has not seen a single piece of action.

As innovative as The Hundred is, it is worth repeating the possible danger to the paying public from the constant crashing of sixes into grandstands and terraces. While ground authorities have a duty of care towards the viewing public, it is also the responsibility of patrons to mitigate the very real threat of injury. With personal protective equipment unlikely to be on the market before the end of the summer, patrons, in the best British traditions of make-do-and-for-God's-sake-look-after-yourself are advised to take all necessary precautions to prevent being mauled by a maximum. To this all-important end we recommend any form of cycling, motorcycling or American football helmet. DIY enthusiasts with an eye to the kitchen might consider a self-padded colander which would certainly help lessen the seriousness of any blow. The volume and solidity of a home perm has long been the go-to safety product for those with a claustrophobic fear of helmets. Full body protection would be provided by a suit of armour more especially if it is part, always a distinct possibility, of a themed costume for the occasion. Finally, given the sheer volume of sheets of discarded perspex since social distancing was relaxed, this would provide both an ideal safety cocoon as well as ensuring a perfect view of the game and action.

While The Hundred stands as arguably the simplest form of the game yet invented – a kind of beach cricket without sand and incoming tide – it should not be taken or treated lightly. From crowd safety to alcohol issues to cricket's already burgeoning lexicon, The Hundred will not go gently into that good night. Forewarned is forearmed.

* * *

Yew Es Hay

One of the many joys of air travel is the distinct possibility – courtesy of a tedious, slow-moving check-in queue or the passenger in the next seat – of striking up a conversation with an American. If so, then there is every likelihood that at some point during the discussion cricket will be mentioned. At which point, better buckle up and prepare for some serious fun. For there is nothing more confusing, more perplexing, more mystifying to our friends across the pond than the sight and sound of leather on willow. By way of opening stanza, it's worthwhile to place on record the very real fact that, at Test level, a solitary fixture is played over five days. *Five days! Are you crazy?* This should be followed by the distinct possibility that, after five days of competitive international sport, the game may well end in a draw. *Get outta here!* Or perhaps that should read: *Ged! Outta! Hair!* Either way, the game is now well and truly afoot.

At this point it's perhaps best, given this may be a long-haul flight, to appease your new best friend with a few similarities between, say, baseball and cricket. For instance, consider the pitcher as the bowler, the batter as the batsman, and the catcher as the wicketkeeper. The relative calm that these similarities have prompted is all too fleeting, however, as you stray into the choppy, uncharted waters of fielding positions. Feel free to offer a little sympathy at this point as the likes of backward point, forward short leg, silly mid-off, gully, deep square, fine leg and third man will fox most Americans. *Silly mid-off? Seriously?* The game-changer, for by now there is a very real need of such, is the civilised and civilising nature of a game that offers the chance during the hours of play for both luncheon and afternoon tea. Even around the shires – the amateur game in full flood – play is halted mid-match in order for tea and buns to be taken.

If that fails to pacify the perplexed and now quite visibly perspiring passenger sitting next to you, then offer up the picture of cricket as an enormous game of chess. A game susceptible to the nuances of atmospheric conditions, to the meteorological mores of rain and bad light, and the clear and present danger while batting of being poleaxed by a thunderous blow to the groin that will simultaneously take the wind out your sails, while at the same time reducing the opposition to gales of laughter.

Having had your sport for the day, it's time, in an effort to restore the equilibrium, for some home truths from the pavilion, which will surely make your new American chum's chest swell with pride. Be careful, though, for at any moment he may feel the need to unbuckle his seat belt, stand loud and proud, and launch into a chorus of Yew Es Hay, Yew Es Hay.

For whether we like it or not the game of cricket has sold out to all things Stateside, in particular the new kids on the block: Twenty20 and The Hundred. In both instances it is as if the creators were handed return air tickets to the US together with a blank canvas on which to map out a new sporting format of which Americans would be proud. Thus, Twenty20 and The Hundred were created purely with primetime TV slots and attendant wall-to-wall advertising in mind, with games to last just long enough for viewers to consume a bucket of chicken wings (other animals and body parts are available), a vat of coleslaw (other diced vegetables are available), and a two-litre bottle of Coke (other brands are available). Written into the fine print of these shortened formats is the condition that every match must produce a winner.

To keep the excitement levels simmering, nubile cheerleaders (pom-poms optional) whoop and holler encouragement. On the basis that you can't have cheerleaders without music, a DJ is part of the package along with decibel-deafening music. And if the frenzy appears to be falling short of expectations, then simply activate the fireworks and flamethrowers. To mirror the heroes of gridiron, batsmen now walk to the crease as if a cross between RoboCop and Mad Max. Player identification among the fielding side is little improved as cricketers today, as if a demented strain of Midwich Cuckoos, meld into one with their evenly tanned features, close-cropped hair and, by way of further tribute to American sport, more tattoos than the City of Edinburgh. In their efforts to leave no turn unstoned, both Twenty20 and The Hundred come complete with an array of statistics of every size, shape, description, graph, bar, and pie chart.

And just when you thought it safe to leave the lounge for a call of nature, up pops another blazered or bouffanted expert or slick, silver-tongued summariser with more breaking news that you simply can't miss. Fear not, though, your bladder has been catered for courtesy of sponsored strategic timeouts. The final part of the production package sees a raft of new network speak to keep players, pundits, and public on their toes. Thus, a long hop is now seen in terms of a slow bouncer, the full toss is a strategic death over delivery, and cow corner is hitting in the batsman's arc. As for the revolutionary free hit, look no further than stuff and nonsense! So while we may take a rise out of our American friends as they struggle to come to terms with the institutions, intricacies, and sheer unintelligible nature of the game of cricket, be careful of such fun and games. For scratch the surface of both Twenty20 and The Hundred and you'll find formats built on foundations as American as Hershey Bars and Macy's Parade. What have we done?

* * *

Chin Music

One of the many side effects of the pandemic on the game of cricket – over and above the hard-to-stomach suspension of club teas – has been the rampant growth of facial hair. The cumulative effect of lockdown and home office has seen a steady falling off in the need or desire of men in general, and cricketers in particular, to commit themselves to hot water, shaving cream and razor. Cricket has a long history in matters involving facial hair. The very first England XI to tour Australia in 1861/62 were only too happy to promote side whiskers, with skipper H.H. Stephenson leading from the front and sporting an imposing full beard. The next to fly the facial flag was the undisputed Father of the Game, W.G. Grace. One can imagine the good doctor casting the same withering gaze on barber and razor that he saved for bowlers who dared threaten his occupation of the crease.

From the Great War onwards whiskers fell out of fashion as cricket became a game for the combed, clipped and closely shaved. When this was threatened, as with the spat over Bodyline and the potential harm to the Commonwealth, it was reassuring to note that the main protagonists – Bradman, Jardine, Larwood, Voce and Bowes – were all clean-cut individuals with barely a five o'clock shadow to call their own. Wind the clock forward to the 1970s and cricket historians note a sudden and significant outbreak of moustaches in the Australian camp led by a man looking to audition for the role of silent movie villain, Ian Chappell. Aided and abetted by the likes of Dennis Lillee, Max Walker, Rod Marsh and Ashley Mallett, it began to look like facial hair was a key attribute to selection along with a stockpile of expletives of mass destruction.

In the decade that followed, while not going down the bushranger route of a bearded Ned Kelly (although his armour plating would have been useful to combat the West Indian pace attack), certain Australians took the moustache to the next level with a bushy Zapata style as favoured by both David Boon and Merv Hughes. More commercial than cricket-based, this immediately marked the players as identifiable and thus more marketable whether it be advertising fast food in the case of Boon or beer with Merv the Mighty. Fearing failure on the follicle front, England countered with several acres of designer stubble as championed by Graham Gooch. Leading as always from the front, the Essex and England captain would only appear before the cameras or attend a press conference if he had at least three days' growth. This look soon caught on and was the accepted practice among England players for both home and away series. There was a counter movement, briefly led by Mitchell Johnson, who turned the clock back to the Lillee era by sporting a large, black, and ever-threatening moustache. As a tactical 'tache it worked a treat. Although, as experienced coaches were keen to point out, you could run in with pigtails and a pink, frilly frock just so long as you could bowl in excess of 90 miles an hour.

Despite restrictions on short-pitched deliveries, there is little doubt that fast bowlers are favouring a mid-pitch length these days as opposed to anything full or in the batsman's half. Driven by a proliferation of Twenty20 competitions and the increasing need for disguised deliveries, these same bowlers have taken it upon themselves to produce bouncers of varying speeds in an effort to outfox batsmen. The subsequent deluge of short-pitched bowling, even on the most benign wickets, has not gone unnoticed in the commentary box. It was only a matter of time, then, before the term 'chin music' came into the cricketing lexicon. Whether borrowed from baseball, or the creation of a mischievous former fast bowler, it matters little. The fact is that the term in now embedded in the cricketing psyche thanks to the likes of the Indian Premier League.

Fighting fire with fire, or in this instance chin with chin, batsmen looked to a combination of heavy stubble and firm jaw to combat the new menace. While their new trophy hairstyles were denied public access and adoration by the use of protective helmets, this did not stop them making a statement that was both defiant and designer with facial hair. Thus, the shorter and faster the delivery, the greater reliance on stubble and steadfastness. This was the state of play – the hair and now – until the onset of the pandemic, lockdown, and home office. As has become abundantly clear of late, 12 months is a long time in respect of facial hair and habit, a point graphically illustrated at the start of the 2021 season with a mass outbreak of beards at all levels of the game from club cricket to the Test arena. All of which begs the question – with few if any chins on display, could this be the end for chin music? If so, where now for commentators and expert summarisers? Given that chins have simply been replaced by beards, and short-pitched bowling has never actually gone away, then there is every likelihood that the media will simply tweak their text to suit the new facial formula. To this end, and without wanting to encourage, they may care to consider: sideburn sonata, hirsute hip-hop, five o'clock fandango, lulla-Lillee-by, follicle folk song, and whiskers a go go. Sky Sports and *Test Match Special* – over to you.

* * *

Revolution

'Let the world change you and you can change the world,' said Che Guevara during what I suspect was another sticky jungle night with Fidel Castro as they indulged in a spot of plotting and planning before getting stuck into the Cuba libres. While difficult to think of Fidel and Che in any form of cricketing context, you do have the sneaking feeling that, as they proved in the 1950s and '60s, they would have made a formidable opening partnership. It might have been difficult to get them to don whites or club caps, but who's to say that their catchy jungle camouflage and berets would not have caught on, especially in light of some of the more garish IPL uniforms.

In this day and age, however, it is not their potential prowess on the pitch that holds sway, but their message about change. Because whether we like it or not the game of cricket is set for further transformational tinkering with a second season of The Hundred competition in the offing in 2022. It may be, like many of the paying public, that your preference is for white clothing, white sight screens, red balls, and 90-plus overs in a long and leisurely day. It may also be that while adjusting over the years to 60-, 50- and 40-over competitions and even, at a push, the bun fight that is Twenty20, you may see The Hundred as a competition too far. Given everything that has happened to the game since the pandemic this is perfectly understandable and a natural reaction.

While I was not around when cricket's powers that be added a third stump, you can only imagine the consternation on the batsman's part as his job just got that much more difficult. A different proposition of course for the bowler who now had more furniture at which to aim. And just when our batsman had mastered the trials and tribulations of a third stump the bowling – Shock! Horror! Probe! – changed from underarm to roundarm to overarm. And not a helmet, thigh pad or arm guard in sight. Little wonder recourse to strong liquor and insurance policies spiked. Monumental change, then, and yet the game not only survived but positively prospered.

Move the pavilion clock forward to the late 1970s and revolution was again on the table in the form, the very large form, of Kerry Packer and his World Series Cricket. Now I can hold my hand up as a witness to that. Indeed, within a few weeks of arriving in Melbourne in January 1978 I journeyed out to VFL Park in Waverley. In a vast concrete bowl of a stadium holding 75,000, we 3,000 hardy souls made for a curious sight among the wide-open spaces. Albeit with a decidedly Australian accent, and encompassing players and supporters alike, this was cricket's 'give me your tired, your poor, your huddled masses' moment. To the tired, poor, and huddled you can add drenched as, almost as if on cue, at the end of the game a storm of biblical proportions broke over the stadium leaving we huddled masses longing for shelter and a dry towel. Within a season or two of World Series Cricket we were happily perched on Sydney's Hill watching day/night cricket under a full moon wondering what all the fuss was about and why coloured clothing and fielding restrictions hadn't happened years earlier.

If the Packer revolution taught us anything – other than greedy billionaires buying up the sport we know and love – it is that cricket will continue to evolve, to progress, to advance. As such, a feet-dragging approach to change is not recommended as a) it's not a great look and is likely to scuff that new pair of brogues you just bought, and b) it will not make a blind bit of difference. So with The Hundred set in stone, it's a case of finding ways and means to limit the shock, calm the anger, and embrace the hype and hoopla. A quick and convenient way to achieve this – you can try this at home – is to integrate limited-overs terminology into everyday speech. To this end, morning tea or elevenses should now be referred to as a strategic timeout. A pinch, teaspoon or larger measurement of a particular herb is a Dilscoop. To over-step the mark in a social or work setting and thus risk a slap across the face is very much a free hit. An enthusiastic yet ageing family dog is a slow bouncer. A thoughtful yet slightly overbearing mother is a maximum. To clumsily bump into or inadvertently graze your shin on an electric plug is nothing more than a switch hit. On the rare occasions it is necessary to strike a thief in an effort to prevent a crime is to be a pinch hitter. For the calorie conscious, a daily or weekly record of chocolate bar consumption is known as a snickometer, or for the slightly older a Wagon Wheel. To end a relationship of any duration is to refer to it as being super over. Getting the hang of it? I hope so, because the revolution is upon us.

* * *

Miracle of Moore Park

One of the many initiatives to spice up Australian televised cricket in the mid-1990s was the introduction of a Classic Catches Competition. At the season's end the viewing public would vote for their choice from a shortlist of the extraordinary and outrageous. It could be a horizontal slip fielder clutching a stinging chance in outstretched hand, a pure reaction grab by short leg, extra cover diving low to pouch a certain four, or a fielder in the deep throwing himself every which way to take a miraculous one-handed catch. My own vote that southern summer, however, went not to a Test player or tourist, but an anonymous club cricketer who pulled off a truly audacious piece of fielding with not a single camera on hand to record the moment.

It was a sunny Saturday afternoon. There was a Shield game at the Sydney Cricket Ground. I missed the morning's play and was making my way across Moore Park for the afternoon session. With a dozen club matches in progress cheek by jowl, it was worth whiling away a few minutes on the off chance that a solitary call of 'no-ball' might induce simultaneous false shots in three or four games. These were competitive fixtures at the lower end of Sydney's cricketing pyramid. With no pavilion or changing rooms, players were required to bring their Esky (an Australian portable insulated container for food and drink), kit and folding chair (in that order) along with a picnic table for the scorers.

Having picked my way through the play I approached the northern perimeter of the park with one final game to skirt before Driver Avenue and the SCG. The game was the envy of many that day due to its close proximity to the nearby Captain Cook tavern. Not wanting to walk behind the bowler's arm, I waited for the over to finish. Encouraged by team-mates to increase the scoring rate, the batsman danced down the wicket and lofted a looping delivery high into the pale-blue afternoon sky. Stirred from his slumbers by cries of 'ketch it', long-on set off in token pursuit. It's difficult to say at precisely what point in the chase that ambition took hold. To his credit he never once took his eyes off the ball. This was a feat in itself as he first had to negotiate a path through knee-high grass, discarded pizza boxes and last night's tinnies. On a couple of occasions, he stumbled as the ground fell away alarmingly, but managed to retain his balance.

The next obstacle, for it was fast turning into that sort of chase, was a series of rutted sandy tyre tracks left by vehicles of the Sydney City Parks Department. And still his eyes remained transfixed on the ball, which by now had reached the top of its arc and was set for gravity to take hold. Sprinting for all his worth, urged on by team-mates, he took his eyes briefly off the ball to deftly sidestep a telegraph pole that promised untold harm. Refocused, he increased his pace. Starting back on a leisurely second run, the batsman looked nervously over his shoulder as ball and fielder appeared to lock coordinates at long-off. Negotiating the last tufted yards of terrain, the fielder dropped to his knees as if beseeching The Almighty and, with arms extended and palms cupped, scooped the ball inches off the ground. There was silence, but it didn't last. A split second later an explosion of noise brought whooping, cheering, screaming team-mates proclaiming their catcher in the rye.

The lack of cameras to record the occasion was the only downside to a stunning piece of cricket. This was more than offset, however, by the likelihood of team-mates standing him beers for the entire night (if not season) in the Captain Cook. I suspect too that, now 25 years on, should the bar-room banter start to flag then he's only too happy to reprise the Miracle of Moore Park.

* * *

Ahmedabad: The Movie

I don't buy into the outrage and uproar following the truncated 2021 India vs England Test in Ahmedabad. A seasoned Indophile, I've long held the belief that out of adversity comes opportunity. Indeed, I dare say that, even as you read this, a Bollywood producer is already hiring scriptwriters to work on a cricketing cross between *Gone with the Wind* and *Brief Encounter*. Think about it: Ahmedabad had it all including five sessions of play that already corresponds to the running time of a Bollywood blockbuster. As for the choreographed song and dance routines so beloved by the Indian film industry, look no further than the countless orchestrated appeals for leg before and the ballroom ballet if answered in the affirmative. Set to be part-funded by the Board of Control for Cricket in India, the script – certainly when talk turns to the future of Test cricket – can be guaranteed to include the line: frankly, mem sahib, I don't give a damn! As to the bewitching tug of love, we already have the very Cricket India ménage à trois of Ravi Ashwin, Axar Patel and the Ahmedabad pitch. Indeed, as the final delivery explodes, Ravi and Axar can be seen gazing longingly at each other and then at the pitch. As their images are lost in a cloud of red Gujarat dust, a faltering voice laments: don't worry, we'll always have Ahmedabad.

Strategic Timeout

April
The Guardian, Friday, 16 April 1999

The signs are unmistakable: a general stretching, yawning, and flexing among the population. Eyes, glazed for much of the winter, now sparkle as if sensing a juicy half volley, while nostrils, still full of runs, twitch with expectancy. Over the length and breadth of the country, from park bench to penthouse, tower block to Tudor mansion, the club cricketer is set to re-emerge. The great awakening, a new season, is close at hand. As if to emphasise the end of hibernation, stirrings at grassroots level appear unusually advanced for the time of year. Grown men have already been sighted measuring run-up and delivery stride as they walk purposefully to bus stop and tube station; the more daring, a furtive glance over shoulder, have taken to perfecting the perfect doosra with an imaginary ball. The Indian Premier League has much to answer for.

Yes, with fixture card and tea roster newly arrived, the tankard returned to the clubhouse, and the indiscretions of last August with a pretty visiting scorer all but forgotten, the odyssey, that of a new campaign, has almost arrived. There only remains the task, now part of the Duke of Edinburgh's Award scheme, of locating last season's kit. Mercifully, some come immediately to hand. The visor from the club helmet is in the sewing basket, a valuable aid apparently in the unravelling of wool. As for the helmet itself, look no further than the potting shed. 'Ideal for that troublesome hardy annual,' is all the wife or girlfriend will offer on the subject. With the search set to begin in earnest, our cricketer recalls the forgotten resolutions of September last: of flannels washed, boots whitened, and bat oiled.

Confidence, never high in relation to such quests, falters still further – setting off alarm bells at the World Health Organization – as a fruitless afternoon reveals nothing more than a yellowing, sweat-stained thigh pad, an orphaned sock, and a mildewed batting box of questionable protective quality. The boots, when eventually located, and after summary eviction of an itinerant rodent (plus droppings), bear stark reminder of that final game played amid swirling rain and fading autumnal light. Rock-hard and mud-coated, the answer to a geologist's prayer, they nevertheless rekindle memories of that last, heroic, yet ill-fated single. For the rest of his playing days, he will argue there was a run, maybe even two, to be had. That the umpire's decision rested on yards as opposed to inches, despite a creditable though despairing dive, was a product, he protests, not of error, but of rain-smudged spectacles. Club cricketers never suffer misjudgement, they merely hover (perpetually) between cock-up and catastrophe. The life-and-death manner of that final, fateful lunge is further illustrated by discovery of pads and flannels that relate more to Passchendaele than pavilion.

Though clothing proves elusive, the bat is where all bats spend the winter: doing solitary in the cupboard under the stairs. An inglorious end for such a proud piece of willow. If only he had had time to sponge off the mud, sand away those tell-tale edges, and tape the last shreds of loyal grip that refuse still to depart. The grimmest find of all, however, a half-eaten, long-sleeved sweater, is left until last. No need here to wait for the pathologist; the missing cable stitch eaten and enjoyed (with batting gloves for dessert) by moth and mutt alike. Yet not even a day such as this can dull his enthusiasm or dilute the expectancy. Thus, with faith sorely tested, but still intact, he ends the day with a prayer to St Duncan of Fearnley, 'Thank you for bringing me safe, if slightly soiled, through the winter months and for granting me another season.'

* * *

Sticky Dog

There is little doubt that we English like nothing better than talking about the weather. Fixated by fog banks. Infatuated by isobars. It is part of our DNA. Bugger Brexit: behold the Beast from the East! Pride of place in this Fahrenheit free-for-all is the humble club cricketer. Never, in the history of matters meteorological, has the weekend weather forecast been so keenly perused, and by so many, than during the April to September season. Before climate change came along you could put your house on the fact that as soon as outdoor nets started then temperatures would plummet. So back out came the thermals as you looked to combat single-figure Celsius and snow flurries. One wild and woolly fixture at Burghley Park in late May brought darkening skies and a hailstorm that would have had Noah rushing for his nail bag and four-by-two. Within minutes, the lush green outfield had turned completely white. Fearing a plague of frogs to be imminent, we packed hurriedly and were soon on the road back to Lincoln and the New Testament.

The stock meteorological expression for such early season interruption runs little beyond that of the vagaries of an English spring. Which is climate code for freezing your nuts off and facing chipped bones or broken fingers as a result of collision between leather and limbs. This goes a long way to explaining, certainly in April and May, why the more experienced and wilier of club cricketers, pyjamas or thermals beneath flannels and shirt, make a beeline for the outfield and will not under any circumstances stray within a pitch length of close catching positions. Similarly, all entreaties from the skipper to form part of a suspiciously empty slip cordon will fall on deaf ears. For no good can come of it other than injury and x-ray.

Once the season gets into full swing with hands hardened, muscles flexed, and eyes focused then the very last thing you want to see on the Friday evening is a developing low pressure in the North Sea. For that can mean only one thing: heavy showers mid-afternoon just at the point when the opposition is in disarray and the game is there for the taking. Of course, the fickleness of climate change can just as easily translate into long, hot summers with sunburnt outfields of concrete consistency, where even the most benign push off front or back foot will race to the boundary.

Wind the clock forward and September brings squally rain, strong winds, and the depressing sight of leaves skittering across outfield and pitch. A miserable, chilly end to such promise. In next to no time covers have been herded into a corner as if cattle brought in for the winter, while sight screens, once vertical, now lay horizontal in case autumn gales prove terminal. So passes another season where weather patterns will be remembered long after performances are forgotten.

This fixation with all things climatic is not so pronounced down under. Early season rains in September and October can severely curtail practice and play, but once November arrives the forecast little varies from hot, hotter, and hottest. This may be interrupted by the occasional tropical downpour, but nothing you'd give a XXXX for. This was not always the case, however, and led to the creation of a curious piece of cricketing terminology: a sticky dog. For the uninitiated, a sticky dog is a drying wicket upon which it is almost impossible to bat. Think Headingley in the early 2010s. If caught on the wrong end of a sticky dog then the tactics were simple: get as many runs as possible in the shortest time, even declaring if needs be, just to get the opposition in on a pitch still playing tricks. Eventually, as is the nature of the game, conditions would ease and sanity would return. The hope then was that the damage had not fallen on one team but had at least been shared.

The decision to cover wickets during rain breaks has, in the main, reduced the effect of weather delays. Wet outfields still pose a problem for bowlers, especially in club cricket where sawdust is looked upon as if a bag of magic beans. Recourse at this point is usually made to a handful of towels that mysteriously appear from tea room or tavern. As essential as the coolest brand of sunglasses, the latest weather app will do the rounds among club cricketers long before the onset of April. The division between trust and technology, however, still calls for a second opinion and results in the mass craning of necks in the direction of approaching weather fronts. For despite having survived revolution, innovation, and celebrity, cricket remains a game inextricably bound to the elements.

* * *

Potty Mouth

I suspect that most club cricketers have indulged in one or more of the game's dark arts at some point in their career. In my own case it involved thumbnails and lifting the seam. By way of mitigation, although no such grounds exist, I was never skilled enough to then actually hit the seam. My mentor and main man 'Big Jim' Quincey, never backward in coming forward, relied on outside agents for advantage. To wit: a jar of Brylcreem. I can still see him now walking slowly up from third man or fine leg having already had the ball thrown to him. With cap in hand, he would proceed to rub the ball on the inside lining thereby transferring the Brylcreem from cap to ball, at which point he would innocently hand his cap to the umpire and make his way to the top of his mark all the while rubbing the ball vigorously on his flannels. Little wonder, when faced with a highly polished sheen of near glitterball proportions, that fielders quickly called for sunglasses.

To the best of my knowledge, although time has been known to distort memory, I can't recall a single incident in three decades of club cricket where a Lindum side resorted to sledging. We played hard and to win, but never resorted to the baiting of opposition batsmen. The nearest we came was when a fellow walked out to bat one Sunday afternoon at Fulbeck wearing a blue cap with yellow hand-stitching proclaiming 'NAVY', but with no other insignia. A curious cove of a short leg, I simply enquired whether he had played for the navy or whether the wording just confirmed the colour of his cap. Answer there came none.

Sledging, while not emanating from the mouths of Lindum players, was still out there. Oddly enough, the pattern seems to suggest that the higher up the cricketing food chain the more likely you were to resort to potty mouth. In Joe Price, captain of both Spalding and Lincolnshire, you couldn't wish to meet a nicer, more amiable fellow. And yet, when he crossed the boundary rope, he never stopped chuntering. In his defence, the vast majority of his comments were not actually aimed at the opposition batsmen. Joe started first on his team-mates, followed quickly by the umpires, the sun or cloud cover, the chap in the Ford Cortina parking in the club car park, the drinks wallahs, the orange cordial itself, an errant crisp packet, and only then perhaps the opposition batsmen. The full force of his wrath, however, was saved (and rightly so) for anyone foolhardy enough to walk in front of the sightscreen. And so it would continue for the duration of the innings. Back in the tea room he was his calm, pleasant self again. It was the same in the bar afterwards where he was only too happy to swap a yarn and enjoy the beer.

Higher up the pecking order there was a fixture against Leicestershire seconds at Grace Road. Fielding nine with first-class experience, it was clear that one or two of their number would have preferred a day off instead of a hit-out against a bunch of club cricketers. And we? Well, we just happened to be caught in the crosshairs. West Australian Laurie Potter was not a happy soul. Or, at least, not that day. He was thrown the ball prior to tea and bowled a mix of leg breaks and googlies spiced with an assortment of vivid expletives. Here was a man desperately in need of a foot stool or a golf course. What he plainly didn't want was a club cricketer, me, looking to sweep his every delivery of whatever variety. His whinging continued as we walked off for tea and I suspect long into the interval.

The advance in technology, particularly that of stump cam and microphone, suggests that sledging is alive and flourishing at both first-class and Test level. While old pros laugh it off as banter and part and parcel of the game, there is little doubt that the slip cordon convened by Ian Chappell in the early 1970s viewed sledging as anything but amusing asides. His legacy lives on too as recent Australian sides have taken the art and craft of sledging to unheard-of levels of toxicity, in so doing creating something of a conundrum. For where we in the UK see more sledging the higher up the cricketing pyramid, it appears to be the reverse in Australia where the sledging has blanket coverage at club and park level, becoming more refined and rarefied the higher up the grades you go. Evidence this by the fact that during a decade or more of club cricket in Melbourne, Sydney, and Canberra there were numerous occasions when – a curious amalgam of tall, thin, bespectacled, long haired and wearing a black, yellow, and green hooped cap – I came close to actually sledging myself!

> *Can't you hear, can't you hear the thunder?*
> *You better run, you better take cover*
> Down Under: *Men at Work*

* * *

Touchy-feely

It was like seeing an old friend, who has been out of your life for a very long time. I refer, of course, to the sighting of a pile of sawdust during England's 2020 Test series against Pakistan. Even then I had to look twice. Was Stuart Broad really spreading sawdust on his footmarks? Yes, he was. My goodness. Sawdust. Haven't seen you in a decade or two. The recent advance, certainly in the first-class game, of pitch and outfield covering has pretty much put paid to sawdust sightings. What brought added resonance to the occasion, other than vivid memories of rain-swept cricketing weekends around Lincolnshire, was the fact that it was a part of the modern game with which I could actually identify, there being much currently on show – we won't even mention the free hit – that I fail totally to grasp.

Why, for instance, has the game become so touchy-feely all of a sudden? The ritualised touching of gloves or bats now appears to occupy more time out in the middle than actually facing deliveries. It is as if batmen have taken on the appearance of a Wimbledon doubles duo or a pair of budgie-smuggling beach volleyballers who can barely play a point without feeling the overwhelming desire to touch hands. Perhaps it has something to do with the current Tinder generation and the need for constant unswerving attention that manifests itself in touch. Or is it a sign of reassurance on the part of the batsman at the non-striker's end that despite negotiating a tricky over they are both still at the crease and can continue the fight? I see the point of meeting a new batsman to offer a word of advice, or at an over's end to talk tactics and possible run-scoring opportunities, but why then the obvious urgent need to touch bat or gloves?

If that were not confusing enough, why then the constant chatter among the fielding team after each delivery? Believe me, the batsman knows if he's played a bad shot. Do we really need an inter-ball summary by the slips or cover region to reinforce what we've just witnessed? Similarly, the bowler will know only too well if he's just bowled a rank long hop or wide and needs little prompting to do better with the next. You expect such inane chatter from Sunday League footballers because they know no better. Of course, there are mitigating factors within football: it's the middle of winter, they're skimpily dressed, a first tackle will cover them head to toe in mud, and more often than not they've had a skinful the night before and could easily throw up before half-time. None of which, or almost none of which, can be levelled at club cricketers.

And yet the modern game has more in common with a debating society than a cricket match. At the centre of much of the dialogue is the wicketkeeper-cum-cheerleader. We'll never know whether it's a by-product of Small Man Syndrome, but he appears determined to have the first and last word after each delivery. Lemming-like, the fielders follow suit and so the debate rages. This is not to say that the game should be played in silence. Far from it. Indeed, there is a time and a place for chi'acking opponents, but not by a constant barrage of boorish banalities.

* * *

Beach Cricket

As yet, although it can only be a matter of time, the ICC has failed totally to offer anything in the way of guidelines for the rules and constitution of the most popular form of their sport: beach cricket. Given cricket's place at the top table of sporting pursuit, this stands as a glaring omission. Played on beaches the world over, cricket is the holiday game of choice. Yet there remains a void where there should be procedures and protocols. Where are the guidelines for pitch dimensions, type of bat and ball, numbers per side, ice-cream breaks, lost ball, overarm or underarm, bikini tampering, the six and out rule, sandshoe crushers, free hit for dog or donkey intervention, Kiss-me-Quick helmets, calamine lotion stoppages, escaped beach umbrella penalties, deckchair abuse, tears before bedtime, leading a team off following sandcastle destruction and, perhaps the most conflict-ridden of all, laws concerning an incoming tide?

This would seem the ideal time for discussion as, with the holiday season upon us as this book hits the shelves, British beaches will reverberate with the sound of tennis ball on plastic in the coming weeks. A further area in urgent need of clarification is that involving the giving of catches, a practice that combines an acceptable departure for the outgoing batsman while at the same time encouraging an appearance at the crease of grandmothers, mothers, sisters and girlfriends. I raise this valid point as, many seasons ago, a non-cricketing friend of mine, unable to give catches, batted deep into a fortnight's holiday on the Gower Coast. Indeed, had this been early May instead of late June, reaching 1,000 runs before the month's end was there for the taking. As it was, he boarded the train back to Lincoln at the holiday's end with a contented smile and a batting average of Bradmanesque proportions.

With this in mind, and until the ICC intervene, we suggest that the rules of play are settled before the pitching of stumps along with consultation of local tide times.

* * *

Timing

Long regarded as a cornerstone of the game, if not life itself, timing is cricket's equivalent of the Pommie guest who arrives out of nowhere, eats you out of house and home, emptying the beer fridge in the process, and stays just long enough to cop off with the neighbour's daughter. A nebulous Will-o-the-wisp concept, timing is the meeting of mind and muscle that makes the game in general and batsmanship in particular look ridiculously easy. As you would expect of such a vague notion it little shapes the life and times of club cricketers. This is not to say that yeomen amateurs are devoid of timing. Far from it. But they have little concern for its merits and care even less for its foibles and fancies.

Occasionally the club cricketer will be afflicted by a bout of timing: his feet mysteriously sashay into position, the bat swings through the desired line, the ball arrows in the preferred direction, and all is well with the world. But it is all too fleeting and the muse quickly departs. Thereafter the amateur will revert to the game he both knows and loves, to wit: spending the rest of his time at the crease using the pace on the ball to nudge and nurdle to his heart's content. Not that there isn't timing in both the nudge and nurdle, but these require far less coming together of his admittedly limited resources. And when not deflecting, the club cricketer can revert to type with a meaty combination of heave, scythe, bludgeon, and hack.

At the other end of the cricketing spectrum reside a few gilded youths for whom timing is all. Common to many sporting pursuits, players with such attributes are seen as freaks, luxuries not to be trusted, and whose skillsets will inevitably break down in the heat of battle. As such, recognition is rare and international appearances limited. Too talented for their own good, they are overlooked in favour of the more workmanlike, ten-a-penny professional. And yet. And yet, if you happen upon such treasure then you're in for a day and an innings like no other. Overlooked for many a Test in favour of his less talented but more durable, box-ticking brother, Mark Waugh (media-dubbed the 'Forgotten Waugh') scored a hundred on Test debut against England at the Adelaide Oval in January 1991. An innocent bystander atop the new Bradman Stand, I watched on in time suspended awe. So much more than just an innings, this was a recital, a performance, an exhibition of pure artistry. In fact, so instinctive, so graceful, so nerveless was Waugh's manner that it was easy to mistake debutant for veteran. Ice-cold amid the Adelaide heat, Waugh moved effortlessly towards three figures: persuading rather than punishing; more baton than bat; a masterclass in the art of timing.

The preference today within club cricket for overs as opposed to timed games has seen a steady decline in that other once crucial aspect of timing: the declaration. Should your club side be fortunate in an overs game to score heavily then it may necessitate a declaration and with it additional overs in which to bowl the opposition out. But such instances are few and far between. In an effort to secure an unlikely victory in a rain-affected county game, skippers may lean towards a declaration that is part inspired and part circumstance-driven. Either way, it can brighten and bring unexpected cheer to an otherwise dreary day. International captains, not wanting to be known as the skipper who declared and lost a Test, are naturally more circumspect in their decision-making and tend, in the main, to opt for safety first and inspiration second with the timing of declarations. That said, this particular aspect of timing can leave an indelible mark on both a series, a captain, and a career.

But enough of such rarefied atmosphere. By way of a final example of timing within cricket, look no further than the club game and indeed the clubhouse itself. For no less crucial to a day's play than a finely tuned declaration is the timing involved in the turning on of the tea urn. Too late and the players will already be in the tea room mutinous and mouth-dry gagging for a restorative cuppa and the teapot nowhere in sight. Too soon, and what began as a subtle combination championing both bag and brew will be lost amid a swirling mix more Brown Windsor than Lipton Light. Of course, there are those within the game – rebel factions believed to have sympathisers within both Lord's and the ICC – who contend that stewed tea should be part of the national cricketing curriculum. A lukewarm HQ-backed rite of passage: the preparation and benefits of which are more than worthy of a chapter or two in the latest MCC coaching manual, there being no finer way to launch a youngster in the ways of club cricket, according to a certain vintage of player, than with several gallons – first warm pot – of the cup that cheers. First flush anyone?

* * *

Cricket Teas

In the grand scheme of things uplifting and life-affirming, what could be more uplifting and more life-affirming these dark days than cricket teas? As a survivor of 30 years of club teas I can speak with some experience having consumed countless miles of Battenberg cake, a positive market garden of tossed salad, and a Manchester Ship Canal of stewed tea. Indeed, such was the esteem in which certain cricket teas were held that players were known to rise Lazarus-like from their sickbed to play and, more importantly, to eat. In the heady days of friendly matches, the tea table often carried far greater anticipation than the fixture itself. This is what sets cricket apart. What other game would cease hostilities in the heat of battle for a cuppa and sticky bun?

As you would expect of a cornerstone of the game, tactics and timing play their part in the tea ritual. At the Lindum, for instance, Tim Harding and I, great troughers to a man, could never sit together. We simply placed ourselves at either end of the table and, as if the prototype for *Pac-Man*, munched our way towards the middle. Wicketkeeper and local landlord Brian Clarke, another not shy with knife and fork, rightly deserved a trestle table to himself. Then there were the picky eaters. Our skipper 'Young Jim' Quincey (son of 'Big Jim') would eat nothing but salmon sandwiches. That these arrived with neatly sliced pieces of cucumber mattered little. His plate was easily identifiable at the tea's end by the small, discarded cucumber Alp. And who could forget the steward Sid 'Salmonella' Gott, who produced a rice concoction that appeared to last from May to September and, rather than be consumed, should probably have been sent to forensics and then for carbon dating?

As to the worst cricket tea? No names, no pack drill, but a market town close to Lincoln with a main line station. After an acrimonious afternoon in the field, we arrived to an even more acrimonious tea table that consisted of naught but bread, cheese, and a jar of Branston Pickle! The best? No contest. Away to Spalding in early August with the trestle tables groaning under the weight of locally harvested strawberries.

As a veteran of many summers down under, I can disclose that cricket teas come some way down the pecking order in Australian club cricket. It was as if the entire grassroots game had adhered to the strict teachings of Homer and Bart Simpson in that you don't make friends with salad. As such, austerity cricket saw the 20-minute tea interval used mainly to escape the sun, take a quick shower, or have a change of togs. Cups of tea were available, so too a plate of biscuits assuming that the designated player had remembered to buy them. Of course, this being the land of Foster's, XXXX and VB, what the tea ritual lacked was more than made up for in the dressing sheds and bar at the close of play.

* * *

Skiing With Big Cats in Angola

Without wanting to rain on the club cricketer's parade – the amateur game having suffered more than enough during the pandemic – this does seem an opportune moment all the same to remind players of Quincey's Law of Applied Aches, Ailments and Arthritis, the cornerstone of which states that no matter how successful, lengthy, or countrywide a club career there will always be a reckoning, a price to pay. Despite his passing more than a decade ago, I can still see 'Big Jim' massaging Deep Heat into his battle-weary knees, his only comment, 'Don't worry, it'll happen to you.' He was, of course, referring to the growing list of aches and pains that beset club cricketers who no longer club or cricket.

In Quincey's case it was four decades of bowling that did for his knees, which he happily sent for surgery when in his 70s to ease the pain and aid mobility. This would appear the one silver lining to this whole ghastly growing old experience in that medical science has moved on at such a pace that we now, give or take the odd backlog in surgical procedures, no longer have to suffer in silence. Not that silence was ever Quincey's strong point. Whether a thundered appeal to a quivering umpire or a pleading request to his 80 or so racing pigeons to stop playing silly buggers and land, he was not a slave to silence.

An energetic game played with a hard ball and, if the truth be told, with precious little padding, certainly where fielders are concerned, cricket leaves its players wide open to injury, a good deal of it self-inflicted. A quick audit of my own body reveals three scarred and stitched areas: finger, eyebrow, and shoulder. The finger dates back to September 1972 and a game at nearby Collingham. It was set to be a momentous month as I was just three weeks away from London and a first term of legal text and tome. By the time we made our way into the field after tea, summer had turned to autumn: clouds scudded, leaves skittered, rain threatened. A two-sweater evening, I made my way to deep backward square on the boundary, my only company that of farm vehicles trundling along the narrow lane over a nearby hedge.

With little in the way of action out in the gloaming, I settled upon vigorous bouts of hand-rubbing to generate heat to combat the wind chill. Harnessing a freshening breeze, the batsman swept a delivery in my direction. A low, flat, angry shot, the ball seemed to lock coordinates and home in on me. I didn't have to move an inch, just wait and pouch the catch. As team-mates ran over intent on congratulation something, probably the trickle of blood, prompted me to glance at my left hand. Bad decision. Once straight and perfectly pinky, the little finger now resembled the letter Z. The top joint, as if a crazy golf hole, was at right angles; the middle joint, not to be left out, was clearly visible through broken skin. I wobbled to the wicket growing paler by the second. Back and seated in the small wooden pavilion, a considerate Collingham player brought brandy.

Fortunately my folks were at the game and I was quickly bundled into the front seat of the car and on my way to A&E

at Lincoln County Hospital. The top joint, I can report, clicked back easily, the middle one less so. It took a minute of grappling and Greco-Roman wrestling for the poor doctor to get the confounded thing into place and functioning. To add insult to injury – another brandy plainly out of the question – I was then asked to drop my flannels whereupon a pretty nurse delivered a tetanus shot to my right buttock. With that, my season was over!

Six year later, and 12,000 miles from home, I again found myself in the wars. Fielding in the slips during a Brighton club match in Melbourne, I stuck a hopeful paw in the direction of a thick outside edge. The ball slapped into the fleshy part of my right hand and ricocheted into my right eyebrow, tearing the skin above the eye. Once again dripping blood, I was assisted from pitch to pavilion where a doctor was called, and stitches applied. An hour or so later, Brighton having bowled the opposition out cheaply, I found myself patched, padded, and taking guard. So much for a soft-centred Pom!

Visits to A&E became a regular feature a decade later as three times I was helped off the outfield as a result – once bowling, twice fielding – of a dislocated shoulder. I stayed home one winter shortly after to undergo surgery which would 'tighten' things up. The end product was an impressive scar that, depending on my surroundings and alcohol consumption, was the result of a skiing accident with Team GB or an incident in Angola with a bunch of mercenaries or a big cat circus act that didn't go to plan. If the night was going exceptionally well then it was not beyond the bounds to combine all three and explain that the scar was the result of a skiing accident with big cats in Angola.

As the vast majority of ex-cricketers will confirm, if you're lucky enough to escape fracture, break, tear, dislocation, stitch and scar, there is always a catch-all spot of arthritis to fall back on. This takes no prisoners and afflicts all from Test arena to village green. Nor is there a cricketer's body part – neck, shoulders, back, hips, knees, and ankles – that is likely to remain arthritis-free. Free arthritis with every fifty or five-fer? While unsure of the finer points of *Arthritis and the Armchair Cricketer*, the only possible plus I can report is the ability to forecast a cold snap days if not weeks ahead of the massed ranks of meteorologists. It might be a low-pressure system out over the Azores or something nastier heading our way from the Russian Steppes, either way my knees appear able, through a complicated joint-related system of divining and dowsing, to make an early prediction of its landfall. If this were to work with tornados and hurricanes, then there might be gainful employment for my knees at the National Storm Center. Quincey would have made a fortune!

There is little comeback now for we ailing and infirm ex-cricketers. Of course, we did have a choice and could just have easily turned our back on the game and taken an allotment, or a wife, or skiing holidays with big cats in Angola. We didn't have to play the confounded game. However, and this is why there is no possible hope for old cricketers, for asked if we would do it all again the answer is a resounding YES. Indeed, the growing list of aches and ailments, pains, and possible surgery, pale when set against memories of that diving catch, perfectly executed cover drive, or cartwheeling off stump.

* * *

Smoke and Mirrors

To the New Age Cricketing Lexicon – following hard on the heels of free hit (aka the day the music died) and slow bouncer (nee long hop) – can be added scrambled seam. I'm not sure what Quincey would have made of a scrambled seam.

I suspect, very little. The only things scrambled in his playbook were eggs. Anything else scramble-related would have been over-egging the eggs. His view of bowling in general, and fast bowling in particular, was not to over-complicate what in essence is a very simple art form. Let the conditions – heavy atmosphere, green, flat, or crumbling wicket – sow the seeds of doubt.

Of course, bowling coaches need to keep their jobs, and pundits need something upon which to pundificate. The mantra from both radio and TV is that bowlers need to continually improve their skills so as to gain parity in a game that continues to favour bat over ball. Fair enough. But with much of the game still played in the mind, then a healthy dose of smoke and mirrors should always be the first course of action. Other than the occasional thumbnail to lift the seam or Brylcreem to enhance the shine, Quincey's method was simply to concentrate on line and length and let the conditions do the rest. And if a batsman thinks that – on a sample survey of one – he's bending it like Botham or getting more sideways movement than a season of *Strictly*, then so be it. Smoke and mirrors.

But let's not go over the top in searching for the ultimate deception when more often than not a simple adherence to line, length and limited variation will do the trick. For example, consider the tactic – championed by bowlers and bowling coaches – of a concerted barrage of short-pitched deliveries to remove a tail-ender, when the accepted method since quicks first laced their boots see Trueman, Gough and Malinga – was always the yorker. Nothing curtails ambition more than a full, fast delivery lasered in at the toes. And not a scrambled seam in sight.

* * *

Scarborough Scoff

In search of much-needed downtime a year or two back we headed to the Scarborough Cricket Festival for days two and three of Yorkshire's County Championship game against Somerset. While the rest of the country basked in summer highs, we battled monsoonal weather and temperatures of just 14°C. So much for Scarbados! With warming teas and coffees the order of the day, we could at least look forward to some hearty local food. Or could we? As if the rain, bad light, and Yorkshire's performance were not bad enough, we were confronted over the luncheon interval by the prospect of chips, mushy peas and WARM (be afraid) PORK (be very afraid) PIES! It was fair to say we had neither the courage, constitution nor conviction to attempt such scary Scarborough scoff.

With the cricket mirroring the weather, the highlight of our two-day soiree proved to be the tea room scones with matching jam and cream. On the drive back to the soft south, the weather improving by the mile, we decided there was unfinished business with Scarborough and the Cricket Festival. We'll be back, not this year, hopefully next, when the crisis has passed, and the pork pies have returned to something nearer room temperature.

* * *

Deep Heat

It's difficult to pinpoint the exact moment or place when cricket dressing rooms moved away from rooms in which to dress and became storage units for kit bags. Popular opinion dates it around the time that batsmen started wearing helmets. The size and shape of the protective headwear brought about a complete rethink on the kit front. The first sign of change came with the sighting in many a pavilion of the 'coffin'. A cumbersome affair, the elongated suitcase made it possible for the player to pack all manner of clothing and equipment including, if he so wished, the kitchen sink.

As you might imagine, dressing rooms BC (Before Coffins) were an altogether more spacious affair. With many players having just the basics – flannels, shirt, sweater and boots – a kit bag of any description was all but non-existent. Post-war austerity and the rise of make-do-and-mend cricket saw the shortfall in equipment offset by a bag of 'club kit'. This was a motley and often mildewed collection of cast-offs and hand-me-downs. On average, only the top five, batsmen with ambition, or those with more money than sense would possess their own bat, pads and kit bag. For the remainder the 'club kit' beckoned and with it the very real chance of heading out to the wicket sporting odd pads, ill-matched gloves, and a cracked bat with peeling rubber grip. All of this was tough on the lower-middle order and tail, but was bravely shouldered more especially when set against the extra space generated in and around the dressing room.

And then the helmet happened. Followed quickly by the 'coffin'. And then by giant kit bags, monstrosities that have yet to be fitted with air bags, red lights, and voice-activated warnings when reversing, but it can only be a matter of time. With space at a premium, players have adopted the tactics of German holidaymakers in Marbella by arriving at the ground earlier and earlier so as to put a sweater or helmet on a favoured seat or bench.

The advance in, and desire for, extra clothing and equipment can also be placed at the door of socio-economic conditions and a year-on-year increase in disposable income. And what better way to dispose of increased income than by purchasing the latest state-of-the-art bat or lightweight pads or opting for three sweaters instead of one? That said, the players' need for extra storage space cannot be laid solely at the door of spending power or a craving for the latest kit. For into this equation must be brought the spike in recent years of personal hygiene products and the part they play in the club cricketer's packing process and procedures.

Wind the clock back to the late 1960s and you were lucky if your dressing room had access to a washbasin and toilet. As for showers? In your dreams, buddy. This in turn led to a minimalist approach to personal hygiene. There would be a 'club towel' which would be located next to both the 'club bar of Lifebuoy' and the 'club comb'. These essential items would, certainly in the case of a more far-sighted and free-thinking XI, also come with the 'club truss' and, although believed to be something of an urban myth, the 'club bra'. And that, with a tin of Imperial Leather talcum powder and a can of Old Spice was all you needed to erase the effects of a long day in the field while at the same time preparing for both the clubhouse bar and the possibility of a night on the town.

The only drawback to limited personal hygiene products occurred if a player suffered a tweak or twinge before, during or after the game and had to resort to the 'club tube' of Deep Heat. Every dressing room had one. No one quite understood its healing properties, if indeed any such existed. And yet bowlers, batsmen, fielders, umpires, tea ladies and clubhouse stewards, if not actually swearing by it, were only too happy to rub liberal amounts into ankles, knees, shoulders and backs. As a warning to club cricketers past and present, this would seem an opportune moment to recall an incident that befell a housemate of mine a few decades ago in Canberra. Arriving home in the early hours after a convivial evening at the Press Club, she entered her bathroom with the express purpose of brushing her teeth before bed. At some point in the brushing, it began to dawn that all was not right. In fact, all was very, very wrong. Earlier in the evening she had treated a troublesome shoulder with Deep Heat and left the tube next to the toothpaste. No further explanation is needed other than thank goodness she didn't go in search of mouthwash.

I have no doubt that the tech-savvy makers of Deep Heat – a little like paint manufacturers who have successfully removed all fumes from their products – now produce a more fragrant version, which is just as well given the crowded nature of modern dressing rooms. As a final rose-tinted reflection on dressing rooms of yesteryear, while the increased kit-free space enabled ailing club cricketers to benefit fully from weapons-grade Deep Heat, the full return/risk ratio was difficult to assess or even start to evaluate unless counterbalanced by at least half a can of Old Spice.

* * *

Quincey

In the run up to Lindum's 150th anniversary celebrations in 2006, there was talk of a club publication. As an idea for an article, I spent time with 'Big Jim' Quincey detailing his first season for the club in 1946. Over a chaotic yarn-filled evening, laptop vying with beer, ice-cream and cake, we managed to turn the clock back 60 years. I took the finished piece to him a few days later. He seemed happy enough, not least with the fact that inside a few short paragraphs we'd managed to mention Churchill, Hitler, and Quincey!

Contrary to public opinion, there were no Quinceys wheeling away at the Wragby Road End in 1856. Move the clock forward 90 years, however, and things were about to change. For as post-war Britain was struggling to come to terms with a victory hard won, so a post-war Jim Quincey – 17 years old, 6ft 1in and 12st wet through – was struggling to come to terms with the harsh reality of rationing. One egg a week, 4oz of bacon, 2oz of sweets, 4oz of sugar, and 3oz of meat; was this any way to breed a budding fast bowler? Churchill was no help either, failing totally to mention the effects of powered egg to line and length while warning of the dangers of Soviet expansionism in his 'Iron Curtain' speech.

Around the time that the League of Nations was dissolved – I don't think the two were connected – the cricket committee sent out letters to all youth clubs in the area inviting two youngsters to attend a week's coaching on the Lindum in early July 1946. At the time I was playing youth league cricket on the west common for St Nicholas Boys' Club on Burton Road. The Lindum club and ground that summer was a far cry from today. The old pavilion had survived – dry rot being far more of a threat than Hitler – and continued to house the changing rooms, tea room, and bar, while the adjacent Nissen hut doubled as a shower block. Albert 'Baggy' Kent was the groundsman, alternating evening work at the Lindum with his day job on the broad acres of the nearby Lincoln School. An old fast bowler's lament maybe, but his liberal use of marl on the square made the Lindum pitch, even back then, a batsman's paradise.

Supervised by Lindum players, the coaching sessions were held over three weekday evenings. Despite the combined effects of rationing and Churchill, I was the solitary boy selected and duly made my Lindum debut on 13 July 1946 for the seconds at Newark, with a first home game the following weekend. The passage from youth cricket to the adult game was helped in no small measure by the various characters in the second XI at the time, and none more so than Percy Freeman. Keen to see a chap get on in the game, Percy was always on hand to back up appeals for leg before with those of his own. That these would hail from third man mattered little. A negative response from the umpire would thus be followed by an indignant 'bugger me!' from the boundary.

Loath as I am to return to the subject of food, I should mention, given the family connections, that the supplies for the teas were provided by Stan Rollett from his corner shop in the Bail. The order would normally consist of four loaves, eight eggs, salad, spam, fruit cake (slab for the use of) and tea with ever diminishing amounts of milk and sugar. A purely personal choice, but your bread and margarine could either be used for the salad or, for the more travelled and cosmopolitan, there was a saucer of jam. Which, for the record, was more saucer than jam.

At this time, although in its infancy, I was walking out with young Betty Sawyers of Queen's Crescent. Innocent enough beginnings maybe, but as with many a girlfriend and later wife, this would lead in 1950 to 40 years of tea-making for various Lindum sides. And that, every which way, is an awful lot of spam and scones. If food appears something of a recurring theme in the summer of 1946, then blame it on the trauma of rationing. A trauma, I'm happy to report, I have yet to come to terms with. In George Leachman's case, although a butcher by trade, he was a victim of the little-known condition of piano deficiency. The condition was treatable, however, as he appeared to know every pub in three counties with a piano.

An odd combination, but it was difficult to talk of pubs and pianos that summer without mentioning pork pies. For with 'Wobby' Wilkinson in the side, a visit to a pub – George already installed behind the piano and belting out the tunes – would invariably and miraculously herald the appearance of a 2lb pork pie courtesy of his family pork butchers. And if still hungry, and you could run to threepence (in old money) there was always the possibility of fish and chips on the way home.

During the 1946 season, although national service was a dark cloud fast approaching, I was gainfully employed as a wages clerk at Morrell's pea factory in Bardney. The nine-to-five existence, thanks to the railway, meant I didn't miss a single evening net session. Just as well, too, as this first year of involvement with the Lindum came to an abrupt end on 3 December with my call-up papers. Two inches taller, half a stone heavier and now 20, I was back at the Lindum for pre-season nets and straight into the first team in April 1949, staying for 22 years before dropping down to captain the seconds for another 13, and finally hanging up the boots aged 55 in 1984.

* * *

Seeing is Believing

As if another garish, incomprehensible tattoo to cricket's forearm or frame, the latest edition of what is known to millions as the IPL – the Indian Premier League – is primed and ready to party. Whether you march behind the banner of swash and buckle or that of hype and hoopla, it matters very little as a global audience is guaranteed. While set to win the ratings war, little if anything has been written about the mass appeal of this most limited of limited-overs formats. Those wishing to sweep away cricket's dusty, traditional past in favour of a glossy global future need point only at the game's new and evolving lexicon. To wit: pinch hitter, death bowler, switch hit, paddle scoop, ramp shot, reverse sweep, knuckleball, strategic timeout, free hit, and slow bouncer. To these we can add – hot off the angst – bubble fatigue. This roughly translates to the exhaustion suffered by international cricketers detained in five-star Hilton luxury with little else to do all day but watch Netflix, turn up the air-con, and order room service. Back in the real world, meanwhile, bubble fatigue goes little beyond furlough and food bank.

As innovative as this new cricketing terminology is – aided and abetted by ever-willing pundits – your average club cricketer is no more likely to enter the clubhouse bar and strike up a conversation about the opposition's death bowler's knuckleball than he is about his recently perfected slow bouncer. Which, for the record, was last seen half an hour ago and has still to come within the Earth's gravitational pull. From this we can deduce that, small sections of the cricketing public apart, it is not the allure of a new language that accounts for the rise and rise of Twenty20 cricket.

Few would argue that the three-hour, made-for-TV format is the real winner here. Indeed, this accounts for a good many of cricket's 'new audience'. With attention spans not quite what they used to be, the games fill the void once occupied by *Midsomer Murders*, *Poirot*, and *Morse* with, certainly in the case of the former, far fewer stiffs. That said, the formula and plot lines remain much the same and, barring a late swash and buckle, we know whowonit long before the game's end. While format is part of the popularity it's still not the crucial x-factor that appeals to, and can be identified by, millions across the generational and social divide. All of which suggests that the missing ingredient is a particular shot; a stroke that resonates, not just within the IPL, but among every form of the game. In which case look no further than the slog-sweep.

A slog with career aspirations, the shot is given legitimacy in its relationship to, and close connection with, the sweep. No one at the top of cricket's pyramid seems interested or game enough to divide the shot into percentages of slog or sweep just so long as the ball clears the boundary and another maximum is recorded to the accompaniment of cavorting cheerleaders, pounding music, and fiery pyrotechnics. And yet remove one aspect of the slog sweep, in this instance the sweep, and you are left with, if not a whole new ball game, then a brief insight into the appeal of Twenty20. While franchise owners might be unhappy to have their product tainted with such a crass term, the slog nevertheless remains the most identifiable shot for cricketers of all ages and ability. And nowhere more so than in England where the slog is as much a part of club cricket as the tea urn or hand-pulled roller.

It is a classless shot, too, in that it is just as easily the domain of commoners as kings. Of the latter, you may recall a picture of Kate Middleton on a tour of India some years ago. When in Mumbai she and William tried their hand at cricket. There is one particular image of Kate advancing down the wicket and swinging the bat in her natural arc. The first recorded 'slog by royal appointment' and one, had she connected, that would have sent the ball high in the direction of those wide acres between deep midwicket and wide long-on. I'm reluctant at this point, given the place of the cow in Indian religion, to refer to it in terms of cow corner as this would do a huge disservice to all concerned. Suffice it to say that this shot was executed by a member of the royal family and will be re-enacted many times over in the IPL.

The confusion arises, however, in the case of the royal family in general, and Kate Middleton in particular, in that it's difficult to know whether this whole head-in-the-air, arms flailing approach is anything cricket-related or whether it is just a part of normal royal protocol? Without wanting to incur an appointment at The Tower, the much-publicised Middleton mow offers further insight into the mass appeal of the IPL among its fan base. Whether the slog carries a high-risk tariff is inconsequential. Success or failure matters little. The plain and simple truth – irrespective of whether commoner or king – is that we can all execute the exact same shot. We may not have a lucrative IPL contract as proof of our ability, but for a brief, glorious second, we can identify; feel the same rush of adrenalin; the same explosion of connectivity; and follow the same arcing trajectory as the ball disappears into the late evening sky. Either that, or the brief disbelieving suspension of time before cartwheeling stumps, flying bails, and the long, lonely walk back to the pavilion. Chipping Norton seconds or the Chennai Super Kings: small margins. Seeing is believing.

* * *

Gone Too Soon

A champion sportsman, Tim Harding arrived in Lincoln in the early 1980s to take up a teaching post in the sports department at Christ's Hospital School. A rampaging number eight, he quickly made his mark at Lincoln Rugby Club where he performed with distinction for the first XV. Having spent the winter around the broad acres of the Lindum it was only natural that he should join the cricket club the following spring. A proud Devonian and talented junior cricketer, Tim represented his county at under-19 level. During that summer the bowling unit acted as net bowlers for a Gloucestershire County Championship side that included Pakistan Test star Zaheer Abbas. Midway through the session Tim decided to bounce Zaheer. Barely had the ball left his hand than Zaheer pivoted and hit it out of the net, out of the ground and, in Tim's own words, 'Out of the county!'

A genuine all-rounder, Tim bowled at a lively medium pace, batted with courage and panache, and added greatly to Lindum's fielding with his athleticism. His enthusiasm and sense of fun was as infectious in the dressing room as out in the middle and, with the game over, it was into the clubhouse and then on to pub or party. Tim's arrival at the Lindum coincided with a period of unprecedented success with a second South Lincs & Border title, Albion Cup wins, Sunday League success, and twilight trophies courtesy of midweek league and cup competitions. To celebrate the SL&B win Lindum held a team dinner at the Flying Pizza in Lincoln's Bailgate. To encourage dessert sales the restaurant offered a second XXL profiterole free of charge to anyone who, having consumed a first, was game enough to attempt a second. Quick to volunteer, his prowess at the tea table legendary, Tim, to the accompaniment of cheering team members and astonished fellow diners, demolished both in a twinkling.

Supremely fit, his strength and stamina were tailor-made during his time at University College London for the 400m hurdles. He later brought these attributes to the marathon by clocking a hugely impressive two hours and 50 minutes around the streets of the capital. His passion for the outdoors continued with orienteering, canoeing, triathlons and arguably his greatest love, climbing. Having already scaled Mont Blanc, he brought his undoubted talents to bear in and around the city of Lincoln by completing the first known ascent of the North Face of Alfred Lord Tennyson's statue in the grounds of Lincoln Cathedral. This was doubly impressive as it was completed without oxygen and with only minimal recourse to cans of Australian lager. He topped this feat the following year with the solo climb of Newport Arch at the conclusion of a friend's stag night.

Tim and I, the last men standing in the clubhouse following an Albion Cup Final win, further celebrated the victory and crowned the perfect evening by requisitioning several rolls of pink loo paper. With moonlight our guide we headed back out to the middle where, as a fitting tribute to the heroics of just hours earlier, we edged the pitch in double strength Barbie pink. Tim was again to the fore a season or so later in an Albion Cup semi-final against arch-rivals Hartsholme. With a tight finish looming, a questionable run-out decision brought uproar and recrimination to the middle. Calm amid the gathering storm, Tim made his way to the wicket. With much chuntering still ongoing he took guard and, as if addressing a bunch of truculent fifth-formers, announced, 'OK, let's play cricket.' To emphasise the point, he smashed the next two deliveries back over the bowler's head for four before marching off with a huge grin and bat held high.

Always up for a fight, he brought his single-minded approach to sport to his decade-long battle with a brain tumour. Beset in recent years by the debilitating effects of chemotherapy, he nevertheless took every opportunity to exercise, whether on long walks around Colwyn Bay or an hour or so on the sports cycle he'd customised in his garage. In late summer 2020, by way of a thank you to those who had cared for him in the IC Unit at Liverpool's Walton Hospital, he undertook a tandem freefall skydive, raising much-needed funds in the process. Tim became ill in mid-February 2021 and was admitted to St David's Hospice in Llandudno. He passed away the following evening. The man may have gone, but goodness the memories remain.

Quirky

THE FIRST Commandment of travel states that the more you visit a city or country, the easier it is to survive and prosper. The implication being that you already know the neighbourhood butcher and baker and, should a power outage threaten, the nearest candlestick maker. Which is fine and dandy as commandments and candlesticks go unless the country happens to be India! Current COVID-19 problems apart, India, if anything, raises the degree of difficulty with each passing visit. The reasons for such are simple: growing population, pollution off the scale, traffic gridlock, and temperature and humidity levels that keep on climbing. And yet, if you can summon the strength and fortitude to tough it out then India remains arguably the most magical place on the planet. That said, India has not always been the traveller's boot camp.

My first experience of Bombay was in October 1986. It was not the most auspicious of arrivals, either, with the midnight queue for immigration made all the longer and more debilitating by three flights arriving within a few minutes of each other. Once deplaned, the humidity kicked in. So too the Indian love of bureaucracy. For all that, it still registered low on the Richter Scale of Stresses and Strains. My luggage turned up unscathed, I sorted a cab, and made ready for the journey to Marine Drive and my hotel. The only slight cause for concern was when the cabby stopped in the middle of nowhere, with little if any street lighting, and announced he had to visit his family. So: four o'clock in the morning, pitch black, strange noises and smells emanating from in and around the cab, and not a clue where we've stopped. Welcome to India! The sky was pastel pink by the time he dropped me at my hotel. A hotel booked – in these pre-internet days – by good old-fashioned aerogramme. The night staff quickly found my booking and in little or no time I was unpacking. It was that easy!

Not that there was time to tarry, for once rested there were tickets to be booked. First up was a train to Madras. Despite being a veteran of many a London bus queue, the jostling and crush outside the station ticket office gave sardines and cans a bad name. However, you don't play Sunday League football without knowing how to use your elbows or block an opponent. Once again, the ticket was bought with the minimum of fuss and inconvenience.

More by luck than judgement, my time in Bombay coincided with the final Test of the India vs Australia series. The first fixture in Madras had produced only the second tie in Test history; the final wicket falling with an Indian umpire giving Maninder Singh out leg before to Greg Matthews. That apart, the Test was notable for Dean Jones's 502-minute occupation of the crease in an innings of 210. As each session passed so he was hauled off the pitch, stripped, and pushed under the shower before being dried, dressed, and led into battle again. Jones was not at the ground to witness the pulsating finish as, suffering severe dehydration, he was acquainting himself with a saline drip in a nearby hospital.

The second Test in Delhi was largely rained out with play not starting until late on the fourth afternoon and barely 100 overs bowled in the match. All of which left Bombay. The game, reverting to subcontinental type, proved a high-scoring draw. It did provide the opportunity, however, to witness three Mumbaikers – Gavaskar, Vengsarkar and Shastri – scoring centuries. The proximity of the Wankhede Stadium to my hotel allowed the luxury of heading back for a shower during the lunch interval. With that my week and introduction to India was up and I was winging my way across the Central Plains to Madras. And it all seemed so, so easy.

* * *

My favourite *Fawlty Towers* moment, also one of the briefest, takes place in the hotel bar and involves Basil and the Major.

The Major, 'I must have been rather keen on her because I took her to see India!'

Basil, 'India?'

The Major, 'At The Oval. Fine match, marvellous finish.'

The first time I saw Chennai it was called Madras. That seemed to fit the script as I'd just arrived by train from Mumbai which, when I boarded, was still called Bombay. The great joy of arriving in Madras was that it invariably came at the end of a 24-hour rail trip. Steam trains were still the order of the day for my first visit and for further stays in the 1990s. I would buy an Indrail Pass – US$250 for 30 days of unlimited first-class ticketed miles – from a small travel agency in Wembley. You mailed your proposed itinerary, approximate dates, length of stay and the like, and they'd organise the rest. It worked a treat and with the absolute minimum of effort. The last time I visited Chennai – née Madras – in 2009 I arrived via a domestic flight: not half as much fun, but a good deal less soot!

The 1986 autumn visit was a multi-purpose stopover for around three weeks. I was due to meet the good doctor in Madras. In town to complete the research for her PhD, she booked a modest hotel room for my stay. With the door barely shut, my rucksack still shouldered, there came a knocking. Outside stood a staff member with her right arm extended. Having trouble focusing in the half-light of the hall it soon became apparent that I was being offered, as were all visiting westerners, a toilet roll. An ominous sign. Still, all things considered, a sight more practical than a complimentary fruit bowl. In between bouts of exploring, I would visit the good doctor at the Madras Institute of Development Studies. During one such visit she introduced me to a colleague, Mr S. Subramanian (Subbu).

Arriving in his large, book-filled office a little after midday tiffin it took little time before the two of us were deep in cricket conversation. A published academic and lifelong cricket fan, Subbu was keen to get to grips with the successes and failures of the modern game. And that was it: we were off and running. An hour or so later the *chai wallah* popped his head around the door and Subbu ordered tea. This procedure was repeated twice more. I suspect we would still have been there all these years on had the good doctor not appeared in the doorway a little after 5.30pm. With midday having given way to dusk we reluctantly wound up the debate.

A few years later Subbu put a family bungalow at the hill station of Kodaikanal at my disposal. The detour was well researched but, as with all such plans, never quite worked out. The crazy taxi ride into the hills by an equally crazy driver (one of the scariest rides ever) set the tone. Once there the clouds descended and that was pretty much it for the entire stay. The mist-shrouded terrain led to one of the oddest sightseeing trips of all time. I booked a cab for a couple of hours one morning to drive to the various lookout points. The cabbie was happy to oblige, supplying a running commentary into the bargain. Which was perhaps just as well for at each stop, so dense was the cloud cover that you could barely see beyond your nose.

Before trooping disconsolately off for an early lunch, postcards were bought for no other reason than to give an idea of the views that would never be seen.

The local custodians of the bungalow would arrive early each evening bearing logs and food. Once the fire was set and roaring, and with plates of hot food dispensed, life, panoramic views apart, was not at all bad. The only cloud on the horizon, assuming you could see the horizon, which you couldn't, was the large and troublesome monkey population. Thinking they were the true owners of the property, we had to run the gauntlet each morning and afternoon. This usually took the form of a warning stone or two across the bows before a mad dash for freedom or safety. To prevent nightly raiding parties, a quick sweep of the rooms was made before bedtime to secure all windows and doors.

Over the years I met Subbu several times in Oxford while he stayed with a family member at Wolfson College. We ventured out little during these meetings and were more than content to drink tea and talk cricket, as was the case for my last visit to Chennai in February 2009. I arrived on a Thursday evening flight from Mumbai via Brisbane and Bangkok, and left the following Monday. During the long weekend Subbu and his wife, Prabha, took me to wedding festivities on both the Friday and Saturday. Over the Sunday morning breakfast table, I thought it right and proper to ask, if only for reasons of balance and fair play, whether there might be a divorce celebration we could attend that day.

In many respects, the first meeting with Subbu in 1986 set the bar for all future cricket conversation in India. This was borne out many times over in Mumbai with Ramu and friends or the dizzying evenings with Satya and his merry-go-round of visitors. All of which confirms in spades the words of Andrew Lang:

There is no talk, none so witty and brilliant,
that is so good as cricket talk,
when memory sharpens memory,
and the dead live again – the regretted, the unforgotten,
and the old happy days of burned out Junes revive.

* * *

In the autumn of 1990, I was back in India and briefly resident at the Ashoka Hotel in New Delhi. Better than that, though, I was armed with a 30-day Indrail pass and set for some serious backpacking. The magical mystery tour was briefly put on hold, however, as I set off for 7 Bahadurshah Zafar Marg and the offices of the *Times of India* (*TOI*). Uninvited, this was the ultimate in cold calling. I did dress for the occasion, though: shirt and jeans which, at this early stage of the trip and through squinted eyes, suggested respectability, but little more.

Not that these preparations made an iota of difference to the scrum that surrounded the reception desk. The confusion nevertheless proved a godsend, there being nothing the cold caller likes less than having to make a pitch in stony silence to disbelieving gatekeepers. I was eventually sent on my way with the necessary chit and traversed a couple of dimly lit staircases before entering the chatter and clatter of typewriter in the newsroom. A few heads turned, but with deadline approaching it was the usual heady mix of anxiety and hysteria.

Eighteen months earlier, unbeknownst to me, a BBC film crew had turned up at Zafar Marg to record a documentary on the *TOI* timed to coincide with the 150th anniversary of India's oldest English-language newspaper. Whisper it softly, but in casual wear and sporting a ponytail, I could have walked straight out of Broadcasting House, a point not missed by the *chai wallah* as he brought tea. My pitch, never a strong point, was that I was heading to Australia for the summer, and would the *TOI* be interested in taking freelance cricket copy? For want of reference I handed around a copy or two of *Wisden Cricket Monthly*. Interest aroused, a question followed. How would I describe my style? Good question. Actually, not a good question, a bloody good question!

More saloon bar than Speakers' Corner, my usual pitch was that the fun had gone out of the game. This was a time of austerity cricket. A time of declining sportsmanship and increased mean-spiritedness. We needed to fight back and restore the balance. All that was required was a blunt stick. Yes, a blunt stick to poke the living daylights out of the game's great and good. Not a pointed stick, you understand, that wouldn't be cricket. Something, anything to take them down a peg or two. Make it known that the game was and always would be bigger than them.

While lucid enough for me – lucid enough that is in the early hours of the morning with a few pints under your belt – I wasn't sure that the repeated poking of Test cricketers with a blunt stick was quite how the *TOI* saw it. Acting quickly to remove the stick, and pull back on the poking, I limited my response to the question of style to that of quirky. They liked quirky. In fact, for the next ten minutes everyone who approached the sports desk was regaled with the term as if a eureka moment. To seal the deal the *chai wallah* was called and we toasted a quirky union, with quirky tea, that would last for five quirky years.

Each autumn thereafter, and before embarking on another bout of backpacking, I'd swing by the sports desk to collect my dues. This too erred on the quirky (with just a hint of *The French Connection*) as I handed an empty briefcase to the editor under the desk. He would fill the case with bundles of rupee notes and hand it back. All done in a twinkling with barely a degree of shiftiness. After India and before Australia,

I stopped off briefly in Bangkok to visit friends. While there, and using the heading off a copy of the *TOI*, I had 250 business cards printed; the central feature of which just happened to be a couple of regal tuskers! Quirky is as quirky does.

* * *

It would be fair to say, although whisper it softly, that I never really got out of the habit of being a student. It was a Bedouin life *sans* camels. Or if you prefer something a little closer to home: Gabriel Oak minus both Bathsheba and the sheep. Whatever your glass of tea, it suited. Hence the feeling, deeply migratory, that come the end of September I should be heading, if not to London and legal text and tome, then just packing and moving. Somewhere. Anywhere. Robert Louis Stevenson saw it as 'not to go anywhere, but to go'. This had been the way of it since the early 1970s and I saw no reason, a couple of decades on, to change. An airline ticket, a few clothes, a packed lunch, and I was good to go. It seemed appropriate too, given that Aussies were flooding into the UK and Europe, that at least one poor sap should be heading the other way.

From the autumn of 1990, and thanks to the *Times of India*, I could add to my limited possessions a letter of introduction from the sports editor explaining that I was set to report on the southern summer of cricket for his newspaper and could I be furnished with the necessary accreditation. The request implied, with just a dash of smoke and mirrors, that I was a working journalist. If only. At a push, a very large push using both hands and probably a foot, I might answer to being freelance. This too had a caveat – more smoke and mirrors – in that I appeared far more free than lance. This manifested itself in a variety of ways, not least occasional rupee-based remuneration. Most of which then went on financing that autumn's travels around India or Australia.

Very little had changed five years later when I joined forces with the *Jakarta Post*.

This reluctance to see myself as anything remotely resembling a journalist had much to do with the fact that I'd stumbled on the profession without first doing the apprenticeship or hard yards of flower shows, village fetes, and court circuit. At best, I was an enthusiastic amateur. This was clear from an erratic grasp of spelling, punctuation, and sentence construction. And, depending on whether a good day or bad, a vocabulary of just 14 words of which wheelbarrow was my Saturday night special. Copy was always likely then to err towards the repetitive the repetitive and hold more than a passing reference to horticulture.

In light of such a sketchy employment record, I thought it best to front up at the offices of Cricket Australia in Melbourne sooner rather than later. The thinking being that some sort of presence or face behind the letter of introduction might go some way to establish my otherwise skeletal *bona fides*. The airline ticket out of Delhi or Jakarta would thus read Sydney, my base for the coming summer. From there, and after a night or two of fitful sleep, I would wander across Surry Hills to the Ansett bus depot on nearby Oxford Street. Without the wherewithal to afford air travel I would book a ticket for the daytime service to Melbourne. This would allow another ten or so hours of possible recuperative sleep along with an early and comforting reacquaintance with country Australia. I recall one such trip when, on a 50-or-so-seater coach, the passengers numbered just three: myself and a couple of old ladies. I sat in the seat opposite the driver and, although in contravention of several state laws, gossiped for much of the journey. A snippet included the suggestion that, in light of the scarcity of customers, he might care at some point to swap bus for cab or failing that a motorbike and sidecar.

Resembling more a four for bridge than an interstate bus party, we headed towards Albury Wodonga and the border between New South Wales and Victoria. It was then that I noticed the snow flurries. Having just spent several weeks backpacking in 30°C heat this came as something of a shock. Dressed for a late Antipodean spring, I sported little more than a pair of ageing jeans and an anorexic Fab India cotton shirt. The change of driver at the border did little to improve the weather as the snow got heavier and the mercury plummeted. By the time we made Melbourne and Spencer Street station I was forced to ward off hypothermia with a jog trot to the connection for Flinders Street and then a sprint for the Sandringham line to Brighton Beach.

Over the years I found that, as a visiting Pom and thus an easy, jetlagged target, I normally shouldered the blame for most if not all the maladies that beset Australia. The unexpected and decidedly unseasonal low currently resident over Victoria was no different. The shivering walk from Brighton Beach station along South Road was the coldest I'd ever encountered down under. This was offset by a welcome that warmed the cockles, but did little to hide the fact that I was woefully underdressed. The following morning, in borrowed sweater, jacket and scarf, I hacked along to Jolimont and Cricket Australia for the necessary form-filling. I stayed in town just long enough for my press pass to arrive before heading back to Sydney. By this time, the weather had improved with the low heading out across the Tasman to reap havoc on New Zealand. All that remained now was to settle back into my Surry Hills wheelbarrow and work on a cheap and cheerful travel itinerary for the summer's cricket. Next stop Brisbane.

* * *

I had history, or so I thought, with the Gabba ground. Back in the days before Sky Sports – yes, as hard as it is to imagine, such a day existed – cricket coverage for an Ashes series down under centred almost entirely on the BBC *Test Match Special* radio broadcasts. As an expectant nation tuned in around midnight, so the Under the Bedclothes Club was born. By an odd quirk of fate, these late-night vigils coincided with the pre-duvet era. In an effort to combat both poor reception and falling temperatures, garret dwellers would pile blanket upon blanket until only the strongest (and earthed) could lever open a gap into which to crawl, listen and sleep. Movement of any kind thereafter, as if trapped under a row of postman's bicycles, was impossible.

In the winter of 1974/75, I was hunkered down in a small room on Highbury Terrace grappling with the intricacies of Jurisprudence & Legal Theory. No contest. Do not pick fights with Sophists. Around the same time, albeit 12,000 miles away in Brisbane, Mike Denness and his England tourists were fine-tuning their preparations ahead of what promised to be an exciting Ashes series. Unfortunately, the prep did not extend to the eccentric groundsmanship of the then lord mayor of Brisbane (and Gabba curator) Clem Jones. One could only hope that he was more adept at his mayoral duties because his curatorial prowess was pants! So pants in fact that in the final preparations for the game he managed to roll a ridge into the Test pitch, which Jeff Thomson and Dennis Lillee hit with frightening regularity.

The combination of erratic bounce and blistering pace led to English blood being spilt and bones broken. Amid the carnage, the ball-by-ball coverage made frequent mention of the Vulture Street End. VULTURES! Back in my north London garret, pinned down by blankets, I listened on in horrified silence. I mean, Thomson and Lillee were bad enough but vultures? It took little undergraduate imagination to visualise these sinister creatures circling overhead or stalking unchecked on the outfield waiting their moment to pick over what remained of England's top order.

* * *

Friday, 23 November 1990 was like any other Brisbane day: warm, sticky, and set to get warmer and stickier; it would be a difficult day for gussets. For cricket fans around Australia, this day signalled the first skirmishes of a much-anticipated Ashes series. The first act of a long summer of international cricket was set for the home of Queensland cricket. The hope - 16 years on from the nightmare that was Lillee and Thomson - was for a return to five days of ridge-free cricket. The threat of further bloody consequences to a visiting Pom had been lifted with the arrival of my press accreditation. There was no longer a need to blag my way into Australian Test grounds. I was legit. I had the pass to prove it. And it felt very scary. So where was my stiff upper lip when I needed it most? Easy: doing its best to look calm and collected above a weak, flabby chin.

The press box that Friday morning resembled a classroom of schoolboys returning after the summer hols. There was no flying of paper planes, gum chewing, wrestling, or wedgies, but the chatter was boisterous, good-natured, and animated. Awash with veterans of past Ashes encounters, there was much catching up to be done. Billeted in the Hilton or having flown interstate that morning, there was a warming camaraderie about the swelling numbers, it being highly likely that some had met in the hotel bar the previous evening and were simply elaborating on tales told. In contrast, armed with a press pass but little else, I was lacking both an expenses account and any form of publication-paid accommodation. On the plus side, I was billeted with friends in suburban Brisbane and had the full run of their spare room and mattress. In light of the predicted meteorological gusset warning, I was also packing fresh underwear.

There were many on duty that first morning I knew by reputation or byline, but that was as far as it went. My only ally was the editor of *Wisden Cricket Monthly*, David Frith. I'd contributed questionable copy to his publication for a decade and was happy to see his friendly face. He saw me entering the scrum and called me over to meet a fellow scribe, Peter Roebuck. The former Oxford and Somerset opener had just completed a foreword to Frith's book – *By His Own Hand* – on cricketing suicides. If we had only known.

Twenty or so minutes before play, most having settled and eked out a place to nominally call their own, there was a commotion in the entrance leading to the small press box as two strapping six-footers emerged, both with a twinge of regret perhaps they were not taking the new ball that morning. Squeezing up an inch or two, they settled close by, and it soon became clear that there was another new boy on parade that morning: Jonathan Agnew. Having accepted a brief to cover the series for the *Today* newspaper it was obvious that not only was Aggers new to the press box, but he was also recently arrived in the country. Tasked with taking the new boy through the required practices and procedures was his former Middlesex sparring partner, Mike Selvey. There was much to memorise, too: no running in the corridors, tuck shop hours, teacher nicknames, matron's favourite chocolate, the protocol for packages from home, and the school song.

With little if any room to swing an Olivetti, and thinking I'd donate what space I was occupying to those who actually *had* a daily column to write, I soon took my leave, preferring instead to note take and soak up the atmosphere in the outer. There would be plenty of time to reclaim a seat at the top table with the larger press boxes in Sydney and Melbourne. Still, I'd broken my duck. Taken my place with the great and good. And I had been on hand to witness the arrival of another new boy. By the way, whatever happened to Aggers?

* * *

One of the many reasons that made me such a reluctant reporter was the daunting realisation that I was taking a seat alongside many of my cricketing heroes: players and pundits. This manifested itself from day one when David Frith engineered my entry into the members' area at the Adelaide Oval. A dedicated member of the press corps, it was his practice never to miss a single ball of a session. Thus, after a quick beer and gossip at the rear of the George Giffen Stand, and with the clock edging towards the start of play, he hustled me up a staircase leading to the outdoor press box. On our way up we were passed by none other than Bobby Simpson.

The last time I'd seen the former Australian captain and opener was on our grainy black and white television set in late July 1964 when he scored 311 at Old Trafford. Even for a cricket-mad 12-year-old this was a remarkable innings and one that stayed with me. And now, here, on a staircase at the Adelaide Oval, was the man himself. Clutching a chocolate Violet Crumble bar (a Crunchy for we Poms), Simpson was heading away from the field of play. Spotting the chocolate bar, Frithy said, 'You'll get fat on that, Simmo.' Simmo! SIMMO! The rest of the day is something of a blur as I remained starstruck to stumps and beyond. Not that this giddy state is a recent phenomenon. I can actually trace it back some 20 years before the 1982 sighting of Simmo.

A minor county maybe, but we were fortunate at the Lindum that Lincolnshire chose to play two fixtures each summer on our ground. As a youngster this left plenty of time and opportunity to indulge in autograph hunting of the home or visiting professionals. My earliest memories centre on Johnny Lawrence: the diminutive former Somerset all-rounder was a lower-middle-order batsman and purveyor of leg breaks and googlies. Of his bowling, J.M. Barrie (the creator of *Peter Pan*) once wrote that Lawrence's deliveries were so slow that if he didn't like the look of one he could run after it and catch it. His final game for Lincolnshire was in 1967, aged 56. Another autograph scoop around that time was fast bowler Norman McVicker. Always happy to stop and sign, McVicker would later go on to represent Warwickshire and Leicestershire with a good deal of success. Further cricketing royalty arrived at the Lindum in 1968 with Lincolnshire's signing of West Indian spin legend Sonny Ramahdin.

Courtesy of a fixture against a powerful Yorkshire seconds side, we were treated to an early glimpse of the very raw, very teenage, and very quick Chris Old. Arguably the slipperiest bowler to appear at the Lindum in a long time, Old bowled Lincolnshire out for 72 in their first innings, claiming figures of 6-18 into the bargain. There was to be no reliving the success for Old at the day's end as he was driven straight to the team hotel for an early dinner and even earlier bedtime.

In between sightings of aspiring teenagers and seasoned professionals we were, on occasion, able to go through the looking glass and into the rarefied atmosphere of first-class cricket and cricketers. Having defeated Glamorgan away in the first round of the 1974 Gillette Cup, Lincolnshire were drawn at home to a star-studded Surrey side that contained the likes of Geoff Howarth, John Edrich, Younis Ahmed, Graham Roope, Pat Pocock, Robin Jackman, and Geoff Arnold. Sadly, there was to be no autograph bonanza for me that day as – part of the club work detail – I was assigned to the hastily erected press tent and telephone. It was my job, in the illustrious company of visiting scribes Henry Blofeld and John Thicknesse, to ring the score through at intervals to the Press Association. Having used their quota of fairytales in the previous round, Lincolnshire were well beaten by the Surrey stars.

Despite the second phase of our new clubhouse and dressing rooms being a work in progress, the Lindum was selected as the venue for the three-day fixture in late July 1969 between a combined Minor Counties XI and the touring New Zealanders. A huge game from a financial perspective for the club, the occasion represented a rare treat for the autograph-hunting public with international players on show. Not to be outflanked on this occasion, I was photographed by a friend asking for the signature of left-arm fast-medium bowler Richie Collinge. A combined old-style fast bowler and big unit, Collinge was not too agile in the field as he demonstrated by spilling a relatively easy catch at long-on. The misjudgement brought a little of the North Island to the Lindum as the clipped vowels of Vic Pollard could be heard booming out, 'Git the ball in, Richie!'

A quarter of a century later and, you guessed, still starstruck, there would be a meeting, or more of a collision really, with another far more famous cricketing Richie. During an Ashes Test at the Sydney Cricket Ground, I found myself heading to the M.A. Noble Stand before the start of play to have a quick word with my old mate, Jacko. The shortest route involved passing behind the Channel 9 commentary box. At the precise moment I moved alongside the broadcast position, the door opened, and I just managed to stop myself barrelling into Richie Benaud. Unruffled as ever, Richie, spying my press accreditation but otherwise not knowing me from an Anzac biscuit, wished me a friendly, 'Good morning.' Oh! My! God! Richie! RICHIE! I smiled, offered a faltering and faint 'morning', and did my best to keep placing one foot in front of the other. Once outside, and with breathing and pulse back to near normal, my excited and admittedly one-way conversation went something along the lines of, 'Jacko! JACKO! YOU'LL NEVER GUESS!'

* * *

For close on two decades the first week of January meant only one thing: the Sydney Test. During these years I moved slowly and serenely from The Hill to the members' area to the press box. The journey, a combination of apprenticeship and rite of passage, was worth every last drop of blood, sweat and beers. From a survival perspective, the risk to life and limb, certainly where The Hill was concerned, was much diminished during Test days. The 11am start usually meant that the patrons' first beer of the day was not taken until late morning. In comparison, limited-overs games allowed for three or four hours of drinking before entering the ground. Thereafter it was a topping-up process as day turned into night and night into oblivion. The evening session of play quickly deteriorated into trench warfare as cans and haymakers flew in equal measure. In flip-flops, a pair of dark green rugby shorts, and a NSW University t-shirt, I could, just so long as I kept my mouth shut, pass for one of the locals. In footballing terms, this was the equivalent of sitting with the home supporters for eight hours, your club colours safely stowed away, watching them drink themselves silly into the bargain.

One of the best days on The Hill was 2 January 1986. The Sydney patrons, having sobered up following a riotous New Year's Eve, flocked to the ground to watch their heroes put India to the sword. Tamil opener Kris Srikkanth had other ideas. At lunch he was 88 not out and India hadn't lost a wicket. The noise levels and rowdy atmosphere that had greeted the start of play were becoming increasingly muted, and nor did it get much better as the day drew on. Having pulled a muscle during the morning session, Srikkanth walked out to bat on the resumption with Laxman Sivaramakrishnan acting as runner. With Srikkanth wasting no time in going to his hundred, the two Tamils embraced mid-pitch, their grins as wide as the harbour bridge. Australia took their one and only wicket of the day with the score on 191, Srikkanth falling for 116. Undaunted, Gavaskar (132) and Amarnath (72) continued gaily on as India ended the day 334/1. Dejected and disappointed, the beer tasting of jocks and socks, patrons departed The Hill in near silence.

Graduation from the outer to the members' in the late 1980s, certainly where Sheffield Shield days were concerned, was due almost entirely to the 'requisitioning' of my housemate's Sydney Cricket Ground Gold Card. As far as the SCG gatekeepers and ticket machines were concerned I entered the ground in the guise of a local doctor of good standing specialising in obstetrics and gynaecology. No worries. Or at least no apparent worries unless someone went into labour. To put concerned minds at rest, I had run an eye over some of the doc's text books in our lounge. Which, plus hot water and towels, was a start. I'd also worked as a handyman at a nearby maternity hospital for a couple of weeks. While far from competent to undertake ward rounds – although I did volunteer one alcoholic night in The Brewers on Bourke Street – it showed admirable commitment. And if that failed, then Cath would have been my first call.

A good friend and tip-top nurse, Cath, during our group house days in Surry Hills, more than once turned up from a Saturday night shift bearing fresh croissants in hand and placenta on her shoes. Fortunately for all concerned my limited knowledge of obs and gynae was never put to the test. Unlike the SCG Gold Card – God bless it – that kept on giving deep into the autumn as I could be found contentedly rugged up in the members watching the Sydney Swans Aussie Rules team. The latter provided one of my all-time favourite sporting lines as a Sydney scribe offered, 'I went to a fight and a game of Aussie Rules broke out.'

Three years before the Indian runfest in 1986 England arrived in Sydney for the fifth and final Test of the summer still with a chance of squaring the series thanks in no small measure to a bowel-loosening three-run victory 70 hours earlier in Melbourne. The hype and full house came to naught, alas, as England never recovered from trailing by 77 on first innings and were seven wickets down at stumps on the final day, still 146 shy of the unlikely victory target of 460. The Sydney Test that southern summer was the third in which I'd blagged my way past gatekeepers using my Builders Labourers Federation union card as a press pass. Having entered the ground with the harassed appearance of a working journo, I quickly made a beeline to the nearest loo where shirt, tie and slacks were swapped for casual shirt and jeans. The change of clothing made, the briefcase was then stowed in my daypack and, with the addition of sunnies, the metamorphosis from scribe to spectator was complete.

There was no need for such subterfuge on 1 January 1995 as, in possession of a glossy Australian Cricket Board pass, I made my way to the press box in the M.A. Noble Stand. An exciting draw, as draws go, the game exploded into self-inflicted controversy on the fourth afternoon when the England captain, Michael Atherton, declared their second innings closed on 255/2 with Graeme Hick marooned on 98. Defending the decision, Keith Fletcher, the England manager, insisted that the Worcestershire batsman was well aware that a declaration was imminent and had been given the word. Not wanting to add to the pressure of a touring party already two down going into Sydney, Hick declined to comment. Aided and abetted by rain and a stubborn rearguard action, Australia, seven down at the close, escaped with a draw.

* * *

I don't know what it was about the city and surrounds, but something strange always happened in Adelaide. The bar was set in May 1978 when, late of the Alice, I had a first close encounter with a 'pie floater'. Served in a soup bowl, the meat pie is turned upside down, immersed in mushy peas, and topped off with a dollop of ketchup. As Adelaide as the River Torrens or St Peter's Cathedral, the pie carts are to *cuisine classique* what the *Titanic* was to maritime health and safety.

Twenty pie floater-free months later I found myself criss-crossing Australia by interstate bus, sleeping on friends' floors, or staying in an assortment of youth hostels and seedy hotels following the hurriedly arranged post-Packer reunification series between Australia, England, and the West Indies. In Adelaide over the Australia Day weekend, the youth hostel confirmed three days' accommodation after which there would be no room at the inn. Homeless on the fourth morning of the Test, I decamped to the ground and the hill under the scoreboard waiting for inspiration. It came in the form of local radio station 5DN and guest commentator Henry Blofeld. A Pom in a pickle, I penned a small note to Blowers asking if he would broadcast my plight. Shortly after, a producer was dispatched to take me to the commentary position. Thirty minutes later I left with an address, a phone number, and a ticket supplied by Blowers for a performance that night of *No Balls at the Crease: an evening with Fred Trueman*.

Other than providing accommodation, the Test was remembered for a searing Caribbean performance right from the off. Viv Richards started the carnage with a sublime 70, at one point on the first morning hitting Lennie Pascoe for four consecutive fours. Despite hundreds by Clive Lloyd and Alvin Kallicharran, the best was left for Andy Roberts, who accounted for both Chappell brothers in consecutive deliveries. Already one up in the series, and having long suffered at the hands of Australia, Lloyd delayed his declaration, effectively batting the home team out of the game, series, and arguably Test cricket. Chasing 573 for victory, Australia limped to 131/7 at stumps on that eventful fourth day, eventually losing by 408 runs.

It was in Adelaide three years later that *Wisden Cricket Monthly* editor David Frith, combining confidence and credibility, walked me past a set of gatekeepers and into the members' area of the George Giffen Stand. Having spent the past three southern summers completing a rigorous apprenticeship in the outer amid flailing fists and flying cans, this was a revelation. I immediately felt safe, there being nobody on the manicured lawns about to fell me with a right cross or douse me in beer. In a garden party atmosphere, blazer and Blundstones vied with frock and fascinator. It was all so genteel and cultured. They smelled pretty good too and appeared to speak quietly in sentences curiously devoid of expletives. Having crossed the bridge, I wanted more. That day – apprenticeship over – was my last in the outer. Thereafter, by a combination of blag, bluster and bollocks I walked into and out of every Test ground in Australia using my Builders Labourers Federation union card as a press pass.

A couple of months earlier, in town for England's tour match against South Australia, we few hardy spectators were treated to the rare sight of the tourists, along with both batsmen and the umpires, walking off the pitch midway through the afternoon to watch the running of the Melbourne Cup on TV, a very Australian response to a unique sporting event. The Melbourne Cup brings the whole of the country to a standstill from late morning onwards. Those not taking the day off to head to Flemington will partake in cup breakfasts and lunches with, for many, the party lasting long into the evening. Not wanting to be left out, cricket duly took second place to the main event of the day.

A return to the Adelaide Oval in January 1991 was a bittersweet affair. The city end of the ground now housed the new, albeit ill-conceived, Bradman Stand. Set to honour the great man, the construction looked tacky and totally out of character with the rest of the spectating area. This was to prove the beginning of the end for a ground now totally unrecognisable from once being the most picturesque in world cricket. Sat outside the press box on the top tier of the Bradman Stand, the vantage point proved ideal to witness a hundred on Test debut from Mark Waugh. I was joined that first morning by *Test Match Special* scorer and statistician Bill Frindall. Prior to the start of play, 'Bearders' sprung to his feet and proceeded, in volume both loud and piercing, to act as if piping aboard an admiral of the fleet. I followed his eyeline over the balcony and spotted a waving, beaming Brian Johnston CBE MC. Never less than well dressed, 'Johnners' was resplendent in a brown two-piece suit, enormous tie, and a pair of matching brown and white co-respondent shoes.

My last visit to the Adelaide Oval during England's tour of 1994/95 was a watershed moment in that it brought a first sighting of the Barmy Army and with it the realisation that cricket, especially tours abroad, would never quite be the same again. It was as if Headingley's entire Western Terrace had been transported – football shirts and all – 12,000 miles. A lunchtime circuit of the ground was enough to send me scurrying back to the press box.

At some point during the Test, I was introduced to Sir Lawrence Byford and his good wife, Lady Muriel. President of Yorkshire CCC, Sir Lawrence was a former chief constable of Lincolnshire. While in post he had had a bungalow built on the outskirts of Lincoln. During college vacations I worked as a labourer on the house at Christmas and early the following summer. One of my last jobs on site was to 'recycle' offcuts of floor covering from the downstairs loo and fit them in the privy of my parents' somewhat more modest abode. Twenty years on, and with Sir Lawrence no longer in the force, I thought it an opportune moment, not least because of Australia's penal history, to confess my piece of petty larceny. Sir Lawrence and Lady Muriel thought the tale amusing and decided by a unanimous verdict not to press charges.

Project Front Foot

IT HAS been a long winter on the road – Laos, Thailand, and Australia – at the root of which is the good doctor's lengthy assignment in Vientiane. As keen a camp follower as you could get, I arrive in mid-December 2008 to take up my duties as food taster and gin wallah. With her project breaking for Christmas and new year we head to Bali for a spot of snorkelling around our hotel's house reef. As to my plans post-festive season, these are up in the air. I had thought of two or three months catching up with friends in and around Australia. The good doctor, who would be back in the field by then, is not keen, understandably so given my back catalogue of colonial capers. The matter goes to arbitration. The outcome is a month to wander at a leisurely pace from Melbourne via Sydney to a friend's property north of Brisbane. Underpinning these plans is a writing project that has been nagging away at me for several years and will require a three-week stopover for research purposes in Mumbai on the way home.

Seven weeks after spending a night at the swish Novotel airport hotel en route to Bali, I am back in Bangkok in slightly changed circumstances. There would be no Novotel this night. In fact, no hotel at all. The late-evening arrival of the Brisbane flight has put paid to any thoughts of a hack around the city in search of budget accommodation. There is nothing for it, with Suvarnabhumi airport closing around me, but to find as comfortable a concourse bench as there is, unroll my recently 'acquired' Qantas cabin blanket, and catnap the night away. Not that a blanket is needed for sleeping outdoors in a Bangkok February. Then again, I haven't bargained on getting much sleep. Eventually 6am arrives and I decamp to a nearby café for their 40 baht breakfast of omelette and rice. Fortified, if far from rested, I head back into the airport and, positioning myself in the entrance to the business class lounge, can Skype call the good doctor by hacking into the lounge's wi-fi.

My onward Bangkok–Mumbai connection arrives at Chhatrapati Shivaji airport in the early afternoon. Having cleared customs, I grab the shuttle bus to the domestic terminal for a flight to Chennai. Four sleeps and two wedding celebrations later and it's back to Mumbai courtesy of a 24-hour interstate rail journey. Sadly, there are no steam engines or fading first-class carriages to feast on, not that the locals mourn the loss. They appear more than happy with the second-class air-con carriages.

After an early morning traverse of the awe-inspiring Western Ghats, it's all downhill to Mumbai. I alight at Dadar station and find a cab, or rather he finds me, and we head to Colaba and my modest hotel to catch up on a lengthening sleep deficit. Or, at least, that's the plan until I find my hotel empty, gates locked, a security guard outside, the whole sorry sight awaiting conversion into something corporate. Two or three hotels later I eventually settle on a single room with a confusing mix of minute bathroom, ceiling mirror, gas-fired TV, and an unchanging breakfast of two greasy, apologetic fried eggs, toast, and a flask of lukewarm tea. No Novotel this, either.

Mumbai in February 2009 is simmering on a low heat following the terrorist attack of a couple of months earlier. Part of my hurriedly revised schedule involves a visit to Dharavi.

For the uninitiated, Dharavi is home to South Asia's largest slum. Around a mile square, the suburb is host, on a good day, to around a million souls. On a bad day – well, take your pick – a million and a half, two million? Either way, such visits are not to be attempted independently for as bustling streets morph into narrow alleys and then dark passageways barely shoulder width, all sense of direction and connection disappear.

Fortunately, thanks to the Dharavi-based non-governmental organisation Reality Gives, I have a guide. Midway through the afternoon we take a brief unplanned stop in a school yard to escape the sun and take on water. It should be noted at this point that, as something of a veteran Indophile, I have nothing on my agenda other than completing the research, staying as healthy as possible, and then heading home. End of story. Other than the odd rupee here and there for those less fortunate, I'm harbouring zero charitable or philanthropic thoughts.

Our arrival arouses the curiosity of half a dozen barefooted young cricketers. They shyly wander over. I catch the eye of the kid with the bat, and we embark on an impromptu net session. The action is punctuated with much laughter and ends with handshakes and high fives. The lasting impression of this brief encounter is not so much the kids but, oddly enough, the bat. Where once full size, it had – and I didn't know you could do this to a cricket bat – been worn down to half its original size!

Before I leave Dharavi that afternoon, I decide the very least these kids deserve is some decent kit. I have the name – Project Front Foot – before I make it back to my hotel. That just leaves the bit in the middle. Two days later I meet Chris Way, co-founder of Reality Gives. His take, a little weary perhaps of do-gooders swept along by the experience and shock of Dharavi, is OK – go do it! Over the next ten years in partnership with Reality Gives and working closely with coaches and the Indian Gymkhana club, we build a thriving cricket academy for the Dharavi kids. Moral of the story: beware barefoot batsmen.

* * *

The first priority in the summer of 2009 is the search for recyclable junior kit. This is accomplished by emailing the living daylights out of cricketing contacts. There is also the small matter – already looming large – of social media in general and *the* media in particular. Born into an age of typewriter, carbon paper, and secretaries with stockings and suspender belts I have, like many of my generation, a chronic lack of technology-related knowledge. This covers the spectrum from the mechanics of brassieres to the less onerous, although no less challenging, laptops, microwaves, and CD players. If there is a word for 'beyond Luddite' then I am it! Hence the fervent although fast fading hope – the ultimate long game – that at some point in the future typewriters and Tippex will make a stunning and totally unexpected comeback. In the meantime, this is the worst possible base from which to launch our Kit 4 Kids campaign.

While I suffer increasing bouts of technophobia, I have friends who are better suited to mouse and mainframe. Evidence of this is the quest for a project logo. In the early 1980s I was fortunate to live in arguably the best group house in Canberra. One particular member of this Infamous Five was Vincent de Gouw, latterly of Adelaide, and as talented a graphic designer as you could wish to meet. During his time in Canberra, Vincent was commissioned to design the cover for the ACT telephone directory to reflect the staging of the World Athletics Games at the Bruce Stadium. Not one to miss an opportunity – and, to be fair, without a sporting bone in his body – he proceeded to draw his own face on that of a discus thrower on the back cover. Genius! Today Vincent can be found answering the call of TV networks to pop along to various courts in and around Sydney to sketch the defendants, with his work appearing that same evening on network news programmes.

My request in the summer of 2009 is slightly less demanding. His design of wickets, a ball at pace, and the quirky font with the project's name remains to this day, albeit the colours of the Indian flag have been replaced by the blue background and yellow stars of the European Union.

Not knowing an upload from a download, the search for a website designer is more problematic. I contact Lincoln's relatively new and thriving university in the hope of finding a tech student who would see Project Front Foot as a worthwhile final year project. Unbeknownst to me, my email is forwarded to Lincoln's teacher training college, Bishop Grossteste, and lands in the inbox of Neil Smith. He replies, we meet, and the good doctor and I are soon at work providing pictures and text for Neil. The website goes online in late summer and remains our go-to point of reference for the next decade. During this time Neil performs sterling work for the project despite his increasing frustration at my lack of IT awareness. I have form on this front in that, on her first visit to Lincoln, I innocently ask the good doctor where the film goes in her new digital camera. The defence rests. All the more reason then to salute Neil for a decade of project perseverance. It was he too who introduced Project Front Foot to Facebook where today we conduct all our business.

If a little backward in coming forward on the tech front, I am aware that as a small NGO we need as much publicity as we can get. In September 2009, just weeks before the first

Kitlift to Mumbai, there is a five-minute telephone interview with Chris Florence on BBC World Service radio. This is followed for much of the next decade by annual project updates on BBC Radio Lincolnshire. As the kit collections go further afield so respective county newspapers in Herefordshire, Nottinghamshire, Cornwall along with our own *Lincolnshire Echo* are happy to set aside column inches and pictures of donated kit. A situation helped in no small measure by the fact that Danny Boyle's movie, *Slumdog Millionaire* (filmed in and around Dharavi) is, in these early project days, still part of the public consciousness.

* * *

By September I have enough kit to start the next phase. This centres on the small matter of how on earth I'm going to get all this kit to Mumbai. It's scary thinking back, but it isn't until early autumn that I begin to think in terms of airlines and freight. This is not a case of blind confidence, but more a case of a fledgling NGO winging it for all it's worth. Our self-styled aid on the hoof includes writing to those airlines, around a dozen, who fly the London to Mumbai route. Closer inspection of the British Airways website, and in particular their community investment page, asks charities to provide a business plan. Business plan? WTF! Didn't see that coming. Undaunted, the good doctor writes an impressive aid bulletin while I scribble the crickety bits. To their credit BA reply within a week offering to waive the excess charges of several bags of ticketed kit. We're off and running. Over the next decade, give or take the odd resort to air and sea freight, we take over four tonnes of clothing and equipment to Mumbai and beyond with the national carrier.

During my autumn hack around the airlines, I receive a reply from Mr P.R. Subramanian (Suby) in Mumbai. His company works as a freight subcontractor for one of the large Middle Eastern airlines. While unable to help with our current shipping needs, he urges me to call him in Mumbai if I need help on any other front. As things stand, I have the kit, and Chris, through Reality Gives, has the kids. What we don't have is a ground. Yes, having arrived in Mumbai, I'm still winging it.

Within a couple of hours of making it to Chris's apartment in Bandra I'm on the phone to Suby asking if he knows of any grounds close to Dharavi that we might be able to rent. He calls back a short while later saying that he's teed up a meet with the president and secretary of the Indian Gymkhana Club near King's Circle station in Matunga. Less than 48 hours later Chris, along with his co-founder at Reality, Krishna Pujari, and I turn up bright and early for the meeting and within 20 minutes we have our ground with the rent fixed at the rupee equivalent of £20 a month.

Suby didn't attend the meeting, but is waiting outside the ground as we emerge. He's a little put out that the Gymkhana have charged us anything at all in the way of rent. Delighted with the deal, I didn't appreciate at the time the sheer lack of parkland or public space in Mumbai in general and Dharavi in particular. I assumed, totally wrongly as it turned out, that we would find an open space in the slum for our coaching sessions. The dynamics of slum life suggest otherwise as what vacant space exists does not stay vacant for long before someone appropriates it for either living quarters by constructing a shanty of sorts or uses it for a micro business. In this respect, Suby's intervention, along with the support of the Gymkhana's cricket secretary Mr K. Satya Murthy, proves a game changer. Without their help in securing the Gymkhana we would not have got the project off the ground

I meet with Suby a week later for drinks and dinner. At one point in the conversation, he asks if I have any surplus kit. For sure. Would I care to donate it to a couple of orphanages in Matunga and Chembur? No worries. Thanks to the generosity of British Airways, we have more than enough kit for the first intake of Dharavi kids plus a sizeable amount left over. Shortly after, he and I, along with his driver, Chand, deliver the kit to the orphanages in question.

Little did I realise at the time, but Suby and I had just taken the first steps in what would become the project's Rural Schools Initiative. This is fine-tuned over the next decade into small packages of kit – bats, plastic wicket sets and tennis balls – and, with the help of multiple partners, taken to over 150 orphanages, schools and sporting projects in Mumbai and country Maharashtra. While the Dharavi kids remain our flagship work, the support of rural schools enables us to reach a huge number of kids and communities which, through no fault of their own, have little or no resources for sporting equipment. Thanks to Suby, then, we have our ground, Dharavi Cricket Club is up and running and, although unbeknownst to us at the time, we are well on the way to creating a second country-based string to the project bow.

* * *

The coaching duties for the first intake of Dharavi kids is shared between myself, Chris, Krishna, and another Reality staff member, Asim. When I return to the UK after close on six weeks the coaching reverts solely to Reality Gives staff. My initial thinking on the coaching front evolves around finding a volunteer or retired player who'd be willing to take up the reins. This, along with my grasp of open spaces in Mumbai, also proves groundless. So we muddle through. I return to Mumbai three months later to bring more kit, again with the support of British Airways, and to help out with the coaching. We are ticking over, but no more. My visit concludes with a first inter-club match for the kids at Shivaji Park.

In a city of 23 million (and counting) you would think that every square inch of ground would be sat upon, slept upon, bought, sold and sub-let upon or just simply built upon. Not so. Although many cricket grounds and open spaces remain under constant threat from developers, Mumbai will always have Shivaji Park. Spiritual home to Maharashtrian cricket, Shivaji Park has been enjoyed and endured during their formative years by the likes of Ajinkya Rahane, Rohit Sharma, Sachin Tendulkar, Vinod Kambli, Zaheer Khan, Sunil Gavaskar, Ravi Shastri, Dilip Vengsarkar, Sanjay Manjrekar, Polly Umrigar, Farokh Engineer, Eknath Solkar and Vijay Merchant. Shivaji Park: a lot of heat, a lot of dust, and some of the best cricketers that India has ever produced.

In light of the sheer volume of games in play, the key, whether player or spectator, is all about concentration. In the case of fielders, they have first to locate the ball, and then dodge, weave, and generally lay waste to the mass of humanity that separates them from a textbook long barrier and throw. From a spectator's point of view, it's concentration plus nerve as they sit at backward point or deep gully – often only a matter of yards from the batsman – watching another game. Our efforts that sticky weekday morning prove no less chaotic than the myriad of other games around and about. However, it's a start, we've taken the kids out of their Dharavi environment and in the process given them a taste of Mumbai's rich cricketing heritage.

* * *

If my visit to Mumbai the previous autumn had been key to the creation and content of Project Front Foot, then the mid-season return is no less crucial in that it sees me relocate from Bandra to Matunga, leaving just a two-minute walk to the Gymkhana ground. The previous commute, although short in distance, is not easy and consists of a three-wheeler to Bandra station and then a short train trip to King's Circle all the while battling the wall of early morning or late-afternoon commuters. In an effort to shorten or end the commute altogether I set to one morning after the coaching session thinking I might find a local guest house or lodgings. A couple of laps around Matunga proves fruitless. The suburb, temples apart, is not at all touristy and thus accommodation of any kind is thin on the ground; what there is looks, even by Indian standards, down at heel and decidedly seedy, all of which leaves me hot, sticky, and irritated.

Enter – stage left – a guy in flowing white shirt and pants who asks if I need any help. I explain my predicament and he asks me to follow him to a large building 50 yards away that I've already walked past twice and of which the ground floor is entirely given over to a temple. Having already spied the temple I took little notice of the seven or so floors above it. He takes me to a side office, introduces me to the manager, and explains my dilemma. By a huge stroke of luck, the floors above the temple consist entirely of rooms for rent. Interested, I'm shown a depressingly small, airless box and told the price. Keeping my options open, I feel obliged to head to the adjoining suburb to mix and match. There are far more options in Dadar, but all far too expensive for my meagre budget. A couple of hours later, I'm back at the temple and explaining that, if I could reserve a room, then both I and my bags of kit will be delighted to move in the following day.

* * *

Twenty years after the episode with the *Times of India* I can report that, as if some kind of cricketing Chernobyl, levels of quirkiness in Mumbai remain dangerously high. And nowhere more so than in the suburb of Matunga where, in February 2010, I move into a room on the seventh floor of the Sri Vasavi Kanyaka Parameswari Temple. Bemused friends back in the UK ask whether the room has a mini bar and satellite TV? But why stop there: what about a fluffy dressing gown, slippers, seductive lighting, chocolates on the pillow, rose petals on the duvet, air conditioning, beauty products in the en suite, laundry facilities, complimentary fruit bowl, mineral water, and bottle of fizz? Nope, not even a shower cap or sewing kit. With frills and folderols thin on the ground, it's very much a temple first and lodgings, albeit seven floors of rooms, a long way second.

In what is short-stay accommodation, the rooms are populated by pilgrims, wedding parties, yoga classes, and what sounds like the occasional glee club. Unable to tick any of the boxes, I pin my hopes on six solid years at the Burton Road Methodist Sunday School in Lincoln. Although even that is flawed as my attendance has more to do with the allure of (for those who can remember back to the introduction to this book) my red-headed Sunday school teacher than any great spiritual awakening. At first sight Room 71 calls for paracetamol and pragmatism. The temperature and high humidity immediately negate the need for fluffy dressing gown and slippers. The air conditioning consists of three windows, one fly screen, and a ceiling fan. The seductive lighting proves an interesting mix of strip lighting above the desk and two tired 40-watt tungsten bulbs above the sink and by the loo door. The laundry facilities prove to be a prototype twin tub consisting of twin buckets – one to soak, the other to rinse – and four strips of half-inch dowel that double as the washing line.

The bathroom facilities include a small strip light above the mirror to remind you, lest you forget, just how seedy you're looking. The western-style loo has a detachable seat, an interesting concept which I believe is early Emin during her Armitage Shanks phase. The walls and ceiling throughout are a daring mix of the peeling and the flaking. The perfect storm of one coat of watery paint, monsoon, and high humidity further suggests that the combination of early mildew and late mould may soon produce a crop of watercress, mushrooms, or both. The room's minimalist approach to furniture is Late Functional in period. The mattress on the three-quarter-size bed suggests minimal sleep before urging pilgrims to be up and out pilgrimming. While there's no chocolate on the pillow, I manage to persuade myself that the stain on one of them is little more than a long-discarded and recently melted hazelnut swirl.

On the Home Office front, the rocking motion of the desk, other than likely to tease a spirit level, promises difficult working conditions along with advanced motion sickness. There is better news on the plastic chair front – better news for the planet that is – as all three seem set to biodegrade at any moment. The metal wardrobe, meanwhile, proves unique in that none of the rusting doors and drawers fit or lock. Given its weight and permanence I suspect it arrived first with the temple built around it. While most would see the room as putting the grim in pilgrim, I see only the oo in Pooja. This is vintage quirky, and cool quirky at that. As if to offset the austerity chic, the views from the seventh floor are positively penthouse encompassing Dharavi, Bandra, Mahim and Dadar. Every which way it's love at first sight.

* * *

The autumn exodus to Mumbai is the culmination of eight months' work starting with our annual kit appeal in March. The timing is based on the theory that come spring, parents and clubs will look to buy new kit to replace the old, outgrown or out-of-fashion. We then swing by in September and collect the clothing and equipment for recycling among the Dharavi kids or further afield through our support of country schools. With the appeal emails out of the way the next job is to book the return flight to Mumbai. British Airways offers two options at 9.25, one in the morning and one in the evening. Those with the sort of hotel booking that dispatches courtesy cars or minibuses to the airport opt for the morning flight in an effort to offset both the time difference and resultant jet-lag. The rest of us simply book the evening flight and settle for movies, gin and tonics, and sleeplessness. This being a charity venture, the options on the ticketing front range from economy to economy. The only problem with this is a body shape totally unsuited to narrow seats and negligible legroom. Check-in staff are thus cajoled into leaving messages in the ether about bulkhead seats or an empty row or anything that offers just a little more space. If that fails, then, every which way you wear it.

The lot of the economy flyer is not a happy lot. Little has changed over the years. It once took me three days courtesy of a combined Aeroflot/Garuda ticket to get from London to Sydney thanks to lengthy delays in Moscow and Jakarta. To placate and pacify on Aeroflot, red wine was served in plastic cordial cups. Not that we were game enough to complain, for the realisation soon dawned as to just where the governing body of Russian athletics had relocated its female shot putters and discus throwers who failed IOC sex tests. Thus it was not the drinks trolley that struggled to manoeuvre its way down the aisle, but the thickening thighs of our air hostesses. The intimidatory mood among the cabin crew further suggested that to 'Press Button for Attention' was to invite a one-way ticket to the gulags.

With the Mumbai flights booked the very next email is to Laura and the British Airways Community Investment Team with a request for further bags to be allocated to my ticket. Something of a double-edged sword this as, indirect sponsorship apart, the size, shape and weight of the additional bags exponentially increases the potential for chaos at both the start and finish points of the journey. While just about in control of our destiny at Heathrow, it's the polar opposite in Mumbai. In the form of indirect sponsorship, the additional baggage allowance is worth in the region of £1,000 each trip. Rich in kit, poor in cash, it's no exaggeration to suggest that British Airways' support is pivotal for the project's survival. Occasionally, when demand from other charities is high and our allocation correspondingly low, we bite the bullet and buy additional bags. Hence the mantra: every item and every kilo must count.

Stress levels, as you might imagine, plummet once the bags are checked in only to rise steeply about an hour out of Mumbai. This is due almost entirely to events in Matunga where the temple, base camp for the next few weeks, closes at 1.30pm. Arrive any later and you're destined to wait outside until temple life resumes around five o'clock. A late departure from Heathrow can therefore throw a very large spanner in the works. Into this tricky clock-watching equation is the time it takes to find a BA rep, engage two porters, three trolleys, and then wait, willing the kit to arrive at baggage reclaim. A speedy collection still leaves the potentially hazardous journey through customs which, considering I have out-luggaged returning Mumbaikers by a country mile, is never going to be easy. The x-raying of the kit on arrival only adds to the confusion and delay as officials squint and stare disbelievingly when confronted by the shadowy image of several hundred tennis balls courtesy of the Nottingham Tennis Centre.

Outside on the stifling arrivals concourse wait the guys from Reality Gives. Taking charge of the trolleys and bags, they spirit me to a waiting 4x4 or taxi. The journey from airport to Matunga – a sign of the weeks ahead – takes us directly through the centre of Dharavi. Door to door – Berkshire to Bombay – is 32 long, sleepless hours and counting. Mr Venkat is on hand at the temple and with little fuss or ceremony (my buddy, Ramu, having booked the room several weeks earlier) I'm handed the key to my eyrie. With the help of both temple and Reality staff we manhandle the bags into the lift and up to the seventh floor. There is just time for Reality's Mayur and Ravi to hand me a sim card and internet stick before they dash back to Dharavi.

Closing the door on the world, I turn the ceiling fan to high, stretch out bollock naked on the bed, and let the stillness wash over me. It doesn't last. In India it never does. There's the small matter of provisions to buy: water, fruit, bread, newspaper, soap, and loo paper! This is accomplished at the double in an effort to accommodate headache and impending bowel movement. An hour after my return Room 71 is no longer functional and featureless, but has been transformed into a high-end sports emporium with clothing and equipment occupying every available space. The object in the coming days is to place the kit as quickly as possible in an attempt to improve my living conditions. High ideals but short-lived as, during the latter years of the project's time in Mumbai, I set to purchasing more locally sourced room-cluttering kit for country schools.

Nor is the unpacking quite as simple as you might imagine, for secreted among the various bags is a plethora of survival supplies: food, utensils, books, toiletries, vitamins, storage containers, plugs, adaptors, and medical kit. As I'm set to lose up to 10kg in the coming weeks, the emergency rations are key to the art of survival and include Marmite, soup, coffee, oat cakes and, for pudding, two bags of Sainsbury's dried fruit and nuts. As a means to an end, helmets prove the ideal vehicle for the safe passage of rations. But why go to such lengths? Easy. The supplies are backup. Backup to prevent a potential backup. I mean, six weeks of Indian food, what can possibly go wrong?

* * *

One of the joys of temple life is emerging each morning and not quite knowing what to expect. You could walk straight into a wedding party with the ceremony already under way. Or the forecourt could be awash with chairs, stage, microphone, and sound system for a week-long festival of music and word. Or it might be a posse of lithe yoga types rushing headlong towards their first Downward Facing Dog of the day.

For the first five years of the project, we hold three morning coaching sessions a week – Tuesdays, Thursdays, and Fridays – between 9am and 11am. Having secured funding from Allcargo Logistics in the autumn of 2015 we change these to start at 7.30am, ending at 9am, and add three late-afternoon sessions from 4.30pm to 6pm. The morning sessions bring a six o'clock alarm call. This is conveniently provided by the massed Matunga ranks of cows, crows, and cabs. Not to be left out, the neighbourhood pigeons join in with intricate Fred and Ginger tap routines on the metal cowlings above the windows. And if that is not enough, the water tank on the roof, stirred into action by early risers, commences to gurgle and groan its own greeting.

Over a breakfast of coffee, banana, and nuts, I counter by turning the volume up, especially during the signature tune, on the latest overnight episode of *The Archers*. Goodness only knows what the other guests think as Brian and Adam discuss the autumn ploughing, while Tony and Pat set to work on the veg boxes. In the early days, the kitchen at the Gymkhana provides coffee and breakfast for hungry coaches. My alternative of choice is a stall in Matunga's main drag selling all manner of snacks including samosas. Wrapped in yesterday's news and neatly tied with string, the samosas come with weapons grade green chutney.

In the few quiet moments that Telang Road offers, I ponder on just where all this religious energy coursing through the temple is heading. Six years of Methodist Sunday School leaves me woefully short on answers. Damn those Methodists! All I did know is that the seventh floor and Project Front Foot is its final point before the beyond. And that has to count for something. Stirred into life by a slight fall in temperature, Matunga comes alive early evening with kerbside fruit and veg hawkers vying with cafes and restaurants to feed the family. Local flower stalls, drawn by the close proximity of temples, add to the colour with a kaleidoscope of blooms; marigolds, sold by the yard, proving a particular project favourite. I settle in quickly – how could you not – and am made to feel extremely welcome. Matunga in general, and the temple in particular, quickly becomes the project's home away from home.

* * *

After the early morning coaching session, and unless I have a meeting in Dharavi, then the day is my own until around 4.15pm when it's back to the Gymkhana. The staggered coaching regime from 2015 onwards is to accommodate the kids whether attending morning or afternoon school. The local schools employ a two-shift system. The middle part of my day is taken with emails, phone calls, sorting pictures from the morning session, and the torment of social media. Around lunchtime I might pop out for a spicy omelette. More often than not, though, I pass on the hottest part of the day and content myself with an oatcake and fruit. Mad dog maybe, but there is no way this particular Englishman is going out in the midday sun.

Following the late-afternoon coaching session, and depending on my energy levels, there is always Mani's and the house rice plate, dosa or uttapam. If the day is getting too much, always a possibility, there still remains the need for a final push for provisions in the shape of water, fruit, bread from Hushang at the Parsee bakery and maybe, by way of a treat, a packet of cheese slices. On the cheese front, you can put your mortgage on the pack being past its sell-by date. Ten years in and around the suburb and I never once had a packet that gave the slightest nod to Best Before. To cement the surreal scene, the shop in question plays music on a continuous loop that I swear is the same for my entire decade-long visits to Matunga.

Provisions purchased, it's back to my temple eyrie and chance to collapse under the restorative ceiling fan before summoning the energy to boil water for a minimalist dinner. It's too harsh a statement to say these weeks in Mumbai are a combination of detox and boot camp. A testing time, for sure, and no more so than with the monumental dietary change. To offset this, and if used sparingly, it is possible to eke out my emergency rations for close on a month. From a wellness perspective, I'm thinking here of mental as opposed to physical, it's just nice to occasionally identify a taste or texture that does not require forensics. On average, I lose between seven and ten kilograms each trip without a single day's sickness. Of course, India being India, there are still days when it's advisable not to stray too far from, or at least within sprinting distance of, the nearest loo. But in the main, cast-iron is as cast-iron does. All of which is a roundabout way of saying that you can forget the F-Plan, Hip and Thigh, FAB and Keto diets. For a well-balanced thoughtful approach to weight loss, look no further than the subcontinent.

* * *

As a fledgling NGO, and acutely aware of the pitfalls of misrepresentation, Project Front Foot never once saw our collaboration with British Airways in terms of a main sponsor or partner. At best, the BA logo took its place alongside the likes of the Yorkshire Cricket Board and Lancashire Cricket Foundation under the heading of Project Supporters. That we did, however, interact over a decade suggests that, if not kissing behind the bicycle shed, we were at least holding hands in the park.

Once or twice a year during our decade-long Indian adventure BA would waive the charges on anywhere between five to nine bags of checked luggage. Given that every kilo matters we push the 23kg limit to the maximum, more often than not sneaking in an extra kilo or two. All of that is fine and dandy on paper and via email until, that is, you and a small band of volunteers descend on Heathrow's Terminal 5 with enough trolleys and bags to bring the airport luggage operations to a shuddering halt. By way of tactics, it is my task to turn up early at T5 and recce the various check-in desks, often resorting to a vacant business or first-class counter with a tale of kit and potential chaos. No ordinary check-in, mine is set to involve several queue-blocking trolleys, outsized bags, complicated online ticket adjustments, and waived airline charges, any, or all of which can bring a busy economy queue to a grinding, ill-tempered halt, and significantly raise the concourse temperature in the process.

If that fails, I regale BA staff with tales of slum life and straight drives in an effort to gain a hassle-free check-in that will calm nerves and get the first part of the journey done and dusted with the least possible stress. For only I know what awaits kit and carrier at Chhatrapati Shivaji Airport. Let's just say that the zephyr of disruption at Heathrow is nothing compared to the cyclone of irritation and exasperation in Mumbai. In the main, this pre-flight manoeuvre of getting your retaliation in first works. Which is just as well as, in February 2018, three men, three trolleys, and nine bags snake their way across the departure concourse with all the appearance of a Darwin to Alice Springs road train. Calm amid the growing chaos, the British Airways staff cannot be more helpful. It will come as little surprise to hear that, of the nine bags in question that night, only four were trim enough to travel the conveyor belt. The remaining five 'big boys' were ticketed and toted to the oversize section.

As predicted, life is not so rosy in Mumbai where the entire consignment emerges on the reclaim carousel sporting an ominous yellow chalk cross. The markings are a polite invitation to put all nine bags through an x-ray machine along with my carry-on and computer case before the whole confusion of trolleys, bags, porters, and myself are escorted to a cordoned area to be met by waiting customs officials. Having been party to many such encounters over the decade, best practice is simply to smile and stay calm. After all, the guys are only doing their job. In their shoes I too would want a few answers from a guy who has single-handedly out-luggaged returning Indians and by some distance. Past encounters saw officials, on learning of our work with the Dharavi kids, actually shake my hand and wish me luck before sending me on my way. There are no handshakes today. Just questions, a cursory look in four of the bags, and at my itemised inventory and letters of introduction. After which, and being the primary cause for the hold-up and mounting chaos, our small gridlock of trolleys is ushered towards the arrivals concourse.

* * *

One of the key elements of the project's decade-long tenure in Mumbai is our in-house cobbler. Every NGO should have one. His skillset of stitch, glue and tack enables us to repair and restore damaged items before recycling. Given that donated kit comes in all shapes, sizes, and conditions he is not without work. His remit – as dispenser of cobbled CPR (Cricket Pad Repair?) – is to restore items, not to their former glory, but simply to extend their sporting life: it could be a bat with a hairline fracture, a distressed kit bag, pads requiring sutures or a pair of wicketkeeping gloves with a dislocated thumb. I happened upon this micro-business in early 2010. His kiosk is situated on the pavement outside the Andhra Bank on Bhaudaji Road, just a stone's throw from my temple eyrie. The bank is part of the Woodland Nook building. Trust me, there is nothing remotely woodland or nookish about this part of Matunga, but full marks to architect and landlord for optimism. Around 100 yards from King's Circle, one of Mumbai's busiest roundabouts, the cobbler has plenty of footfall past his kiosk and never seems short of customers waiting for a sole or heel to be reattached to working and walking order. And then I turn up.

I research the subject via various banking expeditions. On the next visit I produce a pair of wicketkeeping pads in need of a little keyhole surgery. He quickly sets about threading needle and the game's afoot. Three bats are proffered a few days later, all, despite being set for a life of tennis ball cricket, in need a spot of glue and a tack or two to keep cracked edges in check. I never offer an opinion as to the job but instead leave it to his expertise and nimble fingers. One of the bigger jobs is a Gray-Nicolls kit bag which is fine in every respect save for a couple of rips that threaten further mayhem if left to their own devices. Once again, barely batting an eyelid, he sets to threading and stitching while I sit and photograph. As you might expect of any micro-businessman, his only English is the price. Yet this never amounts to more than 75p for labour and materials no matter the job or equipment involved. With Mumbai particularly hard hit during these COVID times, I hope his kiosk is still open for business and that he's still sitting cross-legged working quietly away on sandal and shoe.

* * *

A happy home for kids and coaches alike, the jewel in the project crown is without doubt our Indian Gymkhana ground. That said, a first sight of square and outfield on arriving post-monsoon in early October is always something of a shock. Reminiscent of the Thames at Wapping – the wicket table having floated away weeks earlier on an ebb tide – nearby tower blocks strike a reflective pose in the standing water at (very) deep midwicket. A labour-intensive process, the rebuilding of the square starts with the scarifying of what remains of the wicket table, after which several lorry loads of topsoil are unceremoniously dumped on the outfield and sieved by a work party of men and women before being scattered square-wide. The soil is then levelled and tamped by hand before the arrival of arguably Mumbai's heaviest roller.

We did have grass wickets for our first season in 2009/10. Thereafter, a lengthening monsoon season, as annoying as any tiresome tail-ender, prevents the planting of seed. Once rebuilt, pitch maintenance consists of flooding the wicket at regular intervals, rolling late during the drying process, and then leaving it to bake at gas mark seven for several hours of unrelenting afternoon sun. With little in the way of equipment, the *mali* and his groundstaff work wonders.

* * *

Two years into the project and, despite a willing band of volunteers, we still lack continuity on the coaching front. This is remedied in the autumn of 2011 with the recruitment of Bhavana Patil and Harshad Bhojnaik. Having a female head coach also brings a new dynamic to the Dharavi kids in the form of a strong female role model. Within minutes of her first coaching session, Bhavana has won them over with the kids racing around, laughing, and having the best fun. To Bhavana and Harshad's energy and enthusiasm, Reality add the expertise of Peter Woolcock as director of sport. A graduate of Exeter University, Peter makes an immediate mark by introducing fitness tests for the Dharavi kids and, with input from Chris, the coaches and myself, produces an impressive coaching structure.

* * *

In penning the Man Booker prize-winning novel *Heat and Dust*, Ruth Prawer Jhabvala included precious little cricket in the storyline. So, too, did director Ismail Merchant and producer James Ivory in their movie adaptation of the novel. However, had writer, director and producer looked to incorporate just a little leather on willow then they could have done far worse than pop by the Dharavi Cricket Academy. For while deficient in many of the day-to-day cricketing essentials, the project has both heat and dust in abundance. The construction of shade-inducing tower blocks, along with the 7.30am and 4.30pm start times, help shield players and coaches from steepling temperatures. However, even before the mandatory warm-up is over, beads of perspiration gather. Conscious of this and the tireless enthusiasm of the players, the coaches call for regular drinks breaks. Indeed, part of the coaching structure includes advice on rehydration. While we can combat the heat to an extent, we can do little about the dust that the Gymkhana generates. Unique to the modern game, this is grassroots cricket without either grass or roots. In their place we have brown/red soil that, during the monsoon season, resembles the Thames at low tide, and at all other times is baked biscuit hard under an unrelenting sun. Any form of physical activity thereafter generates a film of dust that quickly coats and covers both the moving and stationary.

If our kids and coaches have a tough time combating the prevailing ground conditions, then spare a thought for a band of brothers who go largely unnoticed and unheralded at Gymkhana. Yet the cricket academy and indeed the day-to-day running of club and ground would struggle to function without the *mali* and his dedicated groundstaff. Combining hard work with humour, this loyal and long-suffering team do an outstanding job against vastly unequal odds that just happen to include a four-month monsoon season. The ebb and flow of the Gymkhana's tide times is compounded by the hundreds who use the ground morning, noon, and night. The overuse is a by-product of the surge in redevelopment that has seen cricket grounds in Matunga reduced from seven to just two. A modest selection of tools and equipment do little to ease the toil or toll on the *mali* and his team; no sit-on mower, covers or sprinkler system here. This is groundsmanship at the sharp end with sweaty and calloused hands supplemented only by a ready supply of hot, sweet chai.

* * *

As a game, cricket is not given to the literal. Third man, for instance, has nothing to do with either Harry Lime or Orson Welles. Slip cordons, while prone to slip-ups, rarely if ever slip. Point may occasionally point, but only occasionally, and gully has few connections with a channel formed by the action of water. There are, however, some exceptions. Short leg, for reasons of both agility and self-preservation, is more often than not populated by those with short legs; long leg, the parking position for tall fast bowlers, is similarly peopled by those with inside-leg measurements that the small of stature can only but dream. Which brings us neatly to cow corner, a hitting area much favoured, since the emergence of Twenty20, by both top order and tail.

Not listed in the MCC coaching manual, yet known to cricketers worldwide, cow corner relates to those wide beckoning acres between deep midwicket and wide long-on. Keen to claim, where possible, the literal as its own, I can vouch for and indeed have photographic evidence that the Indian Gymkhana ground near King's Circle station has cows in cow corner. No different to many a Mumbai suburb, Matunga is well populated by the bovine brethren. When not foraging the streets, they occasionally wander into and on to the Gymkhana ground. The outfield, while offering little in the way of grazing, does provide shade around the perimeter along with the occasional discarded entree or main. When not munching or mooching they are prone to settle in their very own cow corner between, you guessed, deep midwicket and wide long-on.

* * *

With time to spare before the afternoon exodus from the city I walk the few blocks to Brabourne Stadium. Once the jewel in the Bombay cricket crown, the Brabourne is a throwback to a bygone age. You can keep the glossy new Wankhede; give me the fading elegance of the Brabourne any day. Without the required pass, I nevertheless manage to wander untroubled through the pavilion soaking up the sepia prints, wicker chairs, marble floors and, in the pavilion foyer, a replica of the Ranji Trophy.

At some point during the afternoon, I strike up conversation with a dapper-looking fellow who introduces himself as Sanjay. He's a diamond merchant. I suppose, if you're going to strike up conversation with anyone then it might as well be a diamond merchant. He suggests drinks so we adjourn to the hushed confines and clinking glasses of the dining room. I decline the offer of food, happy instead to immerse myself in the atmosphere, air-con and occasion. After exchanging numbers and cards, he heads back to the cut and uncut world of diamonds while I linger, not yet ready to throw myself back into the chaos and confusion that is Mumbai's day-long rush hour.

* * *

Such is the blanket coverage of the game today that rarely if ever can you lay claim to a cricketing first. More by luck than judgement just such befell me while wandering back from a meeting with Reality staff in Dharavi. Concentrating hard on traversing the maze of narrow passageways, streets, and alleys I happened upon the first ever recorded incident of goat stopped play! Not only that, but the scene acted out before me went only to confirm the growing gulf between bat and ball, a situation compounded in the modern game by players taking guard with bats of near railway sleeper weight if not proportion.

This particular loophole in the Laws of Cricket had not gone unnoticed in Dharavi where an innovative father had gone a step further and produced the only two-handled bat in existence. The homemade bat, while not quite within the spirit of the game, certainly gave his son an advantage. Indeed, it took the escape of the family goat, and the ensuing chaos, to bring a halt to play. Eventually the goat was apprehended and the innings resumed. While such a move is unlikely to be patented, it does prove that if you want innovation then Dharavi is the place.

* * *

The majority of the 30 or so kids in our first intake of young cricketers in 2009 come from families of pottery workers in the Kumbahwada area of the slum. As the seasons pass Reality staff, Ravi prominent among them, look to enlist kids from various cross-sections of the slum community. For there is as much a structure and hierarchy to slum life as there is to inner-city, suburban, or rural life. As hard as we try, and other than one tomboy, we cannot get any girls to attend, despite the fact we have a female head coach in Bhavana. Depending on the damage reaped by an increasingly late monsoon season, we start our coaching sessions in mid-to-late October. These are basic to begin with as we're unable to use the square until well into November. Undaunted, and let loose after weeks of monsoon-related confinement, the Dharavi kids quickly make up for lost time by hanging on Bhavana's every word and eagerly working their way through skillsets and coaching drills.

Our very first kit appeal brings little in the way of clothing. To this end the Dharavi kids are given a yellow or green Market Deeping CC shirt and matching cap. Later appeals result in an avalanche of clothing enabling us to kit the kids out in white shirts, albeit from a variety of clubs, and flannels. The one item we actually have to buy is cricket boots. Asim is tasked with sourcing the footwear which, given this is most likely the first sports shoes the kids have ever had, adds greatly to the excitement around the project's kit distribution day. On the day itself, early arrivals are placed in a stacking system and, when called, are measured, and handed a shirt, t-shirt, cap, a pair of flannels, and daypack or water bottle if we have them. Not unexpectedly the footwear fitting causes something of a logjam, but all are eventually kitted out. The transformation at the next coaching session is nothing short of miraculous as the kids proudly strut their stuff. The pristine all-white clothing from far-flung clubs in Yorkshire, Lancashire, Northumberland, Cornwall, Wales, Kent, Nottinghamshire, Lincolnshire, and Derbyshire makes for a heart-warming and humbling sight.

* * *

Part of our kit collections during a second year of operations takes us – no names, no pack drill – to a sporting goods company in the south of England. The first box we open on returning to base camp has, written on its side in black felt tip, lacrosse and netball tops. No problem. At the very least they will double as Twenty20 shirts.

Looking more closely at the tops we discover the letter B and then, on the back of the collar, the name Benenden. An independent boarding school, light years away from Dharavi life, Benenden occupies a Victorian mansion, set in 240 acres of parkland, manicured gardens, and woodland in the Weald of Kent. Living, learning, sporting and leisure facilities are clustered around the original 19th-century building. Notable former pupils include Anne, Princess Royal; Basma bint Talal, the Princess Royal of Jordan; Lady Victoria Hervey; Rachel Weisz; and Lady Manningham-Buller. Not a bad top order. The Benenden tops are placed that autumn with kids from the Oscar Foundation and sported proudly around the slum by their football and martial arts players. Project Front Foot twinned with Benenden? Now there's a thought.

* * *

An oasis of calm compared to the chaos and careening outside, the functional two-storey Gymkhana brick pavilion

My mother and grandparents muttering and mutinous after a morning's leather-chasing at Wainlode on the banks of the River Severn. [Vic Mills]

The fledgling 15-year-old off-spinner pictured at the Lindum CC nets in April 1967. [Lincolnshire Echo]

Permed hair just as important as feet placement to the 1980s club cricketer. [Lincolnshire Echo]

Requested to 'harden the f**k up', Australian club cricket converted me into an opening bowler with matching manners and mayhem. [Lincolnshire Echo]

College vacation work as a bin man provided the perfect fitness regime for a budding all-rounder. [Vic Mills]

The Lindum CC's 1976 Pattison Cup winning XI on a grey night in downtown Sleaford. Back row (L-R): Quincey J.P., Roberts, Mills, Emmingham, Stow, Lenton. Front row (L-R) Harvey, Abbott, Quincey J.I. (capt), Gill, Spikings. [Vic Mills]

The Lindum CC's Albion Cup winning XI 1987. Back row (L-R): Goddard, Crookes, Fletcher, Mills, Harding, Cardin. Middle row (L-R): Lawrence, Quincey J.P. (capt), Smith, Coldron, Maddison, Quincey J.I. (scorer). Front row: Sid Gott (Lindum steward). [Lincolnshire Echo]

Last surviving Lindum CC blazer circa 1930s. [Vic Mills]

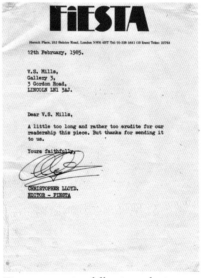

Fiesta *magazine following submission of my one and only attempt at soft porn:* Gardengate – sordid secrets of the soil. *A curious tale combining Watergate and* Gardeners' Question Time. *[Vic Mills]*

My Builders' Labourers' Federation union card that doubled as a press pass for much of the 1980s enabling me to blag my way into every Test ground in Australia. [Vic Mills]

Tour accreditation and with it access to the promised land of press box and party pies. [Vic Mills]

Sort and pack days at Project Front Foot's Berkshire base camp with (L-R) Tim, Fred and Ron. [Vic Mills]

Champion dog and specialist boundary fielder, Zig. [Vic Mills]

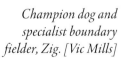

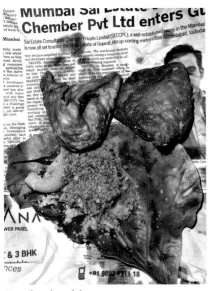

Bombay breakfast: samosas, green chutney, and business news. [Vic Mills]

Gully cricket Dharavi-style. [Vic Mills]

Work party rebuilding the Gymkhana square that had floated away on an ebb tide during the monsoon season. [Vic Mills]

A Mumbai microbusiness more tailor than tailender, where leg theory is reassuringly full, and seam and stitch open to scrutiny. [Vic Mills]

With friend and project supporter, Mr K Satya Murthy, Indian Gymkhana CC secretary. [Vic Mills]

An early season Hurrah! for the project's kit donors. [Vic Mills]

Bring it on: Dharavi Cricket Academy nets February 2018. [Vic Mills]

A first ever pair of sports shoes repacked with loving care by one of the Dharavi youngsters. [Vic Mills]

Shivaji Park early Sunday morning and the game's afoot. [Vic Mills]

The project's unofficial 12th man extending the life of a Lord's Taverners kit bag at his kiosk near the Gymkhana. [Vic Mills]

Key figures during Project Front Foot's decade in Mumbai: (L-R) Mr P. R. Subramanian (Suby) and Mr Vijay Ramuchandran (Ramu). God bless 'em! [Vic Mills]

With Suby the prime mover, we make a November 2011 donation of tennis balls to the Byramjee Jeejeebhoy Home for Children in Matunga. [Vic Mills]

Cricket under the Banyan Tree following a donation of kit to a school near Tarapur. [Vic Mills]

Decision time for the girls of Karnataka High School in Chembur: skirts inside or outside pads, and pigtails inside or outside helmets? [Vic Mills]

Joy unconfined from headmaster and pupils following a Lions Club of Dahisar organised handover of project kit at a tiny village school in Palghar district, northern Maharashtra. [Vic Mills]

Partnered by BBC World Service sports reporter, Seth Bennett, Project Front Foot swaps India for Germany in early 2017 with a vanful of clothing and equipment for refugee Afghan cricketers in Essen. The handover complete, Seth embarks on a final interview with project trustees Vic and Tim. [Vic Mills]

Refugee cricketers of Arras CC in northern France resplendent in their summer 2021 project donated flannels and shirts. [Louise Lestavel]

is home to a lively pair of openers and a solid wicketkeeper in the shape of Messrs Hobbs, Sutcliffe and Oldfield. A cricket pavilion is not a cricket pavilion (certainly in Mumbai) without its resident cats. So it is in Matunga where our specialist short legs – Hobbs and Sutcliffe – appear only too happy to join in the fun. When not employed in keeping the local rodent population down, these Matunga moggies are always up for a spot of cricket. No dead cat bounce here, however, as the use of protective equipment, helmets in particular, is a source of great curiosity and hijinks. Keeping the youngsters in check, and the more experienced member of the pavilion cattery, is Oldfield. His passion and obvious pleasure at perching atop a pair of wicketkeeping gloves quickly sees him christened after the champion Australian keeper of the 1920s and 30s.

* * *

No story about Project Front Foot is complete without mention of Mani's Lunch Home. The favourite restaurant of many in Matunga and beyond, Mani's soon becomes the project's favourite cafe/restaurant of choice. However, as a potential new customer, there is just the small matter of plucking up the courage to enter. That's not as easy as you might imagine given that Mani's is such a popular establishment that weekends and festival days see long queues forming outside and snaking round the small front courtyard. Picking what I hope is a quiet day and hour, I make my move. As if an opening scene from a classic western, the stranger enters, saloon doors swing, pianist stops, the room falls silent. A non-touristy suburb, Matunga hardly sees an Englishman from one month to the next, hence the surprise when, all seediness and shambling, I enter.

This being traditional South Indian cuisine, it is expected that you eat with your fingers. Not a problem, although it doesn't stop my fellow diners judging my progress, style and technique. After the initial shock to management, staff, and myself, we get on like a house on fire. Each return visit to Mumbai brings handshakes and smiles as the owners and staff are genuinely pleased to see me and keen to hear the latest project news.

The restaurant is also the early morning meeting place for Ramu and myself as we plot and plan our school visits. As a likely source of inspiration, the coffee is not to be underestimated as a couple of cups of strong South Indian blend will have you bouncing off the ceiling and creating havoc with an IOC substance abuse test. In 2016 the business moved lock, stock and two smoking rice plates from Matunga to nearby Chembur. Denied the casual coffee scene, Ramu and I popped by soon after the move to renew old friendships and show solidarity with the staff and owners.

* * *

Coffee and tea are as integral to the game of cricket as bat and ball. Evidence this by the fact that the first thing players, commentators and spectators do when attending a domestic or international game is to grab a coffee. Nothing like a shot of caffeine to heighten the senses and focus attention. Tea tends to be an afternoon ritual when the game is starting to take shape.

The ridiculously early start in recent years to the County Championship has added a further dimension to the blended brews in that both coffee and tea now help ward off the onset of hypothermia and those raw, biting northerly winds. Of course, just when you thought you'd seen it all from bean to brew, one of Mumbai's bicycling baristas hoves into view. No skinny latte here. You get both coffee and a floor show for just 20rps. More bikeista than barista, his version of Coffee to Go is to pour, serve and then cycle off into the distance. And all before 7.15am on a Sunday!

Despite producing some of the best teas in the world, India, ever the democracy, has also created a curiously concise cuppa. One for the pot? Don't go there. The *chai wallah* simply spoons leaves into a large pan, adds water, milk, and sugar and then brings to the boil. An acquired taste perhaps but, on a chill early morning at Mumbai Central waiting for that interstate train, this strange brew blends one part comforter with one part heart-starter. For the best part of a decade, this brew proved the perfect pick-me-up after a sweltering early morning coaching session at the Gymkhana.

* * *

In keeping with good business/charity practice it is necessary on occasion to produce reports of a personal nature. The following, a month into the autumn visit of 2015, finds the project principal starting to look and feel a tad seedy.

The prolonged bout of very hot and humid weather has led to the shabby chic of my temple room becoming that much more chic'ier. Overnight yet more paint gave up the wall and flaked clean away. The plaster too is showing grave signs of distress – I know how it feels – with the wall above my bed resembling an Ordnance Survey map of the Lake District. As if to mirror the room I, if not shabby, have taken on a distinct air of seediness. The one skerrick of hope is that I don't actually feel quite as seedy as I look. Well, not at the moment anyway. Depending on where you're coming from, this could either be an advanced case of EMF (Extreme Marmite Fatigue) or the very real prospect of running out of emergency oatcakes early next week.

With or without Marmite, the extreme nature of life in Mumbai, indeed across India as a whole, is never more graphically illustrated for we foreigners than in our bowel movements. There is no happy medium, sadly, as we continually lurch, maybe stumble would be more apt, between constipation and diarrhoea. Die or rear? You just never know when that curry or samosa has your name on it! As you would expect a month into the trip supplies are starting to run low. I'm down to my last can of insect repellent. This is largely due to the very real threat of dengue fever in Mumbai. I'm sure it's not the case, but I like to think that the dusk shift-change between the daytime dengue-carrying mosquitoes and their malarial night stalkers is marked by the mosquito equivalent of a fluttered high five as one clocks in and the other off. So long, and thanks for all the blood!

* * *

Of the numerous visits to Mumbai over a ten-year period, eight of these coincide with my 5 November birthday. If it further coincides with a coaching session then there is every likelihood that one or other of the coaches will appear with a chocolate cake after which the children embark on a noisy life-affirming version of 'Happy Bird-Day'. The evening celebrations prove no less boisterous with my Matunga support team of Satya, Karthik, Kicha, Anil, Shaker, Doc Bharat, Ramu and Ram only too happy to mix cricket with cake. The ideal cure-all – worth perhaps a note to the WHO – in these difficult times. And a cure-all, let us not forget, confirmed by countless cakes and fancies bestowed on *Test Match Special* over the decades.

One particularly surreal birthday sees the assembled team dissecting Jardine's 1932/33 Bodyline tour bouncer by bouncer, bruise by bruise. But that's only the half of it. The more the guys drink the more their conversation strays from English to Hindi. For my part, I give all the appearance of understanding and decline any offer of translation. Indeed, there are occasions when I head home from Satya's convinced that I'm fluent in Hindi and damn near up to speed in Tamil.

Two things I try to avoid during such evenings are politics and, where possible and without hurting his feelings, the offer of a lift home on the back of Anil's ageing motor scooter. When the latter fails, I can be seen white-knuckled and clinging for dear life to the pillion as we head towards King's Circle roundabout (one of the busiest and most ill-disciplined in this city of 23 million). Undaunted, and at a pace only slightly faster than walking, Anil slows, wobbles, enters the roundabout, wobbles again, deftly slips between a fleet of oncoming buses and then, with a semaphore-like hand signal, nonchalantly glides out of the confusion of asthmatic bus horns and cursing cabbies and on to an empty slip road.

* * *

The Old Roshan or Parsee Bakery proves a welcoming bolthole during my time in Mumbai. It can be found in the atmospheric Lanes, a short walk from the temple. A poorly lit dogleg of a shortcut off Matunga's main drag, the Lanes is a tightly knit confusion of four-storey tenement blocks, small tailoring shops, stalls selling college texts, questionable cafes, and just enough space for the kids to play gully cricket. Established in the early 1930s, the bakery is owned and run by Hushang.

I am a regular there along with long-time project supporter Kannan. One particular autumn I'd been teasing Hushang about turning the premises into a sports bar. Even to a non-*Cheers* audience, everything is already in place: a counter over which to order, lean and prop, cabinets for snacks, and a fridge to keep the beer cool. All we need is a flatscreen TV for the cricket.

To his everlasting credit Hushang buys into the idea and one evening – his bread sold – pulls down the shutters and (albeit minus TV) sets out food and drink. The first ever recorded lock-in in bakery history. The evening ends somewhat chaotically with me being offered a job as delivery boy (bicycle included) and Kannan having to be ferried home on the back of Hushang's scooter. Sadly, this part of Old Bombay, along with the bakery, no longer exists. In keeping with much of today's Mumbai, it is now a construction site for two 40-storey tower blocks. Fear not, though, the bakery lives on having relocated to nearby King's Circle.

* * *

On a par with such highlights as finding a ground and the appointment of coaches is the milestone, in the autumn of 2015, of securing sponsorship for our work from the Mumbai-based company, Allcargo Logistics. My main task each February and March between 2010 and 2015 is the soul-destroying task of searching out potential project funding from Indian companies based in the UK and UK companies with a head office in Mumbai. The ultimate in cold calling, this yields few if any responses and zero offers of support. In February 2015 I happen upon a report by the accountants Thornton's, detailing the 30 top Indian-owned UK companies. After six bleak years on the funding front, my pitch that spring has more than a hint of world-weariness about it:

My name is Vic Mills, I run a cricket project for the children of Dharavi slum in Mumbai, and I need help. Heaven forbid that there should ever be a self-help group called Cricoholics Anonymous, but if such did exist, then we would be sat amid a circle of chairs, in a suburban community centre, and you've just heard my opening sentence. As I appear to have the chair, I'll continue. Founded in 2009, a Registered UK Charity since October 2011, Project Front Foot provides kit, coaching and age group matches during the November to May season.

We coach three age groups – U12, U14 and U16 – three mornings a week at the Indian Gymkhana Ground, King's Circle. In addition to our work in Dharavi, we provide basic packages of kit (bats, tennis balls and plastic wicket sets) for schools in and around Maharashtra through our Rural Schools Initiative. Four years ago we took the decision to appoint a female head coach. A radical step given the male-dominated sport of cricket and the perceived role of females in Indian society. The decision has been fully vindicated with Bhavana Patil proving a huge hit with kids and fellow coaches alike.

The various attachments together with our website and Facebook page will help tell the full project story. The galleries in particular paint an atmospheric picture of Mumbai, Dharavi slum, and our work with the children. All very laudable, then, and great fun into the bargain, but not sexy enough in charitable terms when set against clean drinking water, AIDS prevention, drug abuse, malaria eradication, Save the Children, or the 186,000 other

UK charities. But you do what you can do. In our case, bringing fun and enjoyment into desperately difficult lives.

Tapping into Dharavi's recycling mantra, we run an annual Summer Kit Appeal. People around the UK remain incredibly generous with their donations. Last week I sent out 130 Kit Appeal emails and I've already had offers from the Lancashire CCC Foundation, Trent Bridge, and the Cricket Boards of Yorkshire, Leicestershire, Wiltshire, and Derbyshire. Following hard on this, British Airways pitched in with £700 of waived excess baggage charges for my kit run to Mumbai in late October.

Set against this is the fact that the NGO we work with in Dharavi (Reality Gives) has dramatically reduced its funding of the project in order to concentrate on their core work of education. Place cricket against the need for educating the children of Dharavi, and yet again we come out second best. Of course, with more time, I would argue that our project is far more than just a simple sports programme. Indeed, children's participation in sport is a key component of their education and personal development. The potential spin-offs, from a life skills perspective, enormous.

The reduction in funding by the NGO has led to an income shortfall next season of £2,400. Hardly a king's ransom in charitable terms, but more than enough to put six years of work in jeopardy. In past years I've worked tirelessly to seek support from Indian businesses in the UK, and UK businesses in India. All to no avail. In fact, the majority have not even seen fit to reply.

Our years on the ground in Mumbai, allied to expansion with the Rural Schools Initiative, stand testimony to our resolve and commitment. British Airways acknowledged that fact last week with their continued support, so too the various Cricket Boards, Foundations and first-class counties.

In light of this, I would ask you to take a little time to read the various attachments, go to our website, and click on our Facebook pages. And if, having done so, you can help in any respect with our funding needs then do please get in touch. If I can be of any further help with project information, then again do please get in touch. Many thanks for your time.

One of the companies I email is ECU Lines in Southampton, a subsidiary of Allcargo Logistics. Unbeknownst to me the MD forwards my mail to the corporate social responsibility team in Mumbai. Out of the blue one midweek morning in March I receive an email from Allcargo asking for more details of the project. Reality and I put together a response, the outcome of which is a yearly sponsorship package of £7,500. This covers all our costs for cricket clothing, coaching salaries, ground rental, Shivaji Park ground hire, umpires' fees, bananas for our post-session snacks for the kids, and administrative costs. A year or so later Allcargo add a further £2,500 to sponsor the Reality Gives girls' football team.

On the strength of the cricket sponsorship, we add three afternoon coaching sessions a week to cater for those kids who attend morning school. Shortly after, the loosely named Dharavi Cricket Club becomes the more permanent Dharavi Cricket Academy. While the funding relieves me of bringing clothing to Mumbai, save for t-shirts as Diwali gifts, the project remains responsible for providing the cricket equipment – from helmets to pads and everything in between – for the newly established academy.

The head office of Allcargo Logistics in Santa Cruz is said to resemble the superstructure of one of their fleet of container ships. On your way to the main entrance, you pass a large statue of a hand holding the world between its fingers. While happy to believe this version, I can't help but think, from a project perspective, the hand is in fact holding a cricket ball with fingers placed across the seam.

* * *

As a result of obtaining project-saving sponsorship from Allcargo Logistics I take it upon myself to produce a monthly newsletter. This, in part, is a way of showing our new sponsor that they are getting value for money; it also keeps our many donors in the loop with news of practice sessions and matches. Coaches Harshad and Bhavana are charged with providing details along with match reports, scores, and standout performances. Ravi, the conduit between Reality Gives and the Gymkhana, is also on hand to provide photographs of the action and sessions. The reports are emailed to me through the season with the final one set to include the jamboree at the Reality Gives community centre in Dharavi where the much-coveted end-of-season awards are presented. When in town I take over the role of photographer and, combining both our work with the Dharavi kids with that of our rural excursions, can easily snap and save 500 images with another 1,000 or more deleted. The very first monthly newsletter is produced in December 2015 with the last hitting the wires in December 2018.

Although David Frith had long since left *Wisden Cricket Monthly*, the magazine having morphed into the *Wisden*

Cricketer, I did manage to sneak 400 words of project information into an edition as we looked to again focus on media exposure. This came in spades during the autumn of 2016 in the form of a double-page spread in the *Daily Telegraph* by its cricket correspondent, Nick Hoult. In Mumbai to cover England's 2016/17 winter tour, and on the lookout for more offbeat pieces, he came across Project Front Foot. Not long returned from India, and about to set off for Berlin, we had a half-hour phone interview on all aspects of project life. The piece appeared on 5 December with the front cover of the Monday sports section leading with the heading 'Special report – The man giving hope to the slumdog cricketers'. While not too sure about that, the piece – how could it not in such an atmospheric environment – included several pictures, such as one from my battered old Nokia and another from Ramu's altogether more upmarket camera.

We were also getting noticed as a project by the television industry. I turned up one morning early in the project's history to find a Dutch TV crew already ensconced and happily filming away. A year after our alliance with Allcargo Logistics, perfect timing for our sponsor, we had a visit from a Sky Sports team who spent the entire coaching session interviewing players, coaches and Reality Gives staff. The real televisual coup, however, came with the arrival in Mumbai of former England captain Nasser Hussain. He was in town ostensibly filming a documentary about Mumbai cricket with heavy emphasis on the city producing some of India's best batsmen. The hour-long production included extensive interviews with Sunil Gavaskar and Sachin Tendulkar. In contrast to such rarefied atmosphere, Nasser and his team spent a day filming firstly in Dharavi itself, and then holding a coaching clinic for our kids at the Gymkhana. This footage remains available on YouTube and is well worth a visit.

* * *

A sticky Mumbai Saturday. By way of a little downtime, I head to Bandra on the train from King's Circle and then the elevated walkway that deposits me conveniently near Hill Road. Happily observing the bustling street life below I'm suddenly stopped in my tracks by, of all things, a one-room-one-man gents' tailors. Nothing too unusual in that. Not in a city that champions micro-enterprise. But it's not the business that pulls me up short, rather the name above the premises. For whether by accident or design (I hope the latter) the tailor has named his business Bodyline – a series that is universally accepted as the most controversial and acrimonious in Test history. One can only speculate if the tailor, when cutting material for trousers, refers to it as (drum roll) Leg Theory!

* * *

Lest the wrong impression is gained, not every project day in Mumbai is plotted and planned. Indeed, there are days when you simply cast off and go where the current takes you, as this brief diary entry bears out:

09.20. Sunday. 11 March 2018
OK. So here's the deal. I'm in a cab heading to Santa Cruz East (somewhere I've never been), to meet Mahesh (someone I've never met), with a swag of kit (I just about recall), and all this after two days of little or no sleep (this is getting ridiculous!). So: just a normal Mumbai Sunday morning. The small slum community could not be more welcoming and are soon stringing up the Kit Aid banner, while the local MC is already with mic. For one awful sleep-addled moment I think I've walked into a community karaoke. Mercifully, kids and kit soon take centre stage and we're off and running.

* * *

With an eye to the growing traffic problem around Matunga, the local council sanctions a road-widening scheme at the northern end of the Gymkhana ground. As a result, we and the sporting public of the suburb lose a valuable chunk of playing area with long leg now not quite as long as previously positioned and third man little more than second man. That said, it remains a small price to pay when set against other more erratic planning decisions.

When I happen upon the finished work on my next visit it's heart-warming to see that the powers that be have opted for a decidedly local council solution to a decidedly local council problem. As such, no account has been taken of the existing trees and streetlights. Previously sidewalk-snug, trees and lights now find themselves, to their obvious embarrassment, some way out of their comfort zone. Unlike the St Lawrence Lime of Kentish cricketing fame, the Matunga trees are not inside the playing area, not even on the sidewalk, but now, along with the street lighting, find themselves smack bang in the middle of a busy rat run of a road. India. Incredible !ndia.

* * *

As a country, India is a continual assault on the senses which starts as soon as you deplane. A friend of a friend put it another way: plane lands, door opens, trouble starts. Something of an exaggeration, that, but India is anything but a bed of roses. Once you get over the initial shock, and shock is the right word, then slowly but surely the west gives way to the east. Barely noticeable during the days and weeks, this slow, magical process works on the psyche to such an extent that come your time of departure the very last thing you want to do is leave. India is under your skin. And if leave, as leave you must, then you can't wait to get back.

This was always the way with Project Front Foot. High-octane energy during the four, five or six weeks on the ground and then back home and planning the next trip. This is not to say that every waking hour in Mumbai was award-winning. Like everywhere and everything else on the planet you get out what you put in, or at least that's the theory. Just occasionally, however, you hit a brick wall that refuses to yield and around which there is absolutely no way. This happened in October 2011 and led every which way to a bad week in Bombay.

During that summer we put the project on a more professional footing by obtaining registered charity status in the UK for our small, hard-working NGO. In light of this, and after a bumper kit appeal, we decide to transport 500kg of clothing and kit to Bombay by air freight. A bold move for such a fledgling enterprise, but a reasonable enough risk given that we have friends in the air cargo industry who will be on hand to guide us through the minefield of regulation and red tape. Thinking this to be no more than a show and tell exercise, Chris Way and I head out to the airport freight terminal on my first full day after arrival. The kit, by this time, is already in a holding bay and ready for collection. This is Monday. The net result of our day-long occupation is 'nil by kit'. It proves the same on Tuesday and Wednesday. By this time, cooped up in a small airport waiting room, the stress levels are starting to rise. I'm concerned too that we might be racking up some serious storage charges.

The added problem is that nobody seems keen to speak to us. Any normal situation would have us granted access to officials and the chance to plead our case. The bottom line is that we are a small charity, the recycled clothing and equipment has no commercial value, is not for resale, and is destined to support the children of Dharavi along with city orphanages and country schools. All good stuff. But not good enough apparently as nobody is willing to listen. Indeed, the word coming down from a senior customs official that Thursday afternoon is, 'I don't want to talk to the foreigners.' Foreigners! So much for a charity shipment and the beneficiaries being underprivileged Indian children. While no one will talk to Chris and myself, someone is talking somewhere as we are told late on Friday afternoon that the kit will be delivered to our Bandra base camp the following day.

I arrive at Chris's fourth-floor apartment at 9am on Saturday. Fifteen tedious hours later there is still no sign of lorry or kit. A little after midnight we receive a call that the lorry is on Hill Road and about to turn into our courtyard. To add insult to injury, we then have to tote the 30 or so bags and boxes up four flights of stairs. A few days later I receive a bill for around £500. The breakdown includes airport storage, agent's fees, lorry and driver costs, and a single line expense with little or no explanation for the sum of 15,000rps (£200). This, it transpires, is the bribe to customs officials. No bribe, no kit. Done up like a kipper! Given the mind-boggling amounts of air freight arriving in Bombay every day of the year then someone, in what I suspect is a large and impressive pyramid of greasy palms, is making an awful lot of money. I have no idea, nor did the cargo agent, why we were singled out for such treatment. Or is this the way with every cargo shipment entering Bombay? Could it be that the larger concerns simply bypass such treatment by having a standing order to pay a monthly bribe? We'll never know and it was not an avenue down which we were game to look.

* * *

The origin of our far-too-grandly-titled Rural Schools Initiative is a simple question posed by Suby in October 2009. Do I have any surplus kit? The answer, thanks to the generosity of both our donors and British Airways, is a resounding yes. Suby and I place the kit with local orphanages soon after. Returning to Mumbai three months later we repeat the process, Suby sourcing a further four orphanages. On the journey back to Matunga that afternoon he hands me his mobile and says, 'Have a word with Ramu.' This proves a watershed project moment. Ramu lives at the back of the temple in Matunga and is keen to play a part in Project Front Foot. We meet at Mani's Lunch Home for coffee a day or so later and kick around a few ideas; the involvement of his former employer, Galaxy Surfactants, being one.

The following autumn, Ramu and Galaxy staff members Ramakant and Milind source several schools in and around Tarapur in the north of the state. This is the first of many road trips. Galaxy's corporate social responsibility team are already working in these schools, providing a variety of support from new toilet blocks to IT labs to clean water to solar lighting. Project Front Foot simply dovetails this work by adding cricket to the curriculum. The very first school visit leads to an urgent rethink in our approach. First, the narrow, rutted post-monsoon road brings the need to transfer to a four-wheel-drive vehicle. When we arrive at the school 300 kids are already sitting cross-legged under trees with a greeting party of the headmaster and staff members waiting. A kindly welcome and lengthy ceremony follows, but at this rate we're unlikely to visit more than a couple of schools in the day.

Our refined approach sees Ramu liaise with Galaxy to set the date and number of schools. I prepare and pack the kit. On the day, Chand (Suby's driver) expertly combines F1 with off-road skills to get us out of Mumbai as quickly as possible. Ramakant, Milind and latterly Mr Satawee provide further input on schools and a route that traverses narrow country roads, dry riverbeds, and cart tracks. On arrival Chand and I retrieve the kit; Ramakant speaks to the assembled about our work; time permitting the kids and I have an impromptu net. Ramu, meanwhile, oversees the visit, takes pictures and engages staff and kids. Well-planned days, these, but the first Ramu-inspired task before leaving Matunga is always to buy breakfast. Distrust all ventures that do not include food!

As with all such road trips, the Idli, Vada and chutney provide the perfect early morning pitstop. Off the beaten track, these trips represent the perfect opportunity to get out of town and take in a little of country India that few if any tourists see. Long, tiring, sticky days in the back of beyond, the smiles and greetings of hundreds of kids during the day make it all worthwhile. At the end of one particular jaunt in which we manage to distribute kit to six schools over a four-hour period – the largest having around 800 pupils, the smallest just 50 – Ramakant is moved to opine that this is his best day of the year.

* * *

On one particular occasion, with the trusty Chand laying waste to anything remotely resembling the Highway Code, we travel north until pollution finally gives way to warm, scented morning air. Choosing the route less travelled, we happen upon a cricketing tableau that has to be seen to be believed. In a nearby paddock a bunch of young cricketers are gathered, their task for the day to conjure a wicket out of wasteland. Without any of the equipment your own groundsman would use, they are limited to levelling an area as best they can, soaking it with water, and then – barefoot in the park – beating it into submission with a piece of flat heavy wood. The prepared strip is then left to bake in the afternoon sun in readiness for play the following morning. Proof, if any is needed, that there is as deep a passion for the game of cricket in rural India as in the inner city. Indeed, greater love hath no man for his sport than to spend hours in the baking sun, ankle-deep in mud, to produce a wicket for his fellow villagers.

* * *

This would seem an opportune moment to offer a few words on the project's fixer and go-to man in Mumbai, Vijay Ramachandran (Ramu). Ramu's apartment, in the lane at the back of the temple, is perfectly placed for me to pop in for coffee, breakfast, lunch, gossip, televised cricket, and project planning. During later visits, and of an extra-curricular nature, Ramu surpasses himself by finding me a dentist, a GP, and when I'm struggling with eye trouble taking me to a nearby clinic. In between time he is on hand to book my accommodation at the temple, liaise with Lions Club members for our school visits, and oversee all things Galaxy-related. Displaying all the traits of his hero, Jacques Kallis, Ramu proves the perfect all-rounder and first name on the team sheet for Project Front Foot.

* * *

With the good cricketer/bad cricketer routine in mind, it's time for a few home truths from the front. School sport in India is very much for the privileged few. The majority of schools concentrate solely on education with sport either marginalised or simply non-existent. Resources dictate that books come before bats and balls, and rightly so. However, given the country's passion for cricket, you might be forgiven for thinking that sport is a key element of every school curriculum. Nothing could be further from the truth. So, forget all about sports departments, playing fields, gyms, and equipment. They simply don't exist. The only goal set for students is that of grades.

While difficult to argue against, such thinking does undermine the life skills of leadership, fair play, ethics, fitness, mental wellbeing, mutual respect, discipline, and the chance to break down barriers that sport in general, and cricket in particular, promotes. Sadly, resources rule, and this is unlikely to change.

Example A: Ward 43. Turbhe. High Noon. Straight out of a western, three strangers walk down the main street of Navi Mumbai's largest slum. Not that folk run for cover. Why would they? All we're packing is cricket bats, wickets and tennis balls. The street narrows. Eyes flick left and right. Tension. The heat oppressive. A sudden left and there beyond the school gate is the Marathi Municipal Primary School, Hanuman Nagar. Our contact with the school, and our lead today, is Adarsh Nayyar, head of CSR at Galaxy Surfactants. Indeed, it is straight to one of his projects, a new library installed in co-operation with an American NGO. A small presentation follows with the head teacher and then it is straight to the L-shaped school yard to test bat and ball. For once conditions favour the bowlers with Ramu's underarm spin deadly on the challenging surface. One final forward defensive and then pictures, the official handover, handshakes, goodbyes, and we ride out of town and on to Galaxy's HQ for lunch.

Example B: the second part of this PFF/Galaxy co-production sees us truck through seriously heavy industry en route to the village of Wavanje and the Shree Chatrapati Shivaji Vidyalaya School. Some 840 students attend the school from 19 surrounding villages; the furthest entailing an 8km walk for the student through neighbouring hills. Galaxy's presence is immediately evident with a huge shipping container ingeniously converted into an IT lab together with a new art department under construction. Alas, of anything remotely sporty there is none. Not a single bat, ball, whistle, or white line to be seen. Despite such a glaring oversight, teachers are sent to rustle up kids from a nearby class – one can only hope it is double maths – for an impromptu net. It is left for PFF to receive the opening delivery of arguably the first ever game of cricket to be held at the school. Of the two remaining kit packages from the day: one is destined for a street kids community project supported by Galaxy in North Mumbai, the other for a school for underprivileged children south of Pune.

* * *

We never quite knew what to expect on these away days out of Mumbai. It could be a tiny two-room school with 50 kids or just as easily a parade ground of 800 greeting our arrival with the national anthem. Big or small, the common denominator was always a scarcity of sporting equipment.

As you would expect, whether schoolyard or paddock, the pitches came in all shapes, sizes, and situations. Of the many schools visited, one particular image remains. We'd had a brief informal handover with the kids and headmaster followed by a few pictures. As we drove out of the school, I caught sight of a posse of kids galloping in joy unrestrained to a nearby piece of waste ground to road test the kit. Whether mindful of the impending carnage, or keen to improve their fielding skills, the principal had wisely limited them to a single tennis ball.

* * *

The more keen-eyed among the readership will have noticed a glaring oversight in the present chapter. There is, and well spotted, precious little information or in-depth detail on the Dharavi children themselves. There are several reasons for this, at the top of which is language. While we all might have a little French, German, or Spanish, none of us I vouch have even a smattering of Hindi, Marathi, or Tamil. Not that this proved a problem or seemed to matter in the early days as there were always Reality staff on hand to translate where necessary – although many of the skillsets and drills needed little if any explanation – and from autumn 2011 onwards Harshad and Bhavana took over all the coaching duties. This didn't stop the kids, most of whom would have English classes at school or at Reality's community centre, practising a little of their English on this tall, shambling, bespectacled figure who would materialise each autumn bearing all manner of clothing and kit. Which reminds me, one visit I got a few of the kids together and, with Krishna translating, asked each of them which piece of kit they enjoyed most. To a boy the six all said the leather (seasoned) cricket balls, which was a surprise as I thought they'd go for helmets, gloves or bats.

Other than the coaching sessions, Mumbai life left little or no chance for any further contact with the kids. They invariably had to rush off after practice for the start of their school day. I would retreat to the Gymkhana pavilion for a restorative cuppa and maybe a little food. The morning sessions in particular were demanding, whether coaching or not, as the sun was already high and the heat and humidity building. With the kit locked away and order restored there may be a meeting scheduled with both Reality staff and the coaches. This could be at the Gymkhana or occasionally would require a cab to Dharavi. If there was nothing on the agenda, then I'd head back to the temple and wash away the combined session side effects of the morning's heat and dust. With that it was into the day's admin whether meetings with Ramu about our various inner-city or country visits, down to Mehul's sports shop to enquire about our recently purchased kit, or just simply the myriad other tasks and timings that would quickly fill the day.

Early in the piece Krishna asked if I'd like to head to Dharavi one Sunday morning and visit a few of the kids in their home environment. I'm happy to do so and we settle on a date and a very early start time. So early in fact that on the day in question we enter a small one-up one-down dwelling to find several generations of the family still fast asleep on the downstairs floor. Not wanting to step on aunts, uncles, or cousins I'm ushered up a ladder to find an elderly granny sitting cross-legged over a cooking pot. A big unit in a small area, I am quickly asked to sit (wise decision) whereupon tea and hot chapattis are brought for my breakfast. The one question I want to ask, but wait for a more diplomatic moment, is just how many souls are living in this small, confined space. The answer is 22. This is another reason why visits to Dharavi and a closer association with the players is difficult, and always will be where slum life is concerned, there being a fine line between curiosity and intrusion.

In an effort to bridge the divide, and with Bhavana on hand to translate, I attempt a series of pen portraits.

Jiggar has been with the project from day one. Like all the other kids he has a cheeky, impish smile and is alarmingly streetwise. A capable player, he bowls tidy off breaks with a high action and is no slouch with the bat. Keen to progress, we give him extra kit as he graduates to the Indian Gymkhana under-18 and under-23 sides. Unlike a lot of the other small-for-their-age players, Jiggar is a tall, slim young man, polite and capable. Appreciating these qualities, Harshad and Bhavana soon recruit him as an assistant coach. Once his basic schooling is out of the way, however, there is pressure on him, as with all in Dharavi, to contribute to the family income through a better-paid job with prospects. Not long after he pulls up alongside me on Telang Road. Perching on his newly purchased motorbike he explains that he is a trainee manager at a hotel in Dadar. Yes, I could see that. Tall, good-looking, he would make the perfect night manager. More than able to play the part too as his father is a Bollywood film extra.

Rajesh Jaiswar is 14 years old, attends the Sant Kakaya School in Dharavi, and is captain of our academy under-14 side. A serial winner of player of the month awards during his three years with the cricket programme, Rajesh, a talented all-rounder, was voted the best batsman by our coaching staff the previous season. His desire to be in the thick of things whether with bat or ball has made him a natural leader and not shy either to seek advice over captaincy matters. These leadership qualities overlap into family life where he is one of seven children. His joy of cricket and the coaching is heightened by the fact that there is no sport played at his school. As to his favourite piece of kit, look no further than batting pads. The cricket and coaching apart, I ask if he has made new friends through the cricket programme. Strong and clear as if an appeal for leg before, Rajesh replies, 'Lots!'

The Rathod brothers – Narendra and Hiren – have a long association with the Dharavi cricket project. Narendra, an elegant batting all-rounder, is now studying at Mumbai University. In his absence the family colours are now sported by his younger 16-year-old sibling, Hiren. A pupil at Aryan Junior College in Sion, Hiren is another talented product of Dharavi's narrow streets and alleys. Playfully nicknamed 'Chubby' by his team-mates, the younger Rathod is a bundle of hyperactive cricketing ability. Happy to bat, bowl or keep wicket, you have the feeling that if he could keep to his own bowling he would. Without the height of his older brother, Hiren is nevertheless growing into a fine young cricketer. He plays the game in the right spirit too, constantly chattering away to fellow players and coaches, a ready smile never far away. Cricketer and character in one: no project could ask for more.

The real success story to come out of the project, however, is Sameer. One of a family of seven children from Bihar, India's poorest state, his parents sent him to live with his brother in Dharavi some years ago. While attending IT classes at Reality's reception centre he becomes aware of Project Front Foot. A small, reserved youngster, he soon makes his presence felt in the nets and at coaching sessions. As an 11-year-old he represents the project's under-14, under-16 and under-18 sides. Two years on and he is playing for the Indian Gymkhana under-18 and under-23 teams.

Taking it all in his stride, Sameer continues to improve under the guidance of our coaches. Quite simply, he is the project's best player. The classic all-rounder, he bowls lively left-arm, off an economical run-up, bats with flair, and is electric in the field. My dates may be a little hazy here but, in April or May of I think 2015, he attends the Mumbai Cricket Association Area Cricket Camp at Dadar. From various centres around Mumbai each chooses a squad of 25 to represent their area in a series of matches from which the Mumbai under-14 squad is chosen. From this tough selection process – the majority of boys from middle- and upper-class families and private schools – Sameer is chosen as one of the 25 to represent Dadar. A steep learning curve for a boy from Dharavi, the final step to the Mumbai under-14 squad just eludes him. During this time, he represents the MIG (Middle Income Group) Club playing in the same youth team as Sachin Tendulkar's son.

And there, sadly, the story ends. His small stature, a product of background and upbringing, would have counted against him. A foot taller and he would have been near unplayable. I suspect, in the end, that his schooling won out over his cricket. No bad thing as education is far more likely to enable him to shake off the limitations of slum life than the slim chance he might have had of making the grade as a professional cricketer.

* * *

By way of further insight into the life and times of Project Front Foot I have no hesitation in reproducing the various social media posts leading up to and including a final visit to Mumbai in early autumn 2018.

22 September
SORT AND PACK TEN
Undaunted by 40mph winds, heavy showers and a chill September morning, Project Front Foot's intrepid band of volunteers set to at 8.30 to sort and pack the donated clothing and equipment for Mumbai. A process that requires the requisitioning of both sides of base camp's double garage along with an entire forecourt, wall, and lawn. Team PFF toil for seven hours to complete the task. The job not helped by heavy showers late morning that sees a flurry of activity as bags, boxes and equipment are hurriedly carried, dragged, pushed, and thrown under cover.

Just before the first rain hit Jonathan arrives from Brighton to collect kit for a team of Afghan refugees who play their cricket near La Rochelle in France. Talented cricketers, the guys have no kit of their own. They do now! With the seven bags packed for Mumbai all that remains is the typing of an inventory and a slight tweaking of the contents. Huge thanks to Tim, Ron & Fred for their time and energy and for making a difficult job a whole lot of fun.

25 September

PFF IN REST MODE AND AWAITING COUNTDOWN

With a little over fifty hours before PFF heads to Mumbai it's time for the final items to be added to the kit bags including my Mumbai Survival Kit of Marmite, oatcakes, coffee, and two large bags of dried fruit and nuts. It's time too to weigh the various bags and tweak the contents where necessary. Unlike other years that require a manic last-minute repack, this year is more dignified and fully befitting a decade of such flights of fancy. In fact, there is enough space to pack a further three dozen net balls. As ever, the house bathroom scales play a key part as over-large kit bags are wrestled and cajoled upright and into position for the magic numbers (all mercifully around the 23kg mark) to be added to the inventory. With that PFF is now in rest mode and awaiting countdown.

28 September

IN MEMORIAM

Today marks the fourth anniversary of the passing of Mr P.R. Subramanian. A great friend and supporter of Project Front Foot, Suby was a key figure in helping secure our ground in October 2009. Without the use of the Indian Gymkhana at King's Circle there is every likelihood that the project would not have got off the ground. Suby was also a prime mover along with Ramu, Ramakant, Milind, Ardash and Chand, in what has become our Rural Schools Initiative. In October 2011, his advice was of immense value as we took our first unsteady steps in bringing 500kgs of clothing and kit from the UK to Mumbai by air freight. A gentle, soft-spoken man, Suby's contribution to the project proved a key factor in its growth and development.

29 September
PASSAGE TO INDIA

Thursday evening: Heathrow. It's Nightmare at T5 as three men, three trolleys, seven bags + two carry-on cases approach a British Airways check-in desk. Calm amid the growing chaos, Sadath could not be more helpful. Eleven sleepless hours later and, contrary to expectations, life is nothing short of peachy in Mumbai where a first ever E-visa works like a dream allowing speedy passage to baggage reclaim. All seven turn up promptly thanks to priority stickers and surprisingly minus the dreaded yellow chalk crosses.

Uninterrupted, for once, by customs officials, the porters, trolleys, bags, and myself stroll through the Nothing to Declare channel as if a sunny summer's day in Calais. So different to my arrival in February when I'd been hauled off to open bags, produce inventory, letters of introduction, and generally smile and talk my way into Mumbai. In fact, there is barely a customs official in sight today. As a consequence, it takes just 45 minutes (a new Indian all-comers record) from BA199 landing to my appearance on the arrivals concourse. Extraordinary! Ravi arrives five minutes later + off-sider + cab and we manage (just) to cram all seven bags (three on the roof), two carry-on and four adults into the vehicle for the journey to Matunga. As ever, our route takes us along 60 Feet Road and through a crowded lunchtime Dharavi before arriving at my temple eyrie; home and PFF base camp for the next five weeks.

30 September
FOR WHOM THE BELLS TOLL

The proximity of nearby railway lines means that early morning inter-state and suburban trains compete to see who can wake you first: the sedate rumbling of country trains with their baleful horns bound for Dadar and Mumbai Central challenge briefly, but soon lose out to the rattle and hum of their suburban cousins racing to Churchgate.

The trains unnerve light-sleeping crows who see it their given duty to rouse the restless and unwashed. Having preened and pecked their way to wakefulness the huge local pigeon population then perform an intricate tap routine on the metal cowlings above temple windows. The chain of causation continues as early morning cabs with sleepy, unshaven drivers disturb the many resident cows who seem anxious to add to the growing cacophony. Bad, but there's worse to come as at six o'clock precisely a nearby temple embarks upon a bout of frenzied drumming and bell-ringing that, while unlikely to win a heat of *Mumbai's Got Talent*, does put to flight the last vestiges of sleep. Welcome to Sunday morning Matunga-style.'

1 October

TLC

So: what to do in 36°C heat? Easy. Sort out a batch of malcontent bats, remove the frayed and disintegrating rubber, and make ready for a batch of new multi-coloured grips. There's absolutely nothing wrong with these discarded bats other than being in need of a little TLC. Mehul and his team at Ghanashyam Sports will supply that and fix the grips into the bargain. After which the two dozen or so bats will be ready for battle. The other piece of good news today concerns the Byramjee Jeejeebhoy Home for Children. Project Front Foot has long been a supporter of this Matunga orphanage; a connection that has seen us not only donate kit, but also undertake some 'lively' coaching sessions over the years. This coming Saturday we'll donate 60 Kwik Kricket T-shirts (courtesy of Kim at the Surrey Cricket Board) along with a mix of tennis and wind balls.

2 October

MAD DOGS AND ENGLISHMEN

Another HOT! HOT! day in downtown Matunga. The sort of day where it's best to follow the local rules and stay out of the heat. Which is fine and dandy unless you happen to be English. Thanks to Noel Coward we are, whether we like it or not, obliged to go out in the midday sun. There is also the small matter of a shedload of bats to get to Mehul's shop. Revived briefly by hot, sweet coffee and his shop's blessed air-con, we manage to find enough multi-coloured grips for our consignment of soon to be *very cool* bats. While in-house, I take the opportunity to order a further 60 plastic bats (20 each of sizes 3, 4 and 5) along with another 50 wicket sets. Weary, hot, and beginning to feel a little under the weather, I head back to the temple. So: a game of doubles when the heat abates?

4 October

KIT 4 KIDS

Ripped, gripped and ready for action, PFF's collection of rather sad and sorry bats have been transformed in the space of 48 hours by Mehul and his team at Ghanashyam Sports. These bats – after an already long life – will face nothing more daunting from here on in than a tennis ball. Thereby adding another decade (at least) to their useful life and providing a heap of fun into the bargain. Take a bow all of this summer's kit donors.

5 October

SUCH JOY

State of play: thumping headache, dry cough, ticklish throat. Front Foot is now decidedly on the back foot. At least I have company as half of Mumbai seems to be coughing, sneezing or worse. Blame it on the seasonal change aided and abetted by brutal heat. It was hard to say last night – sipping a medicinal home brew of lime, honey, and ginger – whether I had a temperature or not. The confusion caused by the fact that I've been simmering on a high heat (if you can simmer on a high heat) since stepping on to the airport concourse a week ago.

Meanwhile, the trusty ceiling fan is in overdrive, but is doing little more than moving the air around like one of those puzzle games with an empty square. There's no point in taking to your bed either as you're simply replacing hot and uncomfortable in the vertical with that in the horizontal. It is still a workday though, so the morning is taken with a final sort of the kit for Dharavi, Female Cricket, and a Chembur school. There is a little method to this melting madness as at some point next week five large cardboard boxes will arrive with a further shedload of bats and wicket sets. That done, it is into a cab for Dharavi and a 2.15 partners meeting to discuss the upcoming season. Two hours later we're done and dusted, and me only slightly worse for wear, having covered budget, kit, coaching structure, safety, first aid, parents' meeting, and next Monday's stocktake. There is a chance afterwards to hand Reality 30 Kwik Kricket T-shirts and half-a-dozen tennis balls for a small NGO in a Santa Cruz slum. A long difficult day, then, and now (such joy) the prospect of a long and equally difficult night.'

6 October
RETURN TO THE COLOURS
I'm just back from the Byramjee Jeejeebhoy Home for Children where, an hour ago, I handed over 60 Kwik Kricket T-shirts along with two dozen tennis balls. There is also to be a return to the colours for PFF as I agreed (put it down to the fever)

to three coaching sessions with the kids over the coming weekends. Chance for India to take a little revenge for the recent Test series.

7 October
MEDICAL BULLETIN
The following bulletin was pinned to the palace (read: temple) gates at 07.30 Mumbai time on Sunday. The patient spent a fitful night; the sort of night that only Lady Macbeth could truly appreciate. This being a temple in Mumbai and not a castle in Scotland, the patient (more Big Mac than Macbeth) replaced wailing and gnashing with that of hacking and coughing. Indeed, had this been a hotel (and not a temple) the patient would have felt quite within his rights to call reception and complain about himself!

Late Saturday evening the patient, recalling sunburnt days in Sydney, resorted to applying a damp towel to the torso in an effort to draw out the heat and cool both room and himself. While this used to work in deepest Surry Hills, this was sadly not the case in melting Matunga where patient and bed simply turned an uncomfortable amalgam of damp and soggy. There was better news this morning where mentor and fixer, Ramu, will sort a doctor's appointment for tomorrow and has also supplied a portable fan of near industrial proportions. With 37°C predicted for today the patient will now take to his bed and attempt to recover a little of last night's lost sleep. There will be no further bulletins today.

9 October
ON THE ROAD
Having apparently given up on sleep, my alarm merely reinforces the fact that it's 05.30. Oh, five thirty. Alarm? Too right, sport. And Mumbai still crow black outside. Undaunted,

or only a tad daunted, Ramu and I take a cab to Mani's Lunch House in Chembur to collect breakfast. We're joined by JNS Murthy of the Lions Club of Dahisar and his driver whereupon we set off for the southern reaches of Palghar district a hundred kilometres north of Mumbai. Prior to some serious off-road driving we meet with Lioness Saraswati who is the prime mover in this morning's three junior schools. Tiny in comparison with some we've visited, the second and third have registers of barely 50 kids. A long, sticky, bumpy, crickety sort of a morning, then, and yet another example of Project Front Foot (give or take the odd scraped undercarriage) reaching those kids and communities that others cannot. My thanks to JNS and Saraswati for organising the visits and to the inimitable Ramu for getting me up before sunrise.

10 October
MATTERS MEDICAL
'I have an 'itis. Which, although grim, is still markedly better than an 'ism or an 'ology. Pharyngitis! The main symptom of which, other than coughing like a consumptive, leaves you feeling, as Hippocrates might have ventured, as rough as a badger's arse! Collectively I've spent over 18 months pottering around India and have never ever had a weekend like the last. The Mother of All Weekends! Delaying a visit to the doc's didn't help. Monday's medication is slowly kicking in. Something of a miracle in itself as we spent a good part of the consultation talking cricket. Although absent from the prescription, he might well have added ... oh yes, and DON'T! visit Mumbai in October! Wise words. Of course, the jet-lag doesn't help. Nor the pressure cooker heat and humidity. Add in a decidedly unhealthy seasonal crossover and I'm a sitting, make that pale and prone, duck. The lack of sleep is a problem. The bags under my eyes now resemble a matching Gucci set

with vanity case. I fear that that Burberry modelling contract may have gone, too. Bugger! So: eight tablets a day for three days and one solitary but sizeable antibiotic for five days. Oh yes, and don't visit Mumbai in October!

11 October
SPORT AMONG THE SALT PANS

Motor out along the Eastern Express Highway to Tata Nagar, Bhandup (E) and you'll find one of Mumbai's best-kept secrets: 500 acres of salt pans along with a mangrove forest. Filter off the highway on to the service road, take one of the few left turns, and you'll come across the Vidyadhiraja High School & Jr. College, our afternoon destination. Built on reclaimed land, the school has around 550 pupils (65% from nearby slums) with an age range from 3 to 18 years. With no government funding, the staff take only 25% of their salary in order to keep this unique teaching establishment running. The school website (vidyadhirajamumbai.org) choruses Give Us Your Child & Get Back A Worthy Citizen. To this end, principal Mrs. Jayashree Raveendran explains that sport and cultural activities are given just as much time and merit as academic subjects. To assist their sporting programme, we donate a bag of wickets, bats, and balls.

12 October
ALL CHANGE AT THE GYMKHANA

Cricket grounds come in all shapes, sizes, and conditions. Ongoing construction work at the Indian Gymkhana sees the ground qualify on all counts. We're set to lose a ten-metre strip of playing area on the eastern side of the ground as part of the pavilion is converted into a restaurant. With tennis courts and a basketball court already added to the southern end, phase three will see volleyball courts constructed on the

257

western side of the ground. At the northern end, meanwhile, changing rooms and a squash court will be built. All of which will drastically reduce the playing area, but still (we are assured) leave sufficient space to conduct our coaching sessions. If the construction work (due to start after Diwali) becomes dangerous or too restrictive, practice sessions will be transferred to the nearby GSB ground. The message from Matunga, then – the new season's opening sessions tentatively set for Tuesday 16 October – is that come construction hell or monsoonal high water ... we're back. LET'S PLAY CRICKET!

13 October
PFF & FEMALE CRICKET
A frustrating end to the week in that twice we had a day and time pencilled in for a stocktake of the kit at the Gymkhana only for both to be cancelled. On a more positive note, Vishal, from Female Cricket, popped by this lunchtime for a catch-up and was extremely happy with the kit to be donated to his cricket academy. I had hoped to pop by Shivaji Park to watch a session, but the girls don't start their new season until the day after I leave.

13 October
COMMUNITY COUGHING
Another visit to the doc's brings nine (3x3) more pills a day for the next three days plus a small garish bottle of green cough syrup. Nice Bollywood colour combo: pink pills and green syrup. Whereas the other pills were supposed to bring down the fever (how can you tell in 37°C heat?), this current batch should ease the cough ... *he said coughing*. It's not too much of an exaggeration to say that half of Mumbai is down with this particular bug at the moment. A by-product of which

appears to be community coughing such is the chorus in and around Matunga. Memo to Network TV. Subject: idea for new Reality TV show. Forget …. *Snog, Marry, Avoid?* Think …. *Cough, Hack, Spit?* A winner in my book. The ultimate in Saturday night family viewing.

14 October
PFF IN DA HOOD
This morning's coaching session at the Byramjee Jeejeebhoy Home for Children proves no less lively than others in previous visits. Thankfully, Akash is on hand to translate and where necessary restore order. To break the ice, I take along a bag of kit: the helmet is a big hit with wicketkeeping and batting gloves not far behind; a thigh pad proves something of a mystery; while we have to rescue a couple of kids who get stuck in a pair of batting pads. Ice well and truly broken, we move on to batting and bowling basics before some catching and throwing exercises; the hour-and-a-half session ends with a close catching drill. Warm work. Great fun. And we go again next weekend!

15 October
NO CAN NO CURRENT
I'm not altogether sure what a Communications Hub is, or whether I actually qualify, but it certainly feels like it this morning with emails whizzing down the wires to Pakistan, France, UK and several here in Mumbai. Blame the backlog on the bug. There are phone calls too confirming our next kit handover on Friday at the Karnataka High School in Chembur and a meet next Tuesday morning with the Dharavi Cricket Academy's main sponsor, Allcargo Logistics, in Santa Cruz.

One reason I suspect I don't qualify as a Communications Hub is that I currently have a can of LYNX Africa deodorant propping up my laptop cable. This quirky make do and mend approach is a result of a no can no current situation. The card above the socket depicts The Lord of Seven Hills and His Consorts; none of whom look particularly impressed with my Communications Hub. The fact that I've had a morning's admin suggests that all things health-related may be improving. I'm still coughing though, and, as if Central London, remain a tad congested. A situation – turn away those with a nervous disposition – that brought about partial deafness in one ear this morning after a particularly robust blowing of the nose. Given that there are few permutations left for this bug the hope is that after 12 days and counting it will tire of me and move on.

16 October
PETE'S EATS
I pop by Ghanashyam Sports this morning. Our kit has arrived and will be held in Mehul's warehouse until the nine-night Navaratri festival ends on Friday. We'll taxi the gear to the temple on Saturday morning. A former student of Liverpool John Moores University, Mehul spent a lot of weekends hiking Snowdonia. He even knew the world-famous Pete's Eats café in the Llanberis Pass. Of all the things I didn't expect to be discussing on a sticky 36°C Tuesday morning in Mumbai is Pete's *Breakfast of the Gods*. With fried breakfasts a distant memory, I settle on a more modest medicinal omelette on my way back to the temple. The rest of the afternoon is taken with admin and in particular the likely distribution of the new kit; some of which I'll be able to deliver, the balance to be distributed by project partners. The one downside to the day is news that the coaches have delayed the start of our new season with the Dharavi kids by a week. Probably just as well given my still recovering health.

17 October
SISTERS
The changing face of Indian cricket was never better illustrated than an endorsement spotted on a truck in Matunga this morning. Adorning a side of the vehicle, not a picture of Tendulkar, Dravid, Dhoni or even Virat Kohli, but none other than Mithali Raj, the captain of the Indian women's cricket team. In this cricket-mad country, the sisters are quite definitely doin' it for themselves.

18 October
GOING UP THE COUNTRY
Rest day. Sort of. Or the nearest I'm going to get to one. A blessed chance to regroup and recover after a decidedly unhealthy two weeks. The hope is to dodge other such bullets as the next 14 days promise to be the busiest of the entire trip. We head up country again next Wednesday in the company of our friends and partners from Galaxy Surfactants.

19 October
BREXIT-BUSTING PFF TO SUPPORT FRENCH INITIATIVE
In breaking overnight news out of the UK, I can report that Project Front Foot has agreed to support a cricket initiative involving French children. In mid-September PFF donated a substantial amount of equipment to a team of Afghan refugees in the La Rochelle region. In a follow-up to that, and at the instigation of Jonathan and Pradeep of Aunis CC, PFF is delighted to throw its support behind a coaching initiative involving French children. Once again, Project Front Foot reaching those kids and communities that others cannot.

20 October
PIGTAILS AND HEMLINES
Seven months on from our previous visit and we're back at the Karnataka High School in Chembur. An unusual occurrence as we rarely if ever return to a school. However, I'd been so impressed by the staff, students, and play area, that a second allocation of kit was well deserved. Delighted to be excused lessons, it's all hands to the kit. The boys (being boys) soon settle for bowling as quickly as they can and hitting the ball as far as possible which is their every good right. The girls, in contrast, have certain key decisions to make before starting play. Pigtails: to be worn under or outside the helmet? And hemlines: over the pad or tucked inside? A consensus reached, they take to bat and ball with no little talent and huge smiles. The next half-hour proves the most entertaining and amusing of the past three weeks. I'm indebted to Ramu and JNS for organising the visit and to Mala and her Lionesses for their support.

20 October
D'OH!
Saturday morning Matunga and roads close to gridlock. Perfect PFF timing to transfer our swag of recently purchased kit from warehouse to temple. It took around an hour, involved one cab, a couple of trips, four huge boxes, five people, and an awful lot of sweat! Not the most auspicious start, either, as the first box we lifted split. The only other fly in the ointment/ mosquito in the meringue is that delivery has immediately reduced my living space by half. D'oh!

21 October
FOCUSED
It was back to the Matunga children's home this morning for the second coaching session of three. I'm not sure of the value

behind a warm-up routine in such heat and humidity, but it got the troops focused. Kids and coach then embarked on a series of catching and throwing drills before again working our way through the basics of bowling action (already an improvement) and batting stance plus half-a-dozen shots. We put it all together next week with a match.

22 October
TRENCH ARM

Project life is not all about dispensing good cheer and cricket kit. At some point a fellow has to wash his smalls (and bigs!). Mumbai's disgusting October climate does not lend itself to clean living in any respect. Not overly blessed with amenities in the temple (trust me, I'm just happy to have a western loo) my washing machine is more twin buckets than twin tub and pink at that!

Those looking to imitate the workings of a washing machine need only immerse their right arm into the larger of the two buckets and act as if bowling a tidy spell of Jim Laker off breaks. This will sufficiently agitate the water to break down the dirt and give the agitator only a mild case of trench arm. It's then a case of soak, rinse, rinse, rinse, wring and drape. Had there been a rock handy then no doubt I would have tried my hand at a spot of post-wash thwacking. The surviving items, as if an Australian Test captain accused of ball tampering, are then hung out to dry.

23 October
YOU PRANG, SIR

Give or take the odd paragraph on fatwa avoidance, Rushdie's *First Law of Motorised Transport* states that the more you travel by Mumbai cabs, the greater your chance of a prang. So it was this morning on the way back from Allcargo HQ in Santa

Cruz. As we eased gently to a halt at a red light on the inbound Western Highway there was a slight but perceptible nudge in the rear courtesy of a mid-size white van. Highway or no highway, the cabby sprang out and started remonstrating with the guilty party. Having given his spleen a good venting he returned to the cab only to leap out again, inspect the damage, and then presumably ask for the culprit's mobile number and insurance details. Having drawn a blank, he then proceeded to jaywalk through cross traffic leaving me in sole charge of the vehicle as he took his case to a nearby traffic cop. He returned just as the lights turned green, drove across the intersection, and again took his case to the police.

The guilty party, meanwhile, seeing his chance sailed on by and was soon swallowed up in the late morning traffic. The cop, seeing little or no opportunity to solicit a bribe, waved us on our way. There followed a tense couple of minutes as the cabby, weaving in and out of traffic, tried to hunt down the offending driver. All to no avail, thankfully.

Which brings us neatly to Rushdie's *Second Law of Motorised Transport*: don't let the bastards off the hook! There is dramatic news waiting my return to the temple as the coaches, in light of the ongoing construction work at the Gymkhana, have decided to relocate the coaching sessions to the nearby GSB ground. Our tenth season is now set to start on 30 October.

24 October
MERCY
A 5.15 alarm call this morning means that my day is already 13+ hours old and shows no sign of ending just yet. With that in mind, and just a small plea for mercy, I'll save today's spectacular road trip to Tarapur until the morrow.

25 October
THE ROAD TO TARAPUR

Yesterday was PFF's final road trip of the visit; a congested hack to the southern reaches of Tarapur and a frenetic kit handover that included SIX! rural schools amid temperatures in the nervous nineties. With Ramakant joining Ramu, Chand and myself at Borivali we navigate a plethora of flyovers, toll booths and trucks before reaching the open road. Thereafter Chand went into overdrive happy to use all three lanes in no particular order before picking up the last member of our party, Mr Satawee.

Having displayed admirable F1 skills on the drive up, Chand now became more circumspect as the monsoon-rutted roads narrowed. When not skirting potholes there was also the small matter of water buffalo avoidance. It was well worth the effort, though, as we were met by welcoming committees of teachers and pupils at each of the schools along the way. Weary but contented, we made for a happy car on the way back to town as Chand again grappled admirably with Mumbai's late afternoon gridlock.

27 October 2018
SAD NEWS

I have some sad news from Matunga this weekend with the passing of Mr Kannan Rajgopal. A long-time supporter of the project, Kannan was a tall, softly spoken, unassuming man. A graphic designer by profession, he spent many years working in Kenya. One of Satya's Gymkhana warriors, Kannan was a military medium pacer who kept batsmen honest. We met in Matunga's Lanes in the autumn of 2010. I'd just bought some bread and was heading back to the temple when out of the gloom a voice said, 'Mr Vic?' It was Kannan. He introduced himself and we chatted for a quarter of an hour.

Curious to know how he recognised me, I suggested it was because I was the only white guy in the suburb. 'No,' said Kannan, 'Satya just told me to look for a tall guy with a ponytail.' Thereafter the door to his ground floor apartment was always open for tea and cricket talk. Occasionally we'd bump into each other at Mani's as he popped in to buy chapattis for his evening meal. We were also two of the many regulars at the Parsee bakery. I'd visited Kannan a couple of times during my current stay, the last a week ago. Hushang and I had agreed to pop in on Monday as a final visit before I head home. That won't happen now, but we'll raise a glass in Kannan's memory that evening.

28 October 2018
SURREAL
Sunday morning. Sion crematorium. I join half-a-dozen others from the Indian Gymkhana Club, all of us gathered to pay our last respects to Kannan. This is all a bit surreal. Ten days ago, he and I had been happily sharing a yarn and now here he lays garlanded and ready for his last journey. I pay my respects and leave as the pooja begins.

With all life (and death) apparently passing before me this morning I head to the Matunga children's home. I'd promised the little guys a match this morning to round off our short time together, but had cancelled Friday morning on hearing the funeral arrangements. Akash spoke to the kids soon after to head off any disappointment. I ask him to explain again my absence and how sorry I am that we didn't get our game. Sadly, there is no time to reschedule as next week marks the start of the exam season. Apologies made, I wish them well in their exams; they wish me a Happy Diwali. As if to balance a difficult few hours, the morning ends with warm smiles and waved goodbyes.

29 October
WORK IN PROGRESS
With just five weeks on the ground, and a huge amount of kit to distribute, it's obvious that Project Front Foot will not be able to participate at every handover of donated kit. To this end, I've left bats, balls and wicket sets with various partners to place on our behalf: the South Indian Education Society have kit for three village visits, while JNS Murthy and the Lions Club of Dahisar have further school excursions planned for the coming weeks.

In similar vein, Vishal and Srinath at Female Cricket plan to distribute two bags of PFF kit to communities during weekends throughout the autumn. Meanwhile, our friends at Galaxy have several kit packages for schools in and around Navi Mumbai. By the time this kit has been delivered we'll have supported close to fifty schools, orphanages, and village communities making this visit our most successful ever!

30 October
DHARAVI CRICKET ACADEMY
The new season of the Dharavi Cricket Academy – our TENTH! – began this morning at 07.30. Ongoing construction work at the Indian Gymkhana plus the havoc from the recent monsoon has resulted in the opening sessions being moved to the nearby GSB ground. A minor inconvenience as kids and coaches soon get into their work. The opening session also saw the handover of the new season's kit. Our coaching format – morning and afternoon sessions, three days a week – remains unchanged from last season. Player fitness tests will be conducted for all age groups at both the beginning and end of the season. One to one player–coach discussions will be held mid-season to chart the players' progress along with information on nutrition. The much coveted Player of the Month awards

will continue along with an end of season function in Dharavi where the Player of the Season will be announced.

Our coaches will be arranging competitive matches each month during the season, one for each age group and, where possible, to enter Dharavi Cricket Academy sides in local tournaments. The intake for the 2018/19 season has been set at 60 children. With Diwali on the horizon, we end the opening sessions with samosas and gifts of Kwik Kricket T-shirts for the kids. Huge thanks to Lethy, Suman, Nadia and Ravi of Reality Gives and Bhavana of HB Sports for creating a memorable start to the new season, in the process bringing down the curtain on my time in Mumbai.

31 October
ACKNOWLEDGEMENTS
Wednesday evening. Checked-in. Goodbyes said. EXHAUSTED! This has been a tough five weeks. The perfect storm of jetlag, brutal October heat and humidity, a bug that lasted two cough-racked weeks, and a self-inflicted schedule that, while making this our most successful visit ever, has left your correspondent a pale shadow of his former (even) paler shadow. While in dire need of sleep, salad and salvation, there remains the task – before heading to the airport tomorrow morning – to acknowledge all those who helped make this visit such a roaring success. If you are indeed only as good as your support team, then Project Front Foot is particularly blessed. Sincere project thanks to:

UK Support Team: Tim, Ron, Fred, Jane, Jenn, and Sue
Lincoln white van drivers: Gary and Dicky
British Airways: Laura and Sadath
Sri Vasavi Kanyaka Parameswari Temple: Mr
Venkat and staff

Project go-to man and fixer: Ramu
Reality Gives: Lethy, Suman, Ravi, Charlotte, Krishna,
Asim and Mayur
HB Sports: Harshad and Bhavana
Allcargo Logistics: Nilratan
Matunga Support Team: Satya, Kicha, Anil, Doc
Bharat, and Kannan
Parsee bakery: Hushang
Ghanashyam Sports: Mehul and his team
Galaxy's village visits: Ramakant, Milind, Adarsh, Mr
Satawee, Chand, Vinod & Kabir Seth
Female Cricket: Vishal and Srinath
Byramjee Jeejeebhoy Home for Children: Akash,
staff, and children
Lions Club of Dahisar: JNS and Saraswati
WE Club Of Vasant Vihar: Mala and friends
Vidyadhiraja High School & Jr. College: Mrs
Jayashree Raveendran
South Indian Education Society: Ganesh and Dr Shankar
Santa Cruz community: Mahesh
Indian Gymkhana Club: Jayyannt and the
cricket committee
Berlin project support: the good doctor

1 November 2018
DIZZYING
Mumbai: Thursday 05.03. Having given up on sleep for the
last five weeks, I appear to be living the slightly corrupted
Beastie Boys tune of 'No Sleep 'till Blighty'. Talking of
which, I've just checked the BBC weather site: a sticky 35°C
at departure down to a more modest 7°C at Heathrow this
evening. There will now be a short interlude – once Hushang
has kindly dropped me at the airport – while I sleep, eat,
recover, and try to make sense of the past few weeks.

* * *

It would be fair to say that Project Front Foot is a reluctant NGO. We are, in many respects, the worst nightmare for our partners. Why? First up, we have never seen ourselves as a charity or, heaven forbid, as aid workers. Strip away our registered charitable status and you'll find nothing more than a bunch of willing volunteer cricketers. Our world is not that of presentations, donor meetings, spreadsheets, funding, and budgets. We inhabit the slightly less rarefied air of pitch, practice nets and pavilion with the occasional sortie to the bar.

Secondly, we have come late to such ideals as empowerment, sustainability, and life skills. We have nevertheless embraced them as if our own and can, when required, talk both eloquently and passionately about them.

For us, however, the bottom line has never been anything more than seeing kids running around, hitting a ball, and having fun. Our mantra is no less simple: let's have some fun, do some good. This is all very altruistic and well-meaning until you consider the daily demands of running such a project. While we have done our best to play up, play up and play the game, our quirky approach continues to make us a problem partner.

All the more reason, then, to champion the professionalism and fortitude of our flagship Dharavi partner, Reality Gives. For ten long years they indulged our tracksuit management, quietly making good the deficiencies where necessary. In light of this I have no hesitation in dedicating this entire chapter to the many at Reality Gives who helped make our work possible, and to Suby, Ramu and Satya and our many supporters and friends around Mumbai who worked tirelessly on our Rural Schools Initiative. Respect!

Brexit-busting

DURING THE early part of 2018, the realisation began to dawn that our Mumbai cricket project, certainly where the flagship work was concerned in Dharavi, consisted of little more than arriving with kit, photographing coaching sessions, and social media posts. The financial sponsorship by Allcargo Logistics in the autumn of 2015 had negated the need to bring any form of cricket clothing to Mumbai as this was now sourced locally through the funding. The hiring in 2011 of coaches Harshad and Bhavana had further relieved me of any coaching duties. I remained the link between the Indian Gymkhana Club and Reality Gives but even this, after nearly a decade, was of negligible import. As my role with the Dharavi kids waned, I replaced it with an increased workload with our Rural Schools Initiative. The simple idea behind this, however, along with its minimal effort for maximum gains, suggested this was an ideal vehicle for our various partners to take on and expand. The time was right to step back from Mumbai and concentrate our efforts elsewhere.

This appeared ideal timing too as newspaper headlines and news reports spoke of a growing and urgent need for the support of refugees now flooding into Europe. Project Front Foot had dipped its toe into these waters in spring 2017 by taking a vanload of clothing and cricket equipment, in the company of BBC World Service reporter Seth Bennett, from

Harwich to the Hook of Holland and then across the German border to Essen. The various state governments in Germany, in an effort to integrate the flood of refugees, asked for the sporting and social pursuits of the newly arrived. Cricket proved high on the list. However, while sports fields and indoor centres were made available for practice and games this did not necessarily run to the funding or sourcing of clothing and equipment. It was against such a background that Project Front Foot embarked upon a significant sea change.

With a decade of experience in helping get kit to young people, we simply swapped the subcontinent for the European Union and set our sights on a spot of spirited Brexit-busting. For as the prime minister, Conservative government and at least 51 per cent of the UK voting public were pulling back from all things European, we at Project Front Foot were only too happy to be heading in the opposite direction. To reinforce the point, the project logo – Vincent de Gouw again to the fore – was hurriedly redesigned to include, at the expense of the colours of the Indian flag, the blue background and yellow stars of the European Union. That, as it turned out, was the easy bit.

Shorn of the support system of our Indian friends and partners we had to start from scratch, seeking out clubs and communities in need of support. The dynamics had changed too in that our efforts had previously centred on junior and youth cricket. This was not the case with the refugee community where most were young men with the emphasis on senior cricket and senior clothing and equipment. The decade-long project infrastructure in the UK more than compensated for an exploratory first summer in Europe. Our kit donors again rose to the challenge, so too the volunteer drivers and support staff in storing, sorting, and packing a huge amount of donated clothing and equipment.

During 2019, and relying heavily again on British Airways, we shipped kit from the UK to Germany on flights in April, July, and October. In so doing we were able to support refugee cricketers and clubs in Berlin, Halle, Naumburg and Soest. Surplus kit from Soest was later handed to a German NGO for its work with villagers in remote parts of Nepal. Further kit saw its way to France for the support of both refugee cricketers and children keen to try their hand at a new and somewhat curious sport. In the UK, meanwhile, we made another sizeable donation of kit to a cricket project in Croydon run by the Refugee Council. Slowly but surely, we were finding our feet and securing new contacts and friends into the bargain. In light of this growing confidence, we called an early kit appeal for January 2020 with a collection timed for late March with flights booked for mid-April where we planned to take around 20 bags. And then COVID struck.

* * *

The first casualty of the spring 2020 lockdown was our flights and planned kit lift to Berlin. With emails to British Airways in the coming weeks and months going unanswered it soon became clear that the pandemic had claimed another key alliance in the charity sector. British Airways had been with PFF since our inception in 2009. The generosity of the airline in waiving the excess charges for checked baggage continued throughout 2019 as the project looked towards Europe. Given the volume of kit donations – and the need to continually place more where it was needed most – project trustees were due to review our transport options in the autumn of 2020. The pandemic effectively took this out of our hands with the way ahead seemingly van and ferry. A sad, unplanned end to what had been a long, flag-flying partnership. Project Front Foot owes a huge debt of thanks to Laura Phillips and the British Airways Community Investment Team for their generosity and support over 11 years. We can only hope that a return to normalcy in the airline industry is on the horizon.

* * *

These were unprecedented times, as we quickly discovered during our rearranged September 2020 kit collections. We hired vans from behind masks, bought sandwiches and peed (not at the same time) behind masks, bumped fists and elbows instead of handshakes and hugs, and socially distanced as was required of travellers in these uncertain times. If only others had been more distanced and distancing. Right from the Berlin get-go it was challenging. Mercifully, the S-Bahn and bus to Tegel were relatively empty; not so the rapidly filling departure lounge, and disappointingly not so my scheduled BA flight. Having spent the past six months socially sashaying the sidewalks of Berlin, it was a shock to be confronted by a full flight with empty middle row seats no more than a pipe dream. Prior to boarding a guy walked into the departure lounge carrying a briefcase and dressed in full PPE from visor to shoe coverings. This looked promising. I assumed he was tasked with the job of checking temperatures before boarding. No such thing. He was a passenger!

Had it not been for a shedload of clothing and kit gathering dust in garages, pavilions, clubhouses, and offices, then I would have happily stayed at home. But goodwill – with spring turning into summer turning into autumn – will only last so long. The six hours of mask-wearing that Saturday was repeated 48 hours later with an equally cautious journey to Lincoln via three trains and a Paddington to King's Cross tube. There was no time to tarry, either, as the following day we headed to the A1 and the north.

Our first port of call was with Cameron Harris at the Newcastle School for Boys followed by David Artindale at Knaresborough CC. Part of the latter's kit donation came courtesy of the current Yorkshire player, Jonathan Tattersall, and included clothing from his time as England under-19 captain. With rain threatening – this was Yorkshire after all – we headed to Brighouse to be met by Gary (don't worry, he's a softie) the family Boxer dog standing guard over a positive West Riding of kit. Thanks to Steve Archer and the legion of donor clubs affiliated to the Yorkshire Cricket Board we managed, after a spot of untidy scrummaging, to fill the transit and slam the doors. Job done, and there was the chance for a much needed, albeit socially distanced, cuppa over the garden wall before heading back to Lincoln.

Wednesday was scheduled as a rest day but proved anything but as we attempted a pre-emptive sort of the donated items. Neil Lockwood added to the gathering chaos around teatime with four more bags courtesy of Lindum CC. There was another early start the next morning as we headed to Hartshead services on the M62 to collect bags, bats and helmets donated by Peter Dawidowicz and Thornton CC. From there we went to Birch services, north of Manchester, where Martin McEwan had kindly saved us the journey to Crosby and Northern CC by bringing half a dozen bags of clothing and kit to the services. After a brief chat we were back on the road and heading to Mansfield where Charlie Gwillim had yet more bags and boxes.

The final port of call was a warehouse in Newark where, thanks to Peter Mason, The Forty Club, and a hurried repack, we again managed to fill the hire van. A word of thanks at this point to volunteer drivers Gary and Dicky for their time, efforts, and company during the many motorway miles. Following this latest addition of kit, I called Tim at base camp in Berkshire suggesting a larger van for the return trip south.

Throughout these frenetic few days, I'd found myself apologising to donors for turning up sporting an 11-month uncut head-of-hair and matching ponytail: not at all the image for clean-cut cricketing types. It was with no little relief then that I offered myself to Tracey the following morning for a long overdue wash and cut: me behind mask, she behind visor, all of us behind the eight ball! Tim arrived bright and early Saturday morning having set off from Reading at six o'clock. We duly stacked and packed our kit fest before retiring for tea, bacon rolls, and the return leg.

* * *

The day following our return to leafy Berkshire we set about sorting and packing the record 3,000 items of donated kit. The task took two full days and a further two half days before the final shirt was packed and bag zipped. To the bemusement of a procession of dog walkers we requisitioned Tim's front lawn, car port and party wall, the latter proving particularly useful for the housing of helmets, propping of pads, balancing of bats, and sloping of stumps. The side passage bore the brunt of the old, broken, ripped and grubby. Old, broken, ripped and grubby kit, that is, and not the loyal band (Tim, Ron and Fred) of project volunteers. It was also the final resting place – akin to the Lost Sock Laundromat – of a large number of orphaned gloves and pads. For its sins, the lawn was set aside for empty bags and specific kit requirements. Not to be left out, the forecourt became awash with strategically placed dust sheets.

To the recently collected kit was added that from an early September road trip to Newport CC. And to that was added the balance of pads and clothing from last summer's appeal.

And so it began: bags were opened and emptied, their contents allocated to dust sheets, there to be divided into junior and senior sizes. A dust sheet was further set aside for non-cricket items for local charities. Ten years working in and around Mumbai's recycling hub of Dharavi had not been wasted. A day punctuated with teas, coffees, and bacon butties came to a weary close around late afternoon.

Monday saw a repeat performance plus beer. Tuesday brought morning rain and a delayed afternoon start, but by then we were ready to itemise and pack. Fred, a data man from head to toe, was detailed a chair and laptop; his dog, Willow, provided expert systems support. With kit counted and packed, shouted details entered, and bags numbered and stored, the chaos began to clear. By late afternoon, the forecourt was empty save for a light dusting of Stuart Surridge labels, a few errant boot studs, and a handy pile of empty bags. The last men standing, Tim and I completed the project's 13th sort and pack amid light rain on Wednesday morning.

* * *

In the summer of 2020 Project Front Foot made a commitment to provide junior clothing and equipment to Richard Verity and the Lebanese charity Basmeh & Zeitooneh (smile and olive in Arabic) for their cricket project – involving 200 Syrian children between the ages of 7 and 15 – at the Shatila refugee camp in southern Beirut. A tad late in arriving, four bags of project-donated kit reached Beirut on the evening of 5 January 2021, ready for distribution once lockdown conditions eased. In what proved a busy 24-hour period (even by PFF standards) I received an email from Richard early afternoon the day beforehand. He was in London, heading to Beirut the following day and, COVID restrictions permitting, asked if it would be possible to get the bags of kit to him that night.

A hurried Skype call followed between Berlin and Berkshire with project stalwart Tim. Mobile numbers were exchanged, and Tim and Richard spoke early evening. A meet and kit handover duly took place at Junction 5 on the M4 around 7pm. Car journeys were permitted under the West Berkshire Council protocols with people legally allowed to leave home to 'provide voluntary or charitable services'. Sweet. The handover was completed, and Richard arrived at Heathrow's Terminal 2 the following morning.

The four large bags of cricket kit created interest among airline staff, one in particular who, on discovering that the consignment was destined for refugee Syrian children, immediately waived the excess charges. Thirty hours after Richard's initial email to Berlin we received pictures and video footage of the clothing and equipment safe and sound with our new friends in Beirut. In the intervening months, with lockdown measures finally easing, the kit has been distributed among the young cricketers of Shatila and at a series of new cricket hubs established in and around the Bekaa.

* * *

All of that left a considerable amount of clothing and kit safely stowed at our southern storage facility (aka Tim's garage). Poor fellow; since 2009 he has only been able to park his car in the garage between the months of November and until the first consignment of donated kit arrives. Thereafter the garage is requisitioned for project use.

During the early weeks of 2021, when not involved in searching out parking spaces, Tim embarked on a lengthy lobbying process of potential transport and logistics companies with the object of getting our kit into Europe and then to Berlin. His persistence eventually paid dividends and we had our transport. Given that the parties involved have ticked the

'No Publicity' box then, other than our sincere thanks, I'm obliged to accept their wishes.

However, as it transpired, the physical transporting of our bags was the easy part. For from 1 January 2021 a small but plucky NGO like ourselves was now subject to all manner of procedures and protocols involved in the transportation of goods into Europe. It mattered not a tinker's cuss that the kit was of zero value, had been donated free of charge and, had we not collected it, would have found its way at best to a charity shop or at worst to landfill. In the shipment of goods to the continent, charity consignment or not, everything post-Brexit has a value and therefore has to have the corresponding paperwork. Game, set and mayhem.

It had all been so easy in March 2017 with our consignment of kit for Brian Mantle and the Deutsche Cricket Bund in Essen. Back then it was a simple roll-on/roll-off ferry trip from Harwich to the Hook of Holland. The contents of our van were of absolutely no interest to border guards at disembarkation or the German border. In contrast, we now had to have an Economic Operator Registration and Identification number for both the UK and Germany. *Are you kidding me?* No. We were also required to prepare a customs invoice detailing the items to be transported, quantity of each, total weight, the cost of every item in each category, and the country of origin of the items. *Seriously?* Bad, but it gets worse. We were further required to pay import duty of around 20 per cent on the total value of the shipment at the port of entry into the European Union.

The one bit of good news amid the gathering gloom was that we were advised our kit should not attract any further import duty. Draw your own conclusions, but Project Front Foot post-Brexit just got (expletive!) difficult and (expletive!) expensive. As for being a registered UK charity transporting donated goods – forget it! *Shakes head in disbelief and curses – in*

no particular order – Boris Johnson, the Tory government, and the
massed ranks of bloody Brexiteers!

All of that resulted in a total repack of the kit in March 2021 along with the creation of assorted spreadsheets, customs invoices, and led to a sublime half-hour Skype call between Tim and I one Sunday evening as we attempted to place a value on clothing and equipment that, I repeat, if we had not collected would have found its way into charity shops or landfill. *Barking!*

* * *

As a small but determined NGO, Project Front Foot is more than happy to play the long game. This is cricket's equivalent of taking guard, surveying the field, then digging in and making a thorough nuisance of yourself. A combination, if you like, of Geoffrey Boycott, Chris Tavare and, for those with a long enough memory, Trevor 'Barnacle' Bailey.

This was never more evident than during the past 18 months. In January 2020 we started our annual kit appeal with a provisional collection date of late March. One lockdown on and this was put back until early autumn. A brief two-week window in September enabled us to collect, sort, pack and store the kit before the onset of winter, a second wave, a second lockdown, and bloody Brexit. And still we batted on, head down, jaw firm, bat and pad close together. The only ray of sunshine during a bleak midwinter was four bags of project kit finding their way to Beirut and the Shatila refugee camp.

In February and March 2021, sensing a glimmer of hope, there was much toing and froing of emails concerning Brexit procedures and protocols. With a little help from our friends (well, quite a lot actually) the bulk of our kit arrived in Berlin in early May and, after further unpacking, sorting, and repacking, was dispatched to deserving clubs and cricketers in

Hamburg, Dresden, Chemnitz, Kleve, Lippstadt, Wiesbaden, Naumburg, Ludwigshafen, Berlin, and Baden Württemberg.

Great news, but wait, there's more. A couple of weeks later a consignment of five bags crossed the Channel bound for a team of refugee cricketers in Arras and a cricket project for French youngsters in La Rochelle. A year and a half in the making, it would be fair to say that, in a determined Brexit-busting sort of a way, Project Front Foot has made a thorough nuisance of itself.

* * *

On 10 May 2021, Project Front Foot farewelled an old and much-loved project friend. Both sombre and celebratory, there was no lone piper (thank goodness), no tears or flowers thrown as it made its last journey along Berlin's Kurfürstendamm. An integral part of PFF, the black Gunn & Moore kit bag proudly proclaiming 'MCC Tour to Fiji and Papua New Guinea 2003', is now set for a new chapter of kit carrying with the Moorburger CC in Hamburg. The bag, as best any of us can remember, was part of our very first kit appeal in the summer of 2009. It could have been part of a club donation or perhaps part of a vanload of kit courtesy of a sporting goods company in the south. Either way, its size, durability, working zips and wheels saw it quickly become the go-to bag in a dozen trips with British Airways to Mumbai and back. Yes, it always came back, even if empty, such was its standing in the project.

In the early days, its cubic capacity proved ideal for huge amounts of shirts and flannels as we regularly hit the 23kg mark or were cheeky enough to sneak in another kilo or two. And when the bulk of our clothing needs were sponsored by Allcargo Logistics in 2015 it effortlessly switched to bulkier items such as helmets, bats, and pads. The nooks and crannies created by the change in emphasis enabled further crucial items to be packed. Helmets in particular provided the perfect space for stowing the bulk of my Mumbai survival rations including jars of Marmite, oatcakes, instant soups, and bags of Sainsbury's dried fruit and nuts.

The bag's size, shape and cubic capacity led to much fun and games in the transporting of our kit to India. It began at Heathrow as the bag was invariably too large to negotiate the conveyor belt at check-in and so, along with others, had to be wheeled to the over-sized section. But this was only the half of it as the real gilt-edged pandemonium began on arrival at Chhatrapati Shivaji Airport in Mumbai. Prior to renovation the old airport used to x-ray bags as you left the arrivals hall. A curious exercise and one guaranteed, given the odd shape and size of our kit, to land Project Front Foot well and truly in the mulligatawny.

Put yourself in the place of the customs official behind the x-ray screen. More especially when faced with a grainy image of hundreds of tennis balls courtesy of the Nottingham Tennis Centre. I'm not sure how such a serving would appear on screen, but you could put your house on the fact that I'd be quickly waved to one side and asked to wait. Explanations followed, so too letters of introduction, and the opening and foraging among several bags. Eventually, the officials having had their fun, I'd be sent on my way.

The system changed upon renovation with luggage seemingly x-rayed below stairs before being placed on the conveyor belt for baggage reclaim. Any bag, for whatever reason, that didn't pass muster had an ominous yellow chalk cross added, this being customs speak for, ''Ello, 'ello, 'ello what've we got 'ere then?! In the spring of 2018 all nine project kit bags, with Gunn & Moore leading the way, emerged bearing yellow crosses. There followed the spectacle of two porters, three trolleys, nine bags and myself bringing the arrivals lounge to a standstill as we were hauled off for inspection and explanation.

Over the years and visits, the guys at our partner NGO, Reality Gives, had every good reason to remember the Gunn & Moore kit bag if only for the various back strains it caused. First Chris, then Krishna, Asim, Mayur and finally Ravi: all at one point or another had a run-in with the prized black bag, which made its last journey to Berlin in the autumn of 2019 and, due in most part to the pandemic, has stayed on awaiting its moment to return to action. That came with the arrival of our latest batch of kit in early May. Given its size and capacity, it was always going to be the first bag out of town, hence the short walk from cellar to post office and its final journey to Hamburg. We wish it well with its new team and surroundings: a mighty bag in every respect and a great friend and much valued support to Project Front Foot.

* * *

STOP PRESS

A year on from our Brexit-busting encounter and I'm delighted to report a further project kit collection of unprecedented proportions and generosity. During the last week of September 2021, we managed to fill two and a half mid-range transit vans with donated clothing and kit. Whatever doubts existed over the likely extent of our summer appeal evaporated completely in Brighouse where Steve Archer and the massed ranks of clubs in the western region of the Yorkshire Cricket Board all but single-handedly filled the best part of our van on consecutive days.

The long-wheelbase vehicle hired to get the kit down to our Berkshire base camp was similarly packed floor to roof as, towards the end of the repack, items had to be taken out of bags and squirrelled in whatever nooks and crannies still existed.

Extraordinary. On a wet and windy Thursday evening – a long day into night in every respect – Tim and I headed back south. With just a few hours' sleep, and over a four-day period, we set about the sorting, sifting, and separating before packing the kit away for the winter. But not before clothing and equipment was set aside for the Refugee Council's project in Croydon, along with five bags packed for a team of cricketing refugees in Paris, and three bags of bats and balls, latterly of the Surrey Cricket Board, for the Shatila refugee camp in Lebanon.

And of the 50 or so bags that remain? The winter will be spent plotting and planning just how we can get this gear from the UK to the continent and, as ever, for the least possible cost. So it begins.

Epilogue: Not Worthy

I DON'T subscribe to the thinking, certainly where club cricket is concerned, that you're a long time retired. Respect to those who play deep into later life, but three decades was more than enough for me. It was also a decision taken out of my hands (but mostly shoulder) by a ball-and-socket joint that was so loose as to have its own Tinder profile. Cricket teas played their part, too, there being only so much stewed tea and scones you can consume before calling time on top spin and tea room. From a scone-free perspective, there was also the fact that I enjoyed watching the game just as much as playing it, if not more so. There is no better way to spend a sunny Sydney Saturday than high in the M.A. Noble Stand with Mark Waugh easing his way to a serene century.

A club cricketer from my coloured cap to my whitened boots, I harboured but a solitary ambition: the briefest mention in an edition of *Wisden Cricketers' Almanack*. Selection for a single minor counties game would have guaranteed a namecheck if only in the Also Batted or Also Bowled section. I'm flattered to think my name may have cropped up at a selection meeting during a stellar season in the 1980s. But it was not to be, and the chance was gone. That said, there were compensations. In 1980, thanks to the generosity of spirit by editor David Frith, I had half a dozen articles in *Wisden Cricket*

Monthly. This was the start of a 15-year association with the magazine. It also placed me, and my questionable copy, just a few pages from my all-time writer-broadcaster hero, John Arlott. To be inside the same cover, albeit a few pages apart, was more than any club cricketer could hope or dream.

An early contribution was a spoof on World Series Cricket in the form of a World Statesmen XI which included the likes of Stalin, Gandhi, Churchill and Ataturk. I still turn pink with embarrassment all these years on when, after a spot of mild GBH on my Remington portable, I managed to hammer Constantinople into Can't-stand-a-no-ball. And this, just a dozen pages from Arlott's essay: Jack Hobbs remembered. The shame of it! Years later, over a few beers with Frithy in Sydney's Paddington, I mentioned how thrilled I was to be just a few pages from Arlott. A fair man and a fine editor, if he'd have known that, he said, he'd have moved me closer. Oh no! No, no, no. Not worthy! Absolutely not worthy!

* * *

Slipcatcher
Wisden Cricket Monthly: December 1987–March 1988

Sunday Times, 12 July 1987. 'On the face of it, life was a mixture of the quaint and the archaic. Every year the office virtually closed to attend the Lord's Test match, where MI5 had an unofficial patch in the Lord's Tavern.' Extract from the book Spycatcher by Peter Wright, the book they tried to ban.

* * *

Wisden Cricket Monthly today publishes extracts from *Slipcatcher,* by Ulysses Wrong, the former MCC administrator. Recently *WCM* has fought a bitter legal battle against the

Marylebone Cricket Club, the latter having opposed publication in an attempt to avoid disclosures of an extremely delicate nature. Next weekend 40,000 copies are being distributed to booksellers across Australia by the Sydney-based publishers Tamara Press. MCC has already gone to court to stop publication of Wrong's memoirs in India, where it lost but has gone to appeal. At courtrooms throughout the free cricketing world, MCC is attempting to stop publication of *Slipcatcher* because it believes that Wrong is in breach of his contract to keep 'administrative' work confidential. Wrong has argued that there is nothing of substance in the book which is of threat to MCC, or which has not already been syndicated, without permission, from an after-dinner speech, having first been the domain of slip-cordon conversation over the years. As to the question of whether two wrongs make a right, only time and the law lords will tell. What is crystal clear, however, is that the extracts we hold for serialisation will blow the lid off cricket's established order.

In a career that spanned 25 years, Wrong swept across the line of many of the game's conventions. Yet, although much has been written of Wrong in the past 12 months, most if not all has centred on the seamier side of his career. In contrast, little has been said about the man himself. Away from the constant glare of publicity, Wrong has settled for a life of comparative anonymity in the politically free climate of Odessa on the Black Sea coast. Here, distanced from the mystery and intrigue that have enveloped Lord's, he can return to the peaceful existence of his retirement, a man ever hopeful that one day his memoirs will be freely available throughout the cricket world. In this first extract from *Slipcatcher* we trace the early days of Ulysses Wrong. Those events, situations and circumstances that fashioned this solitary young man into one of cricket's top administrators.

Part 1: Wrong 'Un

Conceived shortly after close of play at the Scarborough Cricket Festival of 1912, Wrong eventually saw the light of day on a bleak first morning of the Gentlemen v Players fixture at Lord's the following May. A somewhat surprised pavilion official coped expertly with this first delivery of the morning. Rejecting the opportunity to christen their son MCC in honour of his birthplace, yet already aware of a cricket theme developing in his young life, the Wrongs settled upon Ulysses Neville. It was during his prep school days that he acquired the nickname that would remain lifelong. Keen-eyed contemporaries, spying his name listed as 'WRONG UN' in a house match batting line-up, henceforth referred to him as 'Bosey'. In view of a later involvement with the dirty tricks brigade, both surname and initials were to prove inspirational in choice.

It was during his years as an undergraduate at Oxford in the 1930s that Wrong began to witness a hitherto unknown side of cricket. At pre-season nets in April 1933, he made the acquaintance of three young men; a meeting, with hindsight, that would change his life. Guy Burglary and Donald Colgate opened for his college, while Kim Trilby spun an intriguing line in leg breaks and googlies. Already members of a particular group of free-thinking revolutionary individuals known as the non-walkers, they were ever on the lookout to recruit new members. In Trilby's rooms they spoke with chilling fanaticism about lifting the seam with a threepenny bit, using Lipsal to prolong the shine of a new ball, and, with the dust of Bodyline still to settle, intimidatory bowling.

Long into the evening, as the fragrance of gillyflowers mingled with that of honey and anchovy, they considered every conceivable device, from sledging to scuffing the wicket and persistent bat-pad appealing, in an effort to undermine the very structure of the game. While Wrong may have disagreed with the ultimate aim, that of creating new order out of revolution – Kerry Packer eventually completed the task 45 years later – he nevertheless found himself attracted to this win-at-all-costs attitude. Long before the end of that Trinity term Wrong had become a card-carrying Jardineist.

Wrongdoer

Seconded into military intelligence at the outbreak of war, 'Bosey' Wrong was now able to put into practice much of what had been only fanciful theory during his Oxford days. He developed the explodable matting wicket for use throughout the Commonwealth, a device exploited to the full by Mosquito pilot Keith Miller and his RAAF XI. This was followed in 1943 by a call to the War Office and a meeting with Barnes Wallis. Having written his final-year thesis on 'The Psychological and Philosophical Effect of Bodyline on the Colonies', Wrong found himself working on the Dambusters project. The outcome of secret trials on Derwent Water, in the presence of Larwood, Voce and Bowes (all on a 24-hour leave pass), came to be known as the bouncing bomb.

His greatest success, however, came in the field of chemical warfare. It was Wrong who pioneered the mind-numbing gases used on the D-Day landings. Based on a formula that combined the putrid niff of a season-old unwashed jockstrap with a pair of sweat-stained woollen socks, the end-product of a day-long run-feast at The Parks, Wrong had produced the ultimate weapon. Victory would soon be ours.

Wrong turning

It came as little surprise that, at the cessation of hostilities and demobilisation, Wrong opted to join the staff at Lord's and to embark on a career within the twilight world of cricket administration. Prior to recruitment, however, he found himself subjected to an unusually severe security screening. Confronted by a full sitting of the committee with special responsibility for gin-slinging, the questioning came thin and slow. Had he ever been a non-walker? Yes, he had come into contact with it while at university, but no more than any other undergraduate. Had he ever been approached to participate actively with an iron behind the curtain? Yes, but only in a threesome with the maid and a progressively minded nanny, and they had been carpeted by his father three weeks later. Had he ever been queer? No, although he admitted a penchant for leg glances and short balls while at Oxford.

Sat through Roses match

In a manner which impressed his superiors, Wrong set about the practical side of his screening with great courage. As a test of his ability to endure pain, he sat through an entire Roses match, ball by excruciating ball, whereupon he illustrated initiative, this made slightly easier with choice of fixture, by compiling a report in under five words of the positive aspects on view over the three days. Finally, in a demonstration of ruthlessness found in only a few people, he arrived on the eve of the corresponding fixture a year later and dug up not only the pitch but also the entire square and outfield.

For the remainder of this training Wrong flitted between Lord's and a nondescript grey building in Whitehall identified only by the brass nameplate of 'Universal Escort'. Desk-bound for several months, he awaited his first assignment. In the autumn of 1954, with MCC about to set sail for Australia in a bid to retain the Ashes, Wrong's prowess in the field was about to be put to the test.

Part 2: Colonial Brief

The year is 1954. MCC, having regained the Ashes a year earlier, are about to set sail in a bid to retain this most coveted of prizes. In a memo dated September of that year, Wrong is placed on standby, and by the state of play not a moment too soon.

It had been a long, hot, boring, desk-bound summer in St John's Wood. He had chaired meetings, written letters, attended to files, and made the statutory see-and-be-seen visits to the Tests and selected county matches. Yet there just had to be more to cricket administration than this. He became irritable, short-tempered. Even the president's alluring secretary Miss Filthy-Lucre had lost some of her attractiveness.

Then, in late autumn, the balloon went up. England lost the first Test at Brisbane by a staggering innings and 154 runs. After a hastily arranged meeting with E.M. (Sir Edmund Minesa-Gin, MCC president), Wrong was dispatched to the Colonies with a brief to reverse the trend by whatever means necessary. He reached Australia in late December, by which time England had levelled the series, albeit by the slender margin of 38 runs.

The Melbourne Test that southern summer is remembered for one incident in particular.

With play due to restart on the Monday morning, after a rest day that had incorporated a weekend of extremely hot weather, the pitch, to the amazement of all in attendance – especially the curator – was wet. Whether this occurred through natural sweating or by watering has never conclusively been answered, until now. At the centre of events that weekend, unbeknown to players, officials, and curator alike, was Ulysses Wrong.

Wrong's fertility rites

'On arrival in Melbourne I was met by my contact, an old friend from university days, Arthur Dox. It was he, along with Burglary, Colgate, and Trilby, who had preached revolution in those heady days of the 1930s. A discreet and trusted fellow, Dox's fanaticism was matched only by his impetuosity. Once, at the Union, having voted in favour of the motion Alms for the Poor, he promptly severed his right arm, marched to the chair, and handed it (albeit with difficulty) to the president. A legend in his own termtime, he was known around campus as left-arm Arthur Dox.

'With England skittled for 191 on the first day, time was very much of the essence. Over beer at Young & Jackson's on Swanston Street I was introduced to an aboriginal activist by the name of Dick-a-Dick. His personal problems aside, the meeting proved lucrative. A member of the Slabakbmate, his tribe, victims of the petroleum companies' quest for oil, had been forcibly evicted from their settlement. They had journeyed many months, routes their ancestors trod, returning finally to land held sacred in ceremonial fertility rites. Yet even this had been developed, not by multinationals, but by the Melbourne Cricket Ground Trust. The tribe reluctantly moved on, but not without first uttering veiled threats of bad magic.

'The Slabakbmate were not to know, but I had been practising bad magic for years; we had reached common ground. At a hastily arranged corroboree, with the medicine man in attendance, I offered the opportunity to hit back at authority, a chance denied them against the oil companies. The key to the Test lay in the fast-deteriorating wicket. With England still to bat second, the pitch had to last well into the fourth day. Water would help to bind the cracked surface, although quite how this could be achieved without arousing suspicion or claims of "doctoring" still lay unresolved. Dick-a-Dick, with true activist zeal – and a knowing glance at the medicine man – told me not to worry.

'Thus, on the evening of the rest day, on ground baked hard by a day of furnace heat, there assembled a weird and wonderful gathering. The medicine man placed pebbles, pearl shells, tektites, and the bones of animals recently feasted upon, at intervals along the 22 yards. There followed various chants unintelligible to me. I, in turn, offered my own silent prayer. As the chanting stopped, water began to bubble, slowly at first, then burst through the myriad cracks in the pitch.

'There are times, even as an administrator, when questions are best left unanswered. I closed my mind to thoughts of sorcery and the supernatural, preferring instead to focus on the witchetty-grub croissants and goanna tea the Slabakbmate provided for breakfast. At lunch on the fifth day, with Tyson having routed Australia, we parted company, myself to Tullamarine and a flight to London, the Slabakbmate, on the word of friends at the Department of Aboriginal Affairs, to the lower Murray Valley. A successful conclusion to a ticklish situation, yet one awash with irony. For while touring sides appear ever eager to come to the aid of local fertility rites, for once, here was an occasion where local fertility rites came to the aid of a touring side.'

Sonny side up

The unique 'administrative' talents of Ulysses Wrong fostered a spasmodic career in the field. There was simply not the quantity of Test matches to facilitate his expertise. Overexposure too would create suspicion. There would always be a time to lose, and to be seen to lose graciously. The summer of 1957, however, was not such an occasion. On an overcast evening in late May, Wrong was hurriedly summoned to

Lord's. At the eye of the storm was a diminutive windmill of a West Indian by the name of Sonny Ramadhin. With the first Test a day old, England's inning lay in tatters, Ramadhin having spun and woven his way to 7-49. The brief was simple: discover his secret, and quickly, lest England be served Sonny side up.

'In conference with crestfallen English batsmen the following day, they confirmed what I had already gleaned from the morning papers. He bowled off breaks, leg breaks and a straight one without any change to his action. Tricky stuff. As a matter of routine, I called for cinefilm and freeze-frame photographs of his delivery. These were later shown, under blanket security, to a select gathering of the game's top coaches. Alf Gover apart, who thought he recognised a maiden aunt from Tavistock, the exercise drew a blank. Short on inspiration, I returned to my flat and a chapter or two of *Essays in Diplomacy* by Douglas Jardine. Slowly but surely, something began to gel. I considered impersonation, and but for the fact that I was 6ft 3in, Caucasian, had not bowled for 20 years, and had difficulty in disguising my leg break, it might have worked. The Slabakbmate would, with a phone call and a case of beer, have flooded the ground, but it was impossible to get them to Edgbaston for Monday's restart. With cricket still untouched by sex, drugs, and rock 'n' roll, there was just one option left. Omitted from training manuals, spoken of only in hushed tones behind locked doors, there remained the administrator's ultimate weapon – the rules.

'I told E.M. of my decision over coffee in the Long Room. MCC made the rules. Surely, if we could not break them, we were at liberty to bend them, if only slightly. Hiring a homeless aboriginal tribe to cast spells was one thing, but "break the rules", this was something else altogether. In agitated fashion he paced the floor, pausing briefly to mutter something about "the spirit of the game". Given foresight, he would have seen the 1970s and 1980s rob the game of what little spirit existed. The issue was speedily resolved with news that West Indies had posted a first-innings lead of 288. En route to Birmingham that night, I felt strangely elated. If only Burglary, Colgate and Trilby were here, for tonight there was revolution afoot. Twenty years on from Oxford, my Jardinesque ideals had again come to the fore. In 1932/33 he had dispensed with the wickets by bowling at the batsmen. I too would dispense with, with the bat, and play Ramadhin with, with what? Yes! Play him with the pad!

'A novel idea, but in recollecting Gubby Allen's opposition to Bodyline, one unlikely to court favour with the batsmen, especially the amateurs. It would have to be kept from them, suspicion allayed with the selection of just two, then sleep induced, and the technique implanted by the use of autosuggestion. The one problem, how to get them to sleep? I settled on a dinner invitation with Trevor Bailey in attendance, the latter being prompted to recall some of his lengthier defensive innings. It proved a total success. All three fell fast asleep during a rather excellent entrée of garlic prawns.

'After losing quick wickets on the resumption of play, subjects Cowdrey and May duly posted a record fourth-wicket stand of 411. To the assembled press, the batsmen, both amateurs, playing every ball as if an off break, displayed an alarming degree of professionalism. Was this the beginning of the end? Or the end of the beginning? One aspect untouched by hypothesis was Ramadhin's analysis. With 2-179 in 98 overs, his efficacy, with 100 appeals refused, along with his spirit were broken. Harsh treatment for one man, but the wheel of fortune would soon turn West Indies' way. And how!'

It is fortunate for cricket that within its centuries of development there exists a safety valve. While faceless administrators appear to ride roughshod over the sport, they are all ultimately answerable to the very nature and tradition of the game itself. Wrong's slight 'bending' of the rules led shortly after to the lbw law being widened in scope to outlaw persistent pad play. During two days' play at Edgbaston the end all but justified the means. Mercifully, the spirit of the game, if not that of one man, was allowed the last word.

Part 3: Rain, Rough and Revolution

Administrative work can be a dirty and dangerous game: ink smudges on shirt cuffs, telltale coffee stains, and the sheer hell involved in changing a typewriter ribbon. Devoid of rules, casualties are frequent and often heavy. But that is the nature of the game. At the dawn of the 1960s, however, administrative work became even more hazardous.

'From the outset, Lord's rules the cricket world in all matters administrative. MCC made the rules, the others followed. We knew, nevertheless, that this would not always be the case. Infiltration was a fact of life. Once breached, a counter-administrative network could be operational within a matter of weeks. The first signs of this phenomenon appeared in the late summer of 1961. After the events of Hutton's tour seven years earlier, Manchester provided the Australians with a chance to even the score. The turning point, quite literally, of the fourth Test saw Benaud change from over to round the wicket to deliver his leg spin. From this point, despite requiring only 106 to win, England's last eight wickets fell for 51. The Ashes were lost. A quite remarkable victory, yet questions remained: was it inspired or assisted?

'The following week, an innocuous three-line report from the *Manchester Evening Post* arrived on my desk. Over the weekend of the Test, a person or persons unknown had unlawfully entered the Old Trafford pavilion. Fortunately, nothing was stolen. My curiosity was immediately aroused. Why go to all that trouble and take nothing? During the next 48 hours I made it my business to trace and check the kit bags of all those players on Test duty in Manchester. Finally, at Harrogate, I found what I had been looking for: proof positive that Australia now operated a counter-administrative network.

'Someone, most probably a suicide squad, had tampered with Trueman's boots. Removing the studs, they had replaced them with Kakadu scuff sprigs. Although wicketless in the second Australian innings, Trueman bowled 32 overs, in the process leaving three patches of rough at various lengths outside the right-hander's leg stump. Thereafter, Benaud had little to do except select the time at which to revert to round the wicket and direct his line at the rough. Fiendishly contrived, it had been executed to perfection.

'In direct contrast to the sophistication of Australian methods, those of the subcontinent tend towards a somewhat less than subtle approach. Counter-administrative agencies in Delhi and Karachi rely heavily on the Trent Bridge Doctor (as opposed to the Fremantle Doctor) if there is need of "specific" pitch preparation.

'Failing this, the more simplistic methods of rioting and the burning of grandstands will be employed. A slightly more negative approach than those pursued by MCC and the ACB, but effective nonetheless. Indeed, this was the case at Karachi in 1969, where the lawlessness was timed to begin soon after the arrival of Colin Milburn. Whether it was simply the rotund appearance of the player, and with it the threat of nationwide famine should he need feeding for the full five days, or his hundred that triggered the unrest, we shall never know. What did emerge, however, from two and a half days' play, was that it is as difficult to play cricket in a revolution as it is in rain.'

Tit for tat

It has become clear from Wrong's memoirs that MCC's policy of keeping membership at the unusually high figure of 18,000, together with an extensive waiting list, was not for reasons financial but of an altogether more dubious nature.

'Assignments in the field require individual methods to suit the situation. There have been instances where we have been obliged to recruit from outside. In so doing, MCC membership provides the necessary men for all seasons. Normal policy would be to approach those on the waiting list, the inducement being a substantial move forward in their quest for membership. In such recruitment there is always risk, as we were to discover at Leeds in 1975.

'The memo that arrived on my desk read quite simply, "Request pitch assistance – re Underwood, Aug 14-19, Headingley." Australia was already one up in the series, and, after the humiliation of the previous winter, Lord's were desperate for victory. The computer-based waiting list threw out the name of a Mr George Davis, soil engineer! The brief was to widen the cracks in an already wearing pitch so as to assist the Kent spinner. With Mr Davis unavoidably detained, his partners agreed to perform the work. At this juncture, there appeared a misunderstanding over the terms "widen" and "assist".

'The cracks were duly "widened", although quite whether the complete disappearance of Derek Underwood for three days, having fallen down one, constitutes "assistance" is a matter of conjecture. Once out of intensive care, the left-arm spinner went on to confirm that the crude oil allegedly poured on the pitch had in fact materialised from one of the many deep cracks. As a result, BP in conjunction with Yorkshire CCC are hoping to tap the Headingley field sometime early in the new year, so long as Bernard Flack and his countrywide fleet of JCBs do not arrive first.

'The events at Leeds occurred as a direct consequence of a blatant pitch incursion nine months earlier in Brisbane. In what amounted to their first recruitment of an official outside the administrative service, Australia, in true "Fawlty logic", produced a quite enviable degree of success. Short on ideas, yet desperate to take an early lead in the series, the ACB gambled on handing curatorship of the Gabba to the sitting lord mayor of Brisbane, Clem Jones. His skill as a politician had taught him to cut waste, weed out troublemakers, and top dress himself, qualification enough for the position. However, while his civic adeptness achieved much for the city, his curatorial prowess was limited to a window-box, and a small one at that. Unperturbed, Mr Jones set about the pitch with great gusto. Clearly used to "flattening wets" at council meetings, he attempted the very same with a morass of black mud that should have been the Test pitch. In what amounted to GBH with a heavy roller, Mr Mayor proceeded to roll a perfect ridge into the plasticine, a ridge frighteningly exploited only a matter of hours later by Jeff Thomson and Dennis Lillee.

'If the series against Australia in the mid-1970s taught me anything, it was that administration is a young man's game. Errors are fatal. I made one at Headingley, but thankfully escaped with my pension intact. Maybe next time I would not be so lucky. That reckless gung-ho approach of the 1950s had now completely disappeared. Counter-administration had seen to that. The increase in Test cricket, allied to a constantly growing one-day programme, had brought extra pressure. Perhaps it was time to think of retirement.'

Part 4: Light and Bitter

'An MCC tie, akin to a mason's handshake, offers a wide and varied circle of friends. This is especially so throughout Whitehall, where Test match days offer the chance to rekindle that camaraderie of old. Indeed, there is passing reference to this in the little-publicised book *Spycatcher* by Peter Wright, "Every year the office virtually closed to attend the Lord's Test, where MI5 had an unofficial patch in the Lord's Tavern." It was during one such soirée that I was approached "off the record, old boy" to lend assistance.

'Apparently there was trouble brewing in South Africa. I had tried some of their Guinness recently and had guessed as much. It was unsettled, cloudy, the white struggling to keep ahead of the black. What was needed was nothing short of pure genius, but who? David Brown was suggested, but the very name smacked of racial overtones. We were in trouble enough without rocking the boat further. If genius was needed, then Basil D'Oliveira – with MCC due to tour South Africa in the winter – was the man to go to the Cape. He was Whitehall's choice. Hurrah! But our man was not even in the XI for the summer's final Test against Australia at The Oval. For the remainder of the evening, I was left to struggle with my conscience.

'The "unofficial official" word around St John's Wood was that D'Oliveira must not tour. My allegiance, however, remained with my drinking colleagues from the Tavern. With their help we overcame the first hurdle, as Roger Prideaux fell victim of a mysterious bout of pleurisy. Despite scoring 158 at The Oval, there was still no place for D'Oliveira in the touring party.

In a last-ditch effort, I approached each of the tourists and retold of the trouble brewing in South Africa. Tom Cartwright, Guinness devotee of many years' standing, was so overcome that he broke down. It was a relieved D'Oliveira who took his place.

'The events that followed represent cricket's darkest hour. The South African situation became increasingly unstable. This in brewing parlance, was the cause of irregular density levels between black and white. As a result, the predominant colour became light and bitter. Even stout, mild men fled the cities, leaving only bitter men in control. D'Oliveira, the man who could have helped, stayed at home. At the end of the day, I felt only relief: 1968 was not the time, nor South Africa the place, for pure genius.'

'Fot'

Four years on from the D'Oliveira affair, Wrong again found himself in the company of those men from the ministry. This time, and a rare occurrence too, the roles were reversed.

'Following Bob Massie's 16 wickets at Lord's, a performance that caused interdepartmental memoranda to hit new heights, Whitehall placed its entire resources at our disposal. Three years prior to the George Davis fiasco, we were still capable of "preparing" a Headingley pitch of sufficient "help" to Underwood and England. This notwithstanding, official anxiety remained and focussed on one player in particular. Dennis Keith Lillee was on his way to claiming 31 wickets in the series at 17.67 each, and promised to be of much nuisance value in the future. However, at the tender age of 23, he just had to have a weakness.

'Using MCC's Harley Street connection, informed opinion settled on the vertebrae of his lower back. An interesting choice this, for early in the summer Lillee had acquired the nickname of "Fot". "First on tour" was an acknowledgement of his ability to use the undoubted talents he possessed at the earliest opportunity. Had he not returned figures of 6-66 during England's second innings of the first Test? But there was much more. The all-seeing eyes of MCC's administrative network had discovered that "Fot" referred also to something completely different, "First of many tantrums"! This was our chance. If sufficiently enraged, Lillee was prone to hurl objects, sometimes something totally unconnected with the game – Keith Fletcher for instance. On each occasion the sudden movement placed extra stress on his back. For the remainder of the tour every conceivable opportunity to arouse Lillee, whether on or off the field, was taken.

'In line with Whitehall thinking, Lillee's continued use of the tantrum led to a premature halt in his career. Minute stress fractures to two vertebrae kept him out of the game for two years. Only inspired work on behalf of Australian counter-administration, who eventually devised a series of exercises to strengthen the back, returned Lillee to the fray, and honed his tantrums to an art form. A return, I am obliged to say, very much against the odds. Although on second thoughts, did I hear someone mention 500/1?'

Life after Lord's

The Packer affair of 1977 signalled the beginning of the end for Ulysses Wrong, for here was a visionary, a man committed to change on a scale they had only dreamed about at Oxford all those years ago. Forty-five years on, here he sat, establishment written through him as if letters in a stick of seaside rock. MCC's foolhardy stand against the rebels brought a dilemma that would eventually force the retirement of Wrong in the summer of 1979. It seemed only natural that on leaving Lord's he should travel to Sydney at the invitation of Kerry Packer and work as a consultant for his Channel 9 outside broadcast team. It was Wrong's specialist knowledge of bugging devices that led to the installation of effects microphones behind the stumps at day/night matches.

Under increasing pressure to tell his story, Wrong eventually left Australia for Russia, and a chance in the sleepy coastal port of Odessa to unload the burden that had been his for 25 years. Today the stooped shuffle has been replaced by the proud, angular gait of a retired gentleman at peace with himself. The bad old days of cricket administration are behind him now, no more lying and cheating, no more doctoring players and pitches, and no more clandestine meetings with umpires, selectors, and tea ladies. For the life of him, he always had difficulty in differentiating between the latter two. He takes merely a passing interest in the game nowadays, and then preferring only to talk of the 'fun' days in the 1950s. When asked who he would choose to play himself, should the film rights to *Slipcatcher* be purchased, he unhesitatingly replied, 'The only one with any style: Gower.'

* * *

Wide (**Awake**) World of Sports
Wisden Cricket Monthly: August 1989

In the southern winter of 1989, I found myself in Sydney's Surry Hills battling mould and mildew of unprecedented proportions as the rains set in with a vengeance. In any ordinary year I would, this being the second week of June, be back in the UK enjoying another summer of cricket. However, not all was monsoon and misgivings. My housemate's SCG Gold Pass, for instance, would see me rugged up and installed in the members' area to watch Friday night footy Aussie Rules style with the Sydney Swans. Saturday, assuming Randwick were at home, we'd head to Coogee and a virtual Test 15 on show including the Ella brothers and arguably rugby's first superstar, David Campese. That just left Sunday when we'd swap union for league and head to the nearby football stadium where, resplendent in hooped red and green Rabbitohs jerseys, we'd barrack for Souths. Heady days these if you discount the trench foot.

Australian televised cricket at that time was in the hands (and back pocket) of Kerry Packer's Channel 9 and in particular their flagship programme, *Wide World of Sports*. With *Wisden Cricket Monthly* in mind, I thought a night of televised Test cricket – commercials and all – might make for good copy. Not for the sleepy or sociable, *Wide* (Awake) *World of Sports* aka day three of the Headingley Test comes complete with tea, cookies, pillow, duvet, bed socks and a fleeting appearance by tall Swedish Ingrid who wisely departed during drinks in the first session.

* * *

'OH, to be in England now that April's there.' Browning was, of course, referring to an Ashes series. It is likely too that inspiration for *Home Thoughts from Abroad* came after watching Channel 9's coverage of just such a series. If you remain doubtful still, then heed the words of one who now finds himself, and for some little time yet, marooned in Sydney, and thus, at the mercy of Australian television. After the months of inclement weather, and the now compulsory rising damp, how we envy your sunshine and static high pressure, but most of all, as raindrops fall, we envy your cricket coverage. That our transmission begins late evening and runs into the small hours is not the problem. Commercial TV lay at the cornerstone of this misery, for such a network has rights of coverage down under. But why not sit back, relax, and enjoy Channel 9's coverage of Saturday, day three of the first Test at Headingley.

(Warning: the following material is considered unsuitable for the aesthetically inclined or those of a weak or nervous disposition.)

*8.30pm: As if in memory of the sell-out by the Australian Cricket Board to PBL Marketing, this current Ashes series is proudly sponsored by Ampol, Nissan, Wilkinson Sword, and Telecom Yellow Pages. An executive Channel 9 decision has decreed that coverage should not begin until half-an-hour into the first hour of play. This, to preserve the ratings points of such winners as *Hey, Hey, it's Saturday*. Still, it could be worse: the previous evening Sydneysiders were robbed of seeing local boy Mark Taylor's maiden Test century by *Burke's Backyard*, a gardening programme. Enter thus a rather embarrassed Ian Chappell to explain away the Australian declaration of minutes earlier. After a brief summary it's over to Tony Greig and Bill Lawry in the central missionary position. Fighting a brave but losing battle against a throat infection, the former Sussex and England captain remains commendably neutral in comment. In contrast, Lawry is positively jingoistic. Talking in tabloid headlines, he bubbles with the news that England need 401 runs to avoid the follow-on.

*8.38: Wilkinson Sword, and the first ad (infinitum) of the evening. From here on in there will be a commercial break at the completion of each over, with a sudden outpouring of such fare on the fall of a wicket. Should the commercial output appear to be flagging, then advertising, teleprinter-style, will flicker across the screen while play is in progress.

*8.42: A delighted Bobby Simpson, safe in the knowledge that this one Australian innings has ensured his security of tenure, is interviewed by Chappell the Elder. Moving as smoothly as modern technology permits into a commercial break, Simmo is replaced by a husky young thing, showing a little, suggesting a lot, proposing that 'men who like women like *Penthouse*'. Bouncers and fine legs, the evening is not lost, or is it?

*8.50: Just when you thought it safe to increase the volume – enter Geoffrey Boycott. The former champion of the erratic single, eyes glazed at the prospect now faced by the England players of batting for three whole days, blusters through predictable questions with an accent seemingly rather more Yorkshire than is necessary.

*9.00: Cued to perfection, Adelaide viewers join the transmission just in time to discover that Wilkinson's Aquaglide gives the world's greatest shave. Good old Wilkinson, pity it couldn't do anything for our Sydney weather. Outside in Surry Hills the rain lashes down. The recent departure of tall Swedish Ingrid has left only the duvet, hot sweet tea, and a packet of chocolate chip cookies for the long night ahead.

*9.15: With England successfully negotiating the early overs, Richie interviews Ted. Defending stoutly, for perhaps the only time in his career, the chairman recalls a Test against the Windies where England were called upon to field for six wicketless sessions. The moral to this linseed lament of the late 1950s: they still won the series!

*9.45: Benaud emerges next with the much-battered Ian Botham. There appears a distinct lack of Chappell the Elder amid the interview positions. The champion all-rounder looks a sad figure. Decline perhaps, and now fall? In mood positive, a wry smile appears as, in noting the 601/7 declared, he suggests this as a good game to miss.

*10.00: Lunch: England 547 runs behind with nine wickets in hand.

*10.40: Coverage resumes with Simon O'Donnell joining Chappell in the commentary box. As if in response to the *Penthouse* commercial, their pronunciation of the England number three as 'Kim Barr-Nett' is reminiscent more of centrefold than centre wicket.

*11.00: To the embarrassment of Englishmen in general, and a certain Notts opener in particular, Broad falls – CRINGE – to the Merv Hughes 'leggie'. He vacates the scene with the air of a man in search of a deep hole. Pity the poor opener, a victim of unlikely circumstances. Very rarely does this delivery pitch in line; near incalculable too are the chances of it looping gently to the desired yorker length. While silently pondering the opener's dismissal, a man suddenly announces his sale of reef fish has increased 60 per cent by advertising in the Yellow Pages. In light of the recent comic demise, this latest interruption appears as nothing more than a natural extension of play.

*11.15: In what could be mistaken for an episode of *The Magic Roundabout* (with due apologies to Dougal, Dylan, and the gang) Boycott joins Lawry at the microphone. The immediate reaction is to switch to BBC's *Test Match Special* 'call'. The reception, however, is little better as Fred ('Ah joost dorn't oonderstan wot's goin on out th'ear') Trueman attempts, but fails, to follow current England tactics.

*12.30am: Trueman is still bleating about unbalanced attacks. At tea, England have progressed to 189/2; Barr-Nett 77, Lamb 53.

*1.05: As the temperature falls, a red-and-green South Sydney rugby jersey supplements the duvet. More tea, more cookies. The impulse to go in search of a soup kitchen is thwarted by further heavy rain. Twelve thousand miles away a sunny Headingley settles for the post-tea session.

*1.08: As Lamb and Barr-Nett set about Hughes and Lawson, a commercial on the merits of artificial hair implantation rekindles thoughts of a thatchless Boyks.

*1.35: Gower, 7,000 Test runs on, continues to flash away outside his off stump. Whether an addiction, sheer negligence, or simply a side effect of the *Penthouse* commercial, we shall never know.

*1.45: Lamb, convinced that boundaries are the answer to England's cause, continues to plunder a wayward attack. Had he advertised his cover drive in the *Yellow Pages*, the improvement in his Test average would have been as high as 60 per cent.

*2.30: Thirteen overs remain of the day's play, overtime now a certainty; groan, more tea, eyes heavy with sleep.

*3.24: The South African connection, Lamb (103), and Smith (16), sees England safely through to stumps at 284/4. A further 118 are needed to avoid the follow-on. With another and mercifully final plug for the sponsors echoing around a silent house, time for this bleary shamble of duvet, pillow, and cookie crumbs to make a sleepy exit. For those still awake, this has been another presentation from 9's *Wide World of Sports*.

* * *

Bushwhacked
Wisden Cricket Monthly: February 1991

The day Doug Walters came out of retirement to lead the Bradman XI to victory over the England tourists in the country town of Bowral.

* * *

Legendary actor, drinker, fighter, womaniser and professional Irishman, Richard Harris, enlivened a particularly dreary chat show a few years ago recounting a tale of his wild days in London. Horizontal in a Chelsea mews, his one sign of life an outstretched arm, in it a Yale key firmly clutched and pointing Heavenwards. When happened upon by police officers he explained that, as the whole world was passing before his eyes, he was merely waiting for his flat to arrive, whereupon he would enter and retire for the night, if not the century.

The small country town of Bowral, the picture of sobriety it must be stressed, knows that feeling only too well. As the Australian cricket season traverses the continent in frenzied fashion, Bowral has simply waited its turn, safe in the knowledge that eventually all roads would lead to the Bradman Oval. Almost 100 years on from the last visit by an England touring side, their turn had come again. Two hours' drive south-west of Sydney, a mecca to all travelling cricket lovers, the town stands proud as the site of The Don's formative years. Such pedigree has lent an air of quiet confidence to its wide leafy streets and sprawling paddocks. It is a popular location for weekender homes, and the 7,000 population embraces both city and country with a friendly, unhurried ease.

There is much of the West Country in Bowral. A single main street; the scattering of antique shops and tea rooms reminiscent of Stow, Bourton, and Moreton-in-Marsh. Fitting, then, that one of the matchday raffle prizes should come courtesy of Cotswold Garden Furniture. Obliging folk around these parts too. For as England shivered under Arctic blizzards, so Bowral, on the eve of the match, produced a hailstorm of Wagnerian proportions, reducing the lush Oval to an icy lake in minutes. Fortunately, this being summer, the thaw came early; as for idle Cotswold musings, they were put to flight by a heady slice of country Australia. Packed tight behind the white picket fence, singlet and stubbies vied with the height of bush fashion. Under convenient, cooling gumtrees Eskies quickly emptied, while the welcoming breeze brought the confused aroma of sunblock, barbecuing steak and snags, and the statutory Aerogard fly spray. The latter is an essential bush supply, for a hardy and elusive creature is the country fly, far more persistent and irritating that its city cousin.

In the best traditions of bushcraft, the Bradman XI contained an interesting blend of youth and experience, city and country, a combination likely to provide England with a solid workout. Not that the sell-out 5,000 crowd, autographs apart, were too interested in the tourists. Even the return of the long-absent Gooch brought only a polite response. For the majority, certainly by the warm applause that greeted each touch of the ball, were here to pay tribute to another country hero – Dungog Doug! Captain for the day, Walters chanced early to use his lowering arm. Three overs but to no avail for this once ace partnership-breaker.

The England innings, slowed by the loss of John Morris and Michael Atherton, eventually moved into gear. There were attractive fifties for Hugh Morris, Lamb and Alec Stewart. Gooch ventured to the wicket at number five, hit a majestic straight drive, then holed out at mid-off to a full toss. Indicative of current form, runs were shared without anyone dominating. Set to score 230 in 30 overs, the select XI suffered the early departure of Arms and Bayliss to Bicknell. Lehmann should quickly have followed had not Atherton shelled consecutive chances at second slip. Thereafter, the game, very much the way of late, slipped gradually, and then at pace, away from the tourists. Nineteen-year-old Jason Young, a student at the Institute of Sport in Canberra, compiled a stylish fifty, whereupon Lehmann (112) and the fleet-footed Michael Bevan (51) crashed an unbeaten 120-run fourth-wicket partnership in just 16.1 overs.

Victory for Bradman's XI by seven wickets, and a handsome one at that. A result, much to the delight of the crowd, achieved with complete and utter disregard for reason and reputation. Such are the ways of the bush. Disappointed perhaps at not seeing Walters bat, the Highlands nevertheless knows that this festival game is almost certain to become an annual fixture.

* * *

A Cricketing Christmas Carol
Wisden Cricket Monthly: December 1991–January 1992

No introduction needed other than to offer sincere apologies to devotees and disciples of Dickens.

Chapter 1: Gin-sodden

Marylebone was dead, to begin with. There is no doubt whatever about that. The register of his burial was signed by the clergyman, the clerk, the undertaker, and the chief mourner. Stooge signed it. And Stooge's name was good upon 'Change, for anything he chose to put his hand to. Marylebone was as dead as a doornail. Mind! Marylebone had not always been dead; it was just the way he sat. Back in the old days he and Stooge had done a lot of sitting, a lot of wheeling and dealing too, for as partners in a high-flying firm of marketing consultants there was much to be done, fortunes to be made. But this is to get ahead of ourselves.

The time is the 1980s, the place Britain, Thatcher's Britain; for the young, bright, and energetic, a land of opportunity. Find your product, market it for all it's worth, then sit back and reap the rewards. A lad of mixed parentage, old beyond his years, Ebony Stooge found himself one evening in the late summer of 1984 quaffing pints of weak yuppie beer at a bistro in Knightsbridge. He struck up conversation with a suntanned colonial by the name of Jack Marylebone. Despite differing backgrounds, Stooge (English public school) and Marylebone (Sydney's state-school system) each perceived in the other a soulmate, a kindred spirit, a cheap drunk, and, not unusual at this point in English social history, a burning desire to make money, loads of it.

Sharing a bottle of Old Tawny Port on the steps of Australia House, they talked long into the chill early morning. Evicted from his commuter belt box in Cardboard City, Stooge invited Marylebone to a Kennington squat for breakfast. The day long they mused over likely areas of profit. With the sun low in the west, the nearby Oval bathed in the tranquil light of late evening, Marylebone spoke at length of the Australian cricket scene, and the revolution prompted and promoted by PBL Marketing in the late 1970s. At the heart of the 'Packer Empire', PBL, a key element in the much-publicised amalgamation between 'circus' and 'establishment' cricket, had been able to write its own ticket. With the Australian Cricket Board falling for the old 30 pieces of silver trick, PBL effectively controlled Australian cricket. Television transmissions and commercial advertising now lay at the heart of the game, with tour itineraries designed to fit primetime schedules. As Marylebone spoke, so the seed of an idea was sown.

Tragedy

Stooge and Marylebone plc (S&M to their friends) duly came into being. And English cricket? Well, it never stood a chance. Antiquated, arrogant, opinionated, built, and now floundering on the old boy network – and that just the gatekeepers at Lord's – here was a product waiting to be marketed. Conscious of the pitfalls of haste and insensitivity, they adopted a softly-softly approach: a few gin-sodden evenings in the Long Room; access to those hospitality boxes that mattered; tickets for the Gatting Lectures; a sponsorship deal here, a tour to South Africa there. Singularly ineffective, collectively devastating, the headquarters of English cricket moved, at a pace slightly less than that of indecent, from the Dickensian chambers that were Lord's to the palatial, hi-tech offices of S&M in Whitechapel. Success continued unabated throughout the 1990s. With Australia and PBL as their role model, S&M rode roughshod over cricket's traditional values and ideals.

This single-minded desire for profit eventually led to the downfall of Marylebone. An advocate for the further development of night cricket, he was fatally injured – struck by a rogue gritter on the central reservation – while being interviewed by Tony Greig prior to the start of the Natural Gas Challenge between England and Canvey Island. Scheduled to be played under the hazard-warning lights of the M62, the game, as a mark of respect, was settled by bowling at a single traffic cone placed in the fast lane. The tragedy, captured on stumpcam, had a profound effect on Stooge. Consumed by grief, and a crate of rather good Chablis, he withdrew from society. With business now his sole interest, he set himself to squeeze every last penny out of English cricket. In pursuit of this, a young clerk and aspiring cricketer, Bob Crashit, was engaged for the winter months. The poor pay and long hours mattered little. The alternative for Crashit had been nothing better than a two-month tour as the 'straight' man in Graham Gooch's Festival of Fun and Frolic.

To bring our story up to date we must travel forward seven years. It is Christmas Eve, early evening. Outside, in light that would have long furrowed the brow of Dickie Bird, snow is falling. Although London has closed and gone to the pub, the lights in the offices of S&M still burn bright. As Stooge struggles with the commercial aspects of England's 'No Prisoners' winter tour, sponsored by Amnesty International, to China and Iraq, there is a knock at the door. Two distinguished-looking gentlemen enter, their egg-and-bacon ties crisp, deep and even.

Chapter 2: Bah! Hambledon!

'We are collecting for those cricketers who have yet to benefit from the Packer revolution, those poor wretches without a winter tour, coaching contract or Fleet Street column. We aim, with your help, to provide for their long winter of inactivity.'

Unimpressed, Stooge scowled, 'Are there no pantomimes to keep them busy? No guest appearances on *A Question of Sport*?' Having sent them packing, he returned to his work, only to be interrupted by the beaming smile of his fresh-faced nephew.

'Season's greetings, Uncle! I've come to invite you to our house tomorrow to celebrate cricket.'

'Cricket!' snarled Stooge. 'Bah! Hambledon!'

'But Uncle,' began his nephew, 'with series wins against Qatar and El Salvador this summer, and the likelihood of further success in China and Iraq, there is much to celebrate.'

'Celebrate cricket!' snorted Stooge. Having no better answer ready on the spur of the moment, he resorted to 'Bah!' and followed it with 'Hambledon!'

Crestfallen, the nephew departed. Irritated, his train of thought disrupted, Stooge stormed into reception and confronted his clerk, 'And I suppose you want tomorrow off, too?'

Nervously sucking his desk blotter, Crashit looked up from the December issue of S&M's *Bouncers* (the adult cricket magazine) and, in a faltering voice, began, 'Well, er, actually Mr Stooge, I was rather hoping to take the next four months off.'

It took brandy and moistened pages of the *Financial Times* as a cold compress to revive Stooge. His grasp of reality regained, he delivered a volley of expletives worthy of any Australian slip cordon, before repeating, 'Four months?'

'Don't you remember, Mr Stooge?' replied his now ashen-faced clerk. 'I've been chosen for England's winter tour. You helped select the party. We leave for Beijing on Boxing Day.'

Subdued, deep in thought, Stooge recalled the selection meeting. He recalled too a crate of vintage champagne courtesy of the Chinese Embassy. 'A common enough name,' he replied, sulkily. 'Had I known the Crashit in question to have been my clerk, then the nearest you would have got to Asia would have been that takeaway on the Fulham Road.'

Aware that his request for leave might cause problems, Crashit, a *bona fide* touring contract in his pocket, had taken the precaution of calling his agent and solicitor; their arrival led to an animated discussion on the finer points of industrial relations law and in particular breach of contract. Fearing the heavy cost of litigation, Stooge agreed to Crashit's demands, all of them, including a new crutch – to replace the broken president's putter – for his friend and England selector Tiny Ted (Dexter).

Spectre

Shocked by this sudden outburst of player power, Stooge closed the office and retired to his melancholy club for a melancholy dinner. It had been a bad day and, with this tale barely half told, it looked like getting worse. He returned to his penthouse suite at the Dorchester a little before midnight. The rooms had belonged to Marylebone, Stooge having gleefully moved in following his partner's demise. Having fallen asleep in the jacuzzi, he was awoken by a strange moaning sound coming from his bedroom. As the moaning morphed into the clanking of chains, Stooge set off to investigate. Only to be stopped in his tracks as the ghostly presence of his former partner walked through the wall, through the sofa, through the TV, and into the kitchen.

'G'day mate, got any coldies in the fridge?'

'It, you, can't be,' mumbled Stooge, his face the colour of a very raw prawn. 'You're dead!'

'Too right, sport, dead as a dead dingo's donga. Stick us a couple of pies in the microwave.'

Recovering the assemblance of poise, Stooge went on the offensive, 'Cut out that cadaverous, colonial crap, Marylebone. What are you after?'

'You won't wanna hear it mate, believe me, you won't wanna hear it.'

'Try me.'

'Mate, it's the sort of news that even I wouldn't give a XXXX for.' With that he clanked himself to his full height and began to read from pencilled notes. 'I stand before you a man tormented by his former life, a life of uncaring greed. I am that man who stitched up the game of cricket, who let standards drop, traditions go unheeded, and values fall. Each link in this chain is a shonky deal, a broken promise, an ill-gotten gain. But today, mate, you won the chook raffle. I'm here tonight to tell you that you have a chance of escaping my fate.'

Stooge wiped the perspiration from his brow; a thin smile flicked across his thin lips. 'Go on Marylebone, go on.'

'You will be haunted by three spirits, the Ghosts of Cricket Past, Present and Future. Expect the first tomorrow, when the bell tolls one. Heed their message, Stooge, or prepare to grace the pages of the *Sunday Sport*.' At that, the spectre gathered his chains, took a six-pack from the fridge, the pies from the microwave, and clanked off into the Dreamtime.

A shot or two of Scotch later and Stooge, now able to walk, examined the wall through which the apparition had entered. 'Bah!' he snorted, 'Hambledon!' and took himself off to bed. When he awoke it was dark. A nearby church bell rang out a deep, dull, hollow, melancholic … ONE.

Chapter 3: The Mother of all Nights

As if cued by an unseen director, a light show of Spielbergian proportions exploded around the room. Searing waves of psychedelia duluxed everything in sight. Stooge cursed Marylebone's taste in ceiling mirrors. He cursed his taste in four-poster beds too, for at that moment the curtains were wrenched apart revealing a huge, all-enveloping, terrifyingly hairy, black beard. Attached to a man of equally terrifying proportions, beard and man moved closer. As colour uncoordinated as the light show, the spectre wore a Gloucestershire cap, MCC blazer, London County sweater, and carried a bat circa 1890. Stooge shivered. It was 'the Old Man', 'the Champion', 'W.G.' himself.

'Are you the spirit, sir, whose coming was foretold to me?' he queried, wondering too why his speech had taken a hike back in history.

'I am.'

Not one to waste words, unless to plead for his wicket, the spectre clasped Stooge's wrist and set off at a respectable clip towards and through a party wall and into the sparkling sunshine of a midsummer's day.

'Where are we?' whimpered Stooge, not daring to leave the spectre's side.

Ignoring the enquiry, the Old Man stroked his beard and turned, 'You have long plundered cricket, Stooge, offering nothing in return. The game is unrecognisable to the one I played and loved. I have thus returned you to the Golden Age, a time of great skill, beauty, and sportsmanship. Observe, ingest, consider what we once had, and what you have taken.'

Parasols

Invisible to those around him, Stooge wandered freely. It was all so different, so odd, so civilised. The sun shone, turnstiles clicked, tailcoats vied with parasols, and leather was clearly audible on willow. The play – unhurried, graceful, and laced with artistry – mirrored the period. Stooge thought he saw a friend, but it couldn't have been, not him, not Gower. The ground, with every vantage point taken, was brim-full. So too the pots of foaming ale enjoyed by public and players alike. Indeed, beer was in great demand, for with 400 runs or more and 120 overs in the day, a fellow built up a thirst. But whatever the state of play, there was always time for a pipe, a hand of cards, and a glass or two of whisky before dressing for dinner.

Stooge, taking his seat in the pavilion, sat in studied silence. To polite applause, the players, resplendent in baggy flannels, silk shirts, chokers, and the odd solar topee, took the field. The array of talent left him dizzy: Shrewsbury, Gunn, MacLaren, Fry, Bobby Abel, Tyldesley, 'Ranji', Trumper, Darling, Clem Hill, Noble and Macartney, all passed before him that afternoon. Regal cricket; pitches of true bounce; spinners wheeling gently away; Varsity sides beating first-class counties; the amateur game in full flood. Stooge felt weak at the knees. Confused, excited, drained, he was drowning in honey. It was then, as if the answer to his silent prayer, that a solemn voice pronounced, 'And that concludes proceedings for the day.' With stumps drawn, the ground empty, Stooge made an unsteady way to the middle. In measured stride, he was joined by WG. 'Spirit!' said Stooge in failing voice, 'remove me from this place.' Consumed thereafter by an irresistible drowsiness, he reeled, fell, kept on falling and sank into a deep sleep.

Afro-Caribbean

Awaking in the middle of a prodigiously tough snore, Stooge sat bolt upright. He peered nervously at the teasmade. One o'clock. Rivulets of perspiration soaked the duvet. As consciousness came, he recalled the visitation. Could it really have been Gower? Or was it all a dream? As he mused, so the minutes, five, ten, 15, ticked by. Slowly, relief spread. It HAD been a dream. By way of celebration, he rose, poured himself a stiff drink, and was making his way back to bed when he noticed a light in the games room. As he considered his options, a voice called out and bade him enter. Stooge obeyed.

It was the games room. There was no doubt about that. But it had undergone a surprising transformation. The walls and ceiling had gone, replaced by something that looked distinctly like Headingley. The tarmacadam wicket, crumbling committee rooms and newly constructed Afro-Caribbean social club confirmed this indeed as the home of Yorkshire cricket.

'Come in,' exclaimed the ghost. 'Come in and know me better!' With that, Stooge was handed a brightly coloured sponsor's tracksuit, matching visor, and coerced into a punishing circuit of press-ups, squat thrusts and trunk curls, the whole ghastly experience concluding with a six-mile jog.

'Are you,' wheezed Stooge. He never finished the sentence.

'Stand up straight when you address the England manager!' boomed the ghost. 'Eyes front! Head up! Shoulders back! Chest in! Groin out! That's better. We'll make a cricketer of you yet.'

Chapter 4: Pain Meanz Points

Confused, aching from the physical exertion, Stooge eyed his surroundings. The omens were not good. The games room, or what was left of it, reeked of hard, joyless work. In the world of Cricket Present, artist made way for artisan. He was fearful too of this latest spectre. Small, wiry, grey hair thinning on top, a south-London accent, the archetypal no-pain-no-gain county pro.

'I am Sergeant Major Stewart,' began the spirit. 'Mental Micky to some, I believe, but you can call me the Ghost of Cricket Present. It is my task to induce a short, sharp, shock, by way of a brief insight into the modern game. Savvy? Good. Right whe – wait for it – eel! Quick march. At the double yew 'orrible little consultant, yew!'

True to his word, here was cricket at the sharp end. Test match and four-day cricket under threat; dwindling county membership; one-day cricket rampant; rowdy, ill-disciplined crowds; batsmen unrecognisable under protective clothing; intimidatory bowling; slow over rates; bad manners; sledging rife; decisions questioned; declining loyalty; genius despised; underprepared and 'doctored' pitches; medium-pace containment; spinners extinct. Visibly shaken, Stooge had no idea the game had deteriorated to such an extent. He was about to enquire the plight of county professionals when he recalled being asked to contribute to their welfare the previous day. His suggestion – that they seek pantomime work or guest appearances on *A Question of Sport* – left him deeply ashamed. Moved to pity, he sought the fate of Bob Crashit and Tiny Ted.

'A sad end,' replied the ghost. 'Barmaids. Tragic!'

Stooge broke down. The spectre could little console him, although he knew a spirit who could. That spirit now appeared, the Ghost of Cricket Future. Slowly, gravely, silently, the phantom approached.

Crickball

'Ghost of the Future,' sobbed Stooge. 'I fear you most of all. This long, painful night has demonstrated the error of my ways; bring you the final curtain to this sad and sorry tale?'

'Too right,' began the phantom, a curious sight in bright yellow Channel 9 blazer and matching nose. 'Better cop it sweet, Stooge, yer stuffed up! What say we sink a Tooheys or two then take in the Dreamtime?'

Impassive throughout this endless night, Stooge found it hard to contain his revulsion at what followed. Cricket, or crickball as it was now called, evolved solely around the pyjama game. Test matches were long dead; a slow, painful end, so they say. The elements now no longer played their part, as games were restricted to huge American-style indoor venues. Essex played at the Gnome Dome in Chelmsford, Middlesex the Gatt Dome, and New South Wales in the Ken Done Dome. Yorkshire, needless to say, were based at their (self-inflicted) House of Pain near Harrogate. In this artificial environment, grass had given way to astroturf, and groundsmen to a firm of carpet cleaners.

The American theme continued with brass bands, cheerleaders, steroids, congested fixture lists, and nightly primetime exposure. There were substitutions, player transfers, and the right to query a decision, which was then reviewed by neutral referees. Further uncertainty brought polygraph tests for batsman, bowler and fielder. The rules of crickball were based on ten innings per team, ten overs per innings, ten balls per over with a minimum of nine bouncers in each over. All bowlers to be fast, nasty and over 6ft 8in in height. Spin bowlers need not apply. Histrionics are actively encouraged, so too bowling at the body, for as we all know: Pain meanz points and points meanz prizes; prizes; prizzzzz.

Theatre

Christmas morning. In the palatial offices of S&M, the lights once again burn bright. Heady with relief at having survived, as he would later recount, 'the Mother of all Nights', Stooge set about mending his ways. There was much to be done – the return of English cricket to the ECB, discussions with the ICC on the future of the game – but what better way to celebrate cricket than, in his final official act, to appoint David Gower as England manager?

With that, our tale is almost told. Of the young Crashit? Bob gave up barmaids, pursued a successful Test career, and ended his days as cricket correspondent and agony aunt for *Cosmopolitan*. Conspicuous by his absence, Tiny Ted, the hand now steadier, his tee-to-green game improving, continued to make the oddest selectorial decisions well into old age. As for the kindly Stooge, he dissolved S&M, moved out of cricket and into theatre, producing the likes of *Les Bloody Miserables (a short history of Yorkshire cricket)*, and *Get Up, Stand Up!* (all you wanted to know about intimidatory bowling but were too afraid to ask).

* * *

Some Cool Thoughts on a Hot Series
Wisden Cricket Monthly: April 1993

One Short's analysis of the memorable 1992/93 Australia v West Indies series.

* * *

With little more than an outside edge between Australia and West Indies, the recent challenge for the Frank Worrell Trophy always threatened to be a classic confrontation. But few could have scripted the final outcome of this summer of great drama and stunning action, something of a mirror image of the summer of 1960/61, one of the greatest ever. Yet, in the forest of newsprint that chronicled such stirring deeds, there was little on what might be termed the alternative aspects of play. As champion and provider of balance to the modern game, it has fallen to 'One Short' to add the final touches to this remarkable southern summer of cricket.

BRISBANE: Left to work hard to avoid defeat on the final afternoon, West Indies won hands down (make that high-fives up) in the contest that mattered most – that to decide the Kings of Cool. Aware of their dull, dowdy image among sporting trendsetters, the Australians were soon into their stride(s). Shirt sleeves were buttoned fashionably at the wrist, collars high, flannels with just a hint of flare, and all to the accompaniment of designer stubble. On the cosmetic front, Craig McDermott's choice was for lime-green sunblocker to nose and cheeks, reverting to the traditional white as the game progressed. Keen to steal an early march, Border, Boon, and new cap Damien Martyn opted for wraparound sunglasses. Those more conventional among the players settled for squinting. The shades did the trick, all except for Border. His white floppy hat and unshaven look gave him the appearance of a man seeking a white stick and tin can rather than someone embarking on a fashion statement.

For this opening Test, Bruce Reid had removed his wisp of a moustache. It had little effect, other than to make the poor fellow appear like a tree attacked by acid rain. Swapping trees for shrubbery, Merv Hughes sported enough facial hair for the entire team. The Australians did their utmost to swagger, gesticulate, glare, and stare their way to Cool. The only one to succeed, although most of the time he was away with the pixies, was Greg Matthews. He alone stood for Cool. He also jogged, stretched, clapped, cajoled, laughed, chatted and disco-danced for Cool. But in the final reckoning, all to no avail.

The Windies merely watched and waited. No need for designer sunglasses here. The impressionable Arthurton sported a pair, but this was simply the folly of youth. Throughout the Caribbean, cool is genetic. It's all in the genes, man. Have genes will swagger. Gary Sobers was the first King of Cool. His swagger, or a derivative thereof, was handed down, first to Clive Lloyd and then to Vivian Richards. One wonders whether this easy, languid, rolling gait is now an essential element in the West Indian coaching manual. Their fast bowlers, aided and abetted by height and a distinct lack of oxygen, amble naturally. There are occasions, such is their rhythm and movement, that a fielding display will resemble a new work by the Sydney Dance Troupe. The impression of theatre is enhanced still further by the players simply dripping gold. No costume jewellery, this. Rings, bracelets, chains, and pendants abound. Little wonder the Australians took to wearing sunglasses. What the glinting, glistening Wesley Hall began in the 1960s, so the latest generation have added to and built upon. The abiding memory from five days at the Gabba is that their insurance premiums, not for injury, but fire and theft, must be enormous.

MELBOURNE: It started as a typical West Indian dismissal – Martyn caught Simmons bowled Ambrose – one of four during a tense first day of the second Test at the MCG. It ended, however, in a most untypical fashion and the cause of great concern. At the very moment the ecstatic Trinidadian was set to launch the ball into the stratosphere, disaster struck. For reasons best known to him and his maker, the projectile slipped from his hand, hovered indecisively, then dropped gently to his feet. Result: instant confusion. In the general scheme of Caribbean cricket, celebration ranks as the most crucial aspect of play. Recent West Indian sides have taken it to near art-form proportions. Fielding, you see, is only tolerable, indeed only undertaken, on condition that mayhem and madness erupt at the fall of a wicket.

Partytime, the catch taken, is signalled by the return to orbit of the ball. Imagine the dilemma, then, with colleagues set to engulf Simmons, as the ball eludes his grasp, arcs slowly, teasing gravity, only to lose interest and plummet turfwards. Experienced players stopped dead in their tracks. Embarrassment. Dismay. Outrage. Team-mates looked to one another and finally to captain Richie Richardson. Hidden beneath a huge claret sun hat, he too now faltered. A personable fellow, Simmons, his was the cardinal sin, the crime of the century: a solitary act of carelessness that turned joy to sorrow, dream to nightmare and glory to shame.

There were high-fives – for a wicket had fallen – a handshake or two, and thin, humourless smiles: defiance, but little more than damage limitation. A curious game, cricket; barely a fortnight earlier Simmons was proclaimed hero, bowling Pakistan to defeat in a day-nighter. Still there remained a final twist to this tale. With speculation rife over his punishment, a reprieve unlikely, Simmons (Test average a modest 16.26) promptly reeled off a maiden Test century in a single-handed attempt to keep Australia at bay. In view of such heroism his crime, although not his century, was forgotten and a full pardon granted.

SYDNEY: With Australia sporting that lately Lara'd look, there is time to cast an eye around the press box and dwell upon more cerebral matters. Without wanting to plumb the murky depths of metaphysics, it may well be that England's loss in the coming weeks had become Australia's gain this southern summer. As the dispute concerning David Gower's omission from the Indian tour party rumbles on, what of the man himself? Ever one to do his own thing, Gower has merely swapped batting box for commentary box to become an integral part of the Channel 9 television team. As mild-mannered and thoughtfully persuasive with microphone as with bat, Gower brought much-needed calm to the vaudeville stage that passes as the central commentary position.

Anchorman and seasoned professional Richie Benaud remains the team captain, big cheese, all-round good guy, and the man responsible for making sense of it all. Chappell and Chappell bring picket fence and paddock to their version of capable commentary. Chappell the Elder has yet to shed the tag of larrikin and resident *agent provocateur*. Brother Greg, a relative newcomer to TV, is content to ruffle few feathers, remain uncontroversial, and, if needs be, hide behind big brother. The common man, the man in the 'outer', is the domain of Bill Lawry and Tony Greig. Together they shriek, holler, argue and harangue, speaking always in tabloid headlines. More than anyone, they are responsible for the mass migration from television to ABC radio.

Support for the touring team is provided by old 'Whispering Death' himself, Michael Holding. A man of few words in his playing days, the Silent One has a surprisingly deep, bass voice. Remove the Caribbean lilt and the impression is more Covent Garden than cover drive. Relax, however, at your peril. For while the speed of delivery is little more than slow-medium, the threat remains. Little wonder that, amid such mayhem and menace, Gower shines. His style, reflective of many an innings, remains unhurried, typically 'laid-back', fluent, with the occasional dash of spirited recklessness. The joy for Gower and the viewing public is that the rota system brings him to the microphone any number of times in the day, and not, as before, just a couple of times in the match.

ADELAIDE: Out of the bruised bodies and broken dreams of this fourth Test emerged a previously little-known expression. After the most nailbiting of finishes, Allan Border spoke of the 'recent trauma syndrome' or RTS. A highly stressful and sometimes painful condition of mind and body, RTS afflicts the vast majority of cricketers required to play against the West Indies. Indeed, the curious need only target England to find a nation of acute sufferers. The outbreak dates back to the halcyon summer of 1976, when Viv Richards seemed always to be batting and when the ever-diplomatic Tony Greig decided he would make West Indies 'grovel'.

If RTS, as appears likely, is to find a place in current cricket terminology – and as long as West Indies continue to select four fast bowlers it will remain alive and ducking – then One Short would like to submit an associated term for adoption by the free cricketing world. But first, a little by way of introduction. With match figures of 10-120 in Adelaide, Curtly Ambrose proved the prime mover in an unlikely West Indian victory. Yet prior to this fourth Test he had taken just 14 wickets and was in danger of winning the Mike Hendrick Trophy for the 'unluckiest' bowler of the series. The modus operandi for the majority of his wickets lay in a short, lifting ball, delivered at pace; the batsman, anchored on the back foot, is left to defend violently, head jerked back, bat raised protectively high. This reflex action, self-preservation, survival special, more often than not results in a catch behind the wicket, to bat-pad or close in on the off side.

It is submitted that this particular method of dismissal, a regular occurrence these days, should not be recorded as merely caught, but hereafter be known as 'Ambrosed'. This would immediately improve the lot of the spectator, with scorecards being the main benefactor. The latter have much to answer for these days, not the least being their inadequacy of information where a dismissal is concerned. To simply offer 'A.N. Other caught X bowled Y' is of little use to anyone.

However, if the entry were to read 'A.N. Other Ambrosed X bowled Y,' then our connoisseur would knowingly tap the side of his nose and recount to astonished friends and passers-by, 'Vicious short ball, back foot, batsman anchored, self-defence, outside edge, ball looping gently to waiting fielder.'

PERTH: Situation and circumstance this southern summer have pointed to an apparent shift in power (and glory?) away from the 'middle' and into the rarefied atmosphere of both the committee room and private box. Evidence this by the fact that the key characters in the series have not been players but officials. Despite an enthralling finish at Brisbane, the headlines – Border fine signals ICC crackdown – were grabbed by match referee Raman Subba Row. Seven days later, Bobby Simpson and Ian McDonald openly criticised Allan Border for lacking input in team matters.

It took the West Indies a mere seven sessions of play at the WACA ground in Perth to secure a famous series victory. It took ICC match referee Donald Carr just a fraction longer to steal the headlines with his judgment on the indiscretions of Border and Hughes. Add to these the situation in South Africa and New Zealand, where crucial decisions have been adjudicated upon not by the 'standing' umpire but by another official removed from the heat of battle, and this change of emphasis, this shift in power, is clearly visible.

Footnote: 'One Short' is a close friend of Vic Mills.

* * *

The Ultimate Sacrifice
Wisden Cricket Monthly: August 1994

A view, through the bottom of an ale glass, on the 1992 Pakistan ball-tampering controversy.

* * *

Could it be, amid all the claims and counterclaims, surrounding the Pakistan ball-tampering allegations, that the real issue has been clouded, if not overlooked altogether? Cast your mind back to the summer of 1992, fourth day of the Old Trafford Test and an England innings drawing to a sleepy close. The follow-on saved, thoughts were turning to cold beer and supper when the evening suddenly erupted red with controversy. First Aqib then Miandad in company with several Pakistan fielders took exception to the actions of umpire Roy Palmer. In line with the dictates of Law 42, section eight, he had 'called' Aqib for intimidatory bowling.

Upset with the ruling, bowler and captain then became agitated at the manner in which Palmer returned sweater and hat to Aqib. The dispute rumbled on into the final day, with the ICC referee (an unfortunate term) ruling in favour of Palmer and against the behaviour of Aqib and the comments of tour manager Intikhab Alam. With theories ranging from the Shakoor Rana/Gatting incident to collective mob rule, the press had a field day as they sought to dissect the tourists' behavioural shortcomings. Two years on, with ball tampering now the flavour of the month, should we continue to view such allegations in isolation or as part of a more complex problem? As champion of the talented yet misunderstood, it has fallen to your correspondent to defend cricket Pakistan-style, no easy task given the weight of evidence against.

Frustrated

Few would argue that the men on trial (or good behaviour bond) are a group of highly talented sportsmen at the top of their profession. The current holders of the one-day World Cup, Pakistan rank alongside West Indies as the leading Test-playing nation. In accordance with one of the fundamental elements of the Muslim religion, the many stirring deeds that brought such deserved success have all been achieved under alcohol-free conditions. Little wonder, then, with only milk to celebrate, that a combination of heat, humidity, spilled catches, lingering tail-enders (and the prospect of yet more milk) should result in the occasional heated exchange or perhaps the odd bout of alleged ball tampering. For these are men frustrated; men destined never to be intimate with malted hops and barley; men doomed never to wipe the condensation off a pint glass or talk longingly of a creamy head and full body. And on the subject of barmaids – men robbed of the chance to attend the Gatting lectures on social intercourse. In short, and to be brutally honest, men set for a life of lingering unfulfilment.

Attitude

As bat and ball form the essential elements of this particular art form, so too, down the ages, has alcohol become inextricably bound with cricket. Indeed, examples of its part in the development of the game are many and varied. One of the first recorded instances of alcohol and attitude came on England's inaugural tour of Australia in 1861/62. During a successful first colonial soiree, England blotted their copybook against the 22 of NSW and Victoria. Without diminishing the efforts of the opposition, the tourists' defeat was attributable, in part, to off-field events, as scarcely a day passed without invitations to alcoholic breakfasts, luncheons and dinners. The fact was evidenced at a public dinner following a four-wicket win over the Twenty-two of Tasmania when no fewer than 11 toasts were called, with everyone mentioned from the Queen and Prince Consort down to the umpires, scorers, volunteers and even the press. Turn the clock forward a few years and there is mention of a spot of fizz at W.G. Grace's 100th hundred.

With the landmark reached, champagne was brought to the wicket, where his health and no doubt that of cricket were toasted with equal vigour.

The colonial connection reappears in *Crusoe on Cricket*, as Raymond Robertson-Glasgow recalls the career of John Cornish White. The pride of Somerset, White first played for England in Australia during the 1928/29 tour at the age of 37. In the Adelaide Test, in blazing heat, with an oven-breeze, he bowled 124 overs, 37 maidens, and took 13 wickets for 256. England won by 12 runs. Of his performance, White remarked, 'I used a few shirts and several whisky and sodas.'

With Test sides – indeed, whole series – sponsored by breweries, alcohol is now an accepted part of cricket folklore. And still the Pakistanis have only their milk. Imagine the scene at the close of a hard-fought day of Test cricket as they file into the opposition dressing room armed with naught but a crate of homogenised gold top. Devout, courageous, supremely talented, and yet destined to be forever misunderstood, these men should be praised not pilloried. For theirs is the ultimate sacrifice.

Acknowledgements

THERE HAVE been several people over the years who have said that I ought to write a book. Most vociferous among them has been a friend and fellow cricket enthusiast in Chennai, Subbu. I hope it does not disappoint. Many of the tales, whether directly or indirectly, were inspired by the massed ranks of past players of the Lindum CC in Lincoln. May their line and length never waver.

Away from the cricket there were others whose kindness, consideration and no little hospitality allowed me to plough an itinerant furrow. In Lincoln, I'm thinking collectively of the Jollyboys and individually of Gary, Sue, Dicky, Jane, Andy and Sacky. My long-departed parents and sister aided and abetted my lifestyle that they may not have understood, but nevertheless supported through the decades. In Australia, the Gillard family were kindness personified, so too Dr Keith Hollebone in deepest Surry Hills. In Canberra and then Sydney, Hels, Vinny, Trumpet and Fingers produced the most perfect group house an itinerant Pom could hope or wish for. David Frith features heavily in this publication, and I am indebted to him for taking a punt on my erratic flights of fancy in *Wisden Cricket Monthly*.

More recently, I owe a huge debt of thanks to my Mumbai support team of Ramu, Suby, Satya, Anil, Karthik, Kicha, Ram, Kannan, Doc Bharat and Hushang for helping me keep body and soul together. To these I would add Chris, Krishna, Asim, Mayur, Lethy, Ravi, and many others at Reality Gives who we partnered in our decade-long cricket project in India. My thanks too to coaches Harshad and Bhavana for their sterling efforts along with the *mali* and his team at the Indian Gymkhana who worked wonders to provide facilities for the kids and coaches. My thanks to Allcargo Logistics in Mumbai, and Nilratan in particular, for providing life-saving funding for the project. Of our grandly titled Rural Schools Initiative I am grateful to Galaxy Surfactants and in particular Ramakant, Milind, Adarsh, Yatin and Mr Satawee for their work on our behalf. As Ramakant once ventured after a day in the sticks, 'This is the best day of my year.' We were fortunate to have many such days. I must also thank JNS, Saraswati, Mala, and the Lions Club of Dahisar for their help in organising our school visits whether inner-city or country.

No list of thanks in Mumbai would be complete without the admirable Chand who, as Suby's driver, effortlessly combined F1 and Paris–Dakar to ferry us to isolated and far-flung country schools. To the owners and staff of Mani's Lunch Home my eternal thanks for providing much needed sustenance and bringing new meaning to finger food. Thanks too to Mr Venkat and the staff at the Sri Vasavi Kanyaka Parameswari Temple in Matunga who, despite nicknaming me 'Tarzan' (due to my size), played a key part in Project Front Foot.

A long-time friend and cricketing buddy, the project would not have got off the ground in the UK without the support of Tim Gill and his wife, Jenny. The Berkshire support team was bolstered in no small measure by the time and energy of Ron, Fred, and Jane. In the West Country, sincere thanks to my old college chum Sue for her support and calming legal influence when it was needed and to Jane BP who, along with Tim, as a project trustee, was always on hand to offer media advice.

In Berlin, my thanks to Volker, Lissa and Christine for helping with transport, storage, and Battenberg counsel.

Since its inception in 2009 the project has had hundreds of donors, far too many to mention. However, in going the extra yard and more for the project, I must mention Steve Archer at the Yorkshire Cricket Board, Sandy Mitchell at the Lancashire Cricket Foundation, Peter Mason and Barry Aitken of The Forty Club, and Neil Lockwood of the Lindum CC.

On the support front I reserve special thanks for Jennifer in Bath who is without doubt the project's number one fan. The last word rightly goes to Dr Rita Gebert – the good doctor – who has supported both me and the project for a good many years. This book would not have been possible without her belief and encouragement, even if the months in front of my laptop came at the expense of German language classes. Tschüss.

VM, January 2022, Berlin

Bibliography

Books

Arlott, J., *How to Watch Cricket 1949* (London: Sporting Handbooks, 1949)

Cardus, N., *Autobiography* (London: Collins 1947)

Conan Doyle, A. (Sir), *The Adventures of Sherlock Holmes* (Reader's Digest, 1987)

Dickens, C., *A Christmas Carol* (Bantam Classics, 1986)

Fingleton, J., *The Immortal Victor Trumper* (London: Collins, 1978)

Frith, D., *The Trailblazers* (Southlands: Boundary Books, 1999)

Jardine, D., *In Quest of the Ashes* (Hutchinson & Co Ltd, 1933)

Johnston, B. and Webber, R., *Armchair Cricket* (BBC publication, 1957)

Macartney, C.G., *My Cricketing Days* (London: William Heinemann Ltd, 1930)

O'Reilly, W.J., *Cricket Conquest* (London: Werner Laurie, 1949)

Robertson-Glasgow, R., *Crusoe On Cricket* (London: Pavilion Books, 1985)

Ross, G. (editor), *Playfair Cricket Annual 1962* (Playfair Books Ltd, 1962)

West, P. (editor), *Playfair Cricket Annual 1952* (Playfair Books Ltd, 1952)

Wright, P., *Spycatcher* (Port Melbourne: Mandarin, 1989)

Newspapers
Jakarta Post
Lincolnshire Echo
Sydney Morning Herald
The Guardian
The Times
Times of India.

Periodicals
Wisden Cricket Monthly

Songs and Lyrics
Dury, I. and Nugent, S., 'Billericay Dickie' (Ian Dury and the Blockheads, Stiff Records, 1977)
Hay, C. and Strykert, R., 'Down Under' (Men at Work, Columbia Records, 1981)
Harburg, Y. and Arlen, H., 'Lydia, the Tattooed Lady' (Groucho Marx, *At the Circus*, 1939)
Jones, B.T., 'Born Under a Bad Sign' (Cream, Polydor (UK), 1968)
Scaggs, B. and Paich, D., 'Lido Shuffle' (Boz Scaggs, CBS, 1977)
Silverstein, S., 'A Boy Named Sue' (Johnny Cash, Columbia, 1969)
Weller, P., 'Town Called Malice' (The Jam, Polydor (UK), 1982)

Television and Film
Cleese, J. and Booth, C., *Fawlty Towers* 'The Germans' (Series one episode six, October 1975)
Shaffer, A., *The Wicker Man* (British Lion Films, 1973)

Wikipedia
Benenden School
Johnny Lawrence
Stephen Harold Gascoigne (Yabba)
The Sydney Hill

Quotation
Lang, Andrew., *Burned out Junes revived* (Origin and date unknown)